Getting By on the
Minimum

Getting By on the
Minimum
The Lives of Working-Class Women

Jennifer Johnson

Routledge
New York and London

Published in 2002 by
Routledge
29 West 35th Street
New York, NY 10001
www.routledge-ny.com

Published in Great Britain by
Routledge
11 New Fetter Lane
London EC4P 4EE
www.routledge.com

Routledge is an imprint of the Taylor & Francis Group
Printed in the United States of America on acid-free paper.

10   9   8   7   6   5   4   3   2   1

Library of Congress Cataloging-in-Publication Data
Johnson, Jennifer, 1949–
   Getting by on the minimum : the lives of working-class women / by Jennifer Johnson
     p. cm.
   Includes bibliographical references and index.
   ISBN 0-415-92800-1 (hc.) — ISBN 0-415-92801-X (pbk.)
   1. Working class women—United States—Case studies. 2. Poor women—United States—Case studies. 3. Social classes—United States—Case studies. I. Title.
HQ1421 .J65 2002
305.48'9623'0973—dc21   2002016566

Contents

Acknowledgments

A number of colleagues and friends gave me generous support, encouragement, and advice. Doris Entwisle first suggested that I write this book, and from the beginning she has been a generous source of practical and moral support. I also give wholehearted thanks to Doris and to Karl Alexander for giving me access to the families in their Beginning School Study—an act of great generosity as well as trust. Finally, Ilene Kalish, my editor at Routledge, helped make this a better book by urging me to say more.

Transcribing hundreds of hours of interviews felt, sometimes, like grappling with an elephant; funding from the National Science Foundation allowed me to get some professional help with this task, for which I am grateful. I am grateful, too, to Lissa Johnson, who, in a labor of love, relieved me at the transcriber for many hours. Most of all I am grateful to Ken, my best friend and partner, who has kept the faith.

Last, I thank the women who took part in this study: their generosity and honesty are what made it possible—and they are what made it worthwhile.

For Ken,
for our mothers
Betty and Emma,
and for our children,
with love

Money pads the edge of things. . . .
God help those who have none.
—E. M. Forster, *Howard's End*

1.
Introduction

Would sleep ever come? As she lay awake, Joe sound asleep beside her, Phyllis replayed her last few months on the job. It had all started, she thought, when Michael, her boss, quit his job at the supermarket. The new guy who replaced him had been baiting her for months now, harassing her when her speed dropped, forcing her to check with the office every time a decision had to be made, giving her the lousy shifts and break times no one else wanted. What had she done to annoy him? True, she was a bit mouthy, and she'd let him know what she thought of his stupid changes, but so what? Michael had liked her input—and he'd liked her too. This guy seemed to hate her.

And now, by switching shifts with Mary so she could go to her son's game tomorrow, she was about to hand him exactly what he wanted: an excuse to give her a hard time. He'd slap her with a notice, for sure, her second since he came on board six months ago. Just as well she had some new job options. Maybe now she could quit before she was fired. She was never going to make full-time staff anyway, and she was fed up with being treated like a child—a stupid child at that.

In any case, she had no choice. If she missed the game after promising she'd go, how could she look her son in the eye? How could she expect him to trust her? Well, whatever happened, she was not about to miss that game.

Ann had been thinking a lot lately and she had to admit her thoughts were not pretty. In fact, she was downright depressed. Jack and the kids accused her of being moody, and, to be honest, they were right. But here she was, still doing the same things she had been doing for twenty years and did anyone notice? Or care? Maybe it was just menopause: don't women get more cranky and men more laid back as they get older? That fit her and Jack, that's for sure.

Sometimes she wished she could go off by herself—just to think about what she was doing with her life. As if there were time! With her own four kids and two grandkids all at home, not to mention her job, thinking was a luxury she couldn't afford.

Maybe she was just tired—at work, tired of being called a bitch by customers and having returns thrown in her face, and at home, tired of wiping up the same spills on the same floors and complaining about the same careless clutter, day after day. She was tired of daughters who expected her to raise their kids, and sons who expected her to pay their way. She was tired even of herself and of all the mistakes she'd made, since way back when. Why hadn't she gone to a regular high school, for example? Why hadn't she listened when her father said a commercial school was a waste of time? Why did that have to be the only battle with him she'd ever won? If only she had lost that fight, she'd be a professional now, not just a working person. She would not be sitting here behind a customer service counter dealing with the negative attitudes and nasty dispositions of people who thought they could treat her like dirt.

Of course, it wasn't all bad. She liked her job. It was like family. Monday mornings everyone asked how the kids were, and did she have a good weekend? Time off was no big deal. Really, it was a good job. It just wasn't where she'd like to be at this stage of her life. That's all.

Phyllis and Ann are two of sixty-three working-class women whose thoughts, feelings, and experiences of work and family are explored in this book. All but six of these women had remained solidly working class throughout their lives and now at midlife were employed in working-class jobs—as grocery store cashiers, assembly-line workers, school bus drivers, secretaries, clerks, cleaners, and cooks—married to working-class men, and living in poor, working- or lower-middle-class neighborhoods. Also in the book, for purposes of comparison, are eighteen middle-class women whose origins were middle or upper middle class. These women were married to middle-class men, lived in middle- or upper-middle-class neighborhoods and, with one exception, worked in professional or managerial jobs, as teachers, social workers, attorneys, physicians, and entrepreneurs. The book uses the experiences of these two groups of women to explore the difference social class makes in women's lives.

We know that as a group, women have come a long way, but have some women come farther than others? Do shampoo girls at an upscale day spa obtain the same benefits from their work as the clients who come to be pampered? Do secretaries enjoy their jobs as much as attorneys and businesswomen? Do day-care providers feel satisfied with their work? Do waitresses?

Addressing questions such as these is the first purpose of this book. The second is to make the point that social class still matters. In a society whose discourse emphasizes race more than class, it is easy to lose sight of the wide class differences among women. The book explores these differences, with the goal of discovering which problems are common to all women, which not, which rewards are available to all, which restricted to some.

The book has a third purpose, which is to allow the voices of poor and working-class women to be heard as they talk about what *they* consider important. For this reason, throughout the book there are extended passages in which women talk about their past and present lives with very little interruption or interpretation. By listening to their voices, I hope the reader will come to know these women—at least a little—as individuals and will come to discover what matters to *them*.

I can't pretend to have approached the study on which this book is based or the daunting task of writing it with the calm detachment and disinterest of a natural scientist; the subject is too close to my own life, the fragments of their lives, thoughts, feelings, and memories too much an echo of my own. When, for instance, Doreen said, about growing up poor, "No one else was any better off than we were," when Judy said, "We always had warm clothes on our back and food on the table," or Phyllis said, "We might have been poor, but if we were we didn't know it," they chose the same words I might have chosen. Like them, I compared my family with others in our community, most of whose members, including my parents and two of my four siblings, left high school early to earn a living in unskilled or semiskilled jobs. Like a number of the women I interviewed, it was only as an adult living in a very different world that I realized that there were times when we were quite poor.

Like those of many of the women in the study, my own work history is a long and winding road with twists, turns, and dead ends that were not the result of careful planning or "career preparation." My first venture into the world of work came when I was seventeen and took an office job in a factory, a small nail-making concern. I was the only worker in the office, which was a small, dirty shed in the yard behind the factory itself, and there was not enough office work to keep me busy, so I was given nails to sort into boxes. Soon it became clear that my office job was really a nail-sorting job. I hated it, not so much because sorting nails was so terrible, but because I was sentenced to solitude for eight hours every day. Even my lunch breaks were solitary because the men workers lunched in the bar of a nearby pub to which I was never invited (I could not have gone anyway because in those days women were legally not permitted in bars). I had no car and there were no shops in the industrial wasteland surrounding the factory, so I wasn't able to enliven my boring days by window shopping and chatting to salespeople. Later, when women told me that what they liked most about their job was "the people at work," I remembered this job and knew exactly what they meant.

My next job, also clerical, was better. The Australian government was computerizing all its social security files, which required coding basic information onto standardized coding sheets that would later become punch cards. To accomplish this end, about eighty workers sat at long tables in a large room with bundles of files between them. As the day progressed, the files moved from the left to the right of each workstation. The work was repetitive, but had its rewards. One was watching the pile on the left shrink, while the one on the right grew. The other was that my coworkers and I soon devised strategies to while away the hours. There were two main strategies. The first was to talk and tell jokes, keeping only a small part of our minds on the job. The other was to race to see who could earn a beer after work by completing the most files. Even though the rewards of this job were what psychologists and sociologists of work call "extrinsic," it was really not a bad job at all. The conditions were good: the office was air-conditioned, the tea lady came around with tea and cookies at 10 A.M. and 3 P.M., there was an excellent cafeteria, and we were in a downtown building close to the shops.

After a year or so, when most of the files were coded, I went to work in an employment office. It was here that I began to learn about the wider world of work. Trying to match unemployed workers with sales, clerical, and factory jobs taught me more than I could have imagined about what went on behind the blank walls of industrial buildings—that metal was filed, glass was cut, bricks were laid, forklifts were driven, wood was turned, and pallets were loaded, and that this work was performed by process workers, assemblers, laborers, lathe operators, fitters and turners, and machinists who all had complex jobs about which I had known nothing. Later, when I moved on to work only with disabled workers, I needed to delve deeper, gathering every last detail about each job that came into the office. Did the job involve heavy lifting, bending, or reaching? Did the worker have to stand all day, did she need muscle strength, a steady hand, good eyesight? How many different activities were involved? How clearly were directions given? How often was the task changed? What were the job's stresses? Were the bosses and coworkers supportive and understanding? Were enough time and instruction given to learn new tasks? Did the worker have to work too fast? What kinds of performance pressures were there?

This job had intrinsic rewards that I hadn't experienced in the previous two jobs: it involved dealing with people, not files, every day brought something new, and the satisfaction of finding a job for someone who needed it was of a different order from the satisfaction of coding three hundred files. I now realize that I experienced the difference between being satisfied with a job and feeling fulfilled by work—a distinction that I found to be important in this study.

During my years working for the employment service, I learned about the importance of work in people's lives, and about the despair of being unemployed. And although I didn't realize it at the time, I learned about the complicated division of labor in industrial society. The agriculture-based economy of my childhood had not prepared me for this new world, whose complexity has been wrestled with by social theorists since Adam Smith. There were no factories in my small home town; the jobs consisted mainly of farming and its support services. People worked in stores, they repaired cars and machines, they painted and repaired houses, and they installed plumbing—all jobs that were visible and whose purpose was clear. The division of labor was simpler, and the division between home and work was less clear-cut; storekeepers, for example, often lived behind their own shops and opened up any time a customer came around back. Compared with this rural, small-town way of life in which the division of labor was relatively simple, the industrial giant I came to know, its working parts largely hidden away behind factory walls and office doors, seemed complex beyond belief.

Many jobs in the twenty-first century "post-industrial" division of labor are also invisible. Most of us have no idea what, exactly, a software designer does when she goes in to work in the morning, or a statistician, or an economist. Nor is it entirely clear what a human resources specialist does, or a sanitation engineer, or a systems analyst. As industrial areas become more separate from residential, and more products are produced in foreign countries, work becomes even more remote from home and we know less and less about the human labor that goes into creating the products and services that we use every day and take for granted.

Some service jobs, especially those filled by the least educated workers, are visible; we see bored young people flipping hamburgers at McDonald's, for instance, and grocery store cashiers checking us out and bagging our groceries. But we have no idea what these jobs are like for the people doing them. What does the counter salesperson at the 7-11 do when she is not taking our money? What are the main job hassles for women who work in the bakery department of the supermarket? Who chops up the lettuce, fruit, and vegetables that endlessly refill the stainless steel containers at the grocery store salad bar? What is it like, doing this day after day?

We also know little about the strategies these workers use to make their jobs more enjoyable or just to get through the day. My coworkers and I, when we were coding files, made the day go by faster by racing one another, or we socialized. What strategies do other women adopt to make their jobs more enjoyable? What strategies do they develop to fight back when they are faced with obnoxious customers or bosses? What compensations do they find when their jobs lack intrinsic interest? What jobs are most satisfying? These are some of the questions I will address beginning in the next chapter.

The problems of professional women—mommy tracks, glass ceilings, dual-career families, and commuter marriages—have been the subject of countless books and articles in both the popular press and academic journals, but only a handful of studies have focused on working-class women and these studies have concentrated on women in factories or in "non-traditional occupations, who represent only a small minority of working-class women. Too often, working-class women are viewed from a social distance, and through a middle-class lens that filters out differences among them and between them and middle-class women. Because of this social distance and distorting lens, working-class women are often seen as homogeneous, when, in fact, they come from a wide range of economic, cultural, and social backgrounds ranging from prosperous working class to underclass, from nurturing, supportive families to dysfunctional ones.

Also, not all working-class women have the same strengths and abilities or want the same things but their diversity and the complexity of their motivations are rarely appreciated. As Herbert Blumer, the eminent sociologist, points out in his introduction to symbolic interactionism,[1] in all our studies, sociologists need to recall that we too are shaped by our past and by the social and historical context of our lives. We all "have our share of common stereotypes that we use to see a sphere of empirical social life that we do not know. . . . We must say in all honesty that the research scholar in the social sciences who undertakes to study a given sphere of social life that he does not know at first hand will fashion a picture of that sphere in terms of pre-established images."[2] Blumer perceptively observes that the scholar who lacks firsthand knowledge is "highly unlikely to recognize that he is missing anything."[3]

Several books have inspired me as I have written this. One was Studs Terkel's *Working*.[4] I like the way Terkel steps back and gives his interviewees the floor. He seems to say, "I respect these people and the dignity of their lives. I am going to get out of their way and let them talk." Lillian Rubin's *Worlds of Pain* was another—I recognized families I knew in her portrayals of working-class life and respected her refusal to sugar-coat their lives. Two more recent books were also models I admired and emulated; both lay bare the injuries and injustices of class inequality, in and out of the workplace. Written in her characteristically honest, pull-no-punches prose, Barbara Ehrenreich's *Nickel and Dimed: On (Not) Getting By in America*[5] exposes the ugly truth that, in what was at the time of her writing a boom economy, women and men in low-wage jobs still had to struggle for respect and the most basic requirements of a decent life: food, shelter, and adequate health care. And in *Where We Stand: Class Matters*,[6] writing with simplicity, clarity, and grace, bell hooks helps us see that inequality based on class and inequality based on race are two symptoms of the same sickness in our society. The authors of these books have taken the time to know and examine the worlds they describe, and they all make the point that poverty is an equal opportunity experience.

I hope to offer a look at women whose experience is often hidden from view, and whose voices are usually unheard. They offer new insights into the nature of work, the importance of family, the role of education, and the significance of social class as a force to be grappled with throughout their lives. In telling their stories in the pages ahead, I hope to make known their struggles as well as their triumphs. Most of all, I hope to show the dignity with which they live their complex and often difficult lives.

The Meaning of
W o r k   a n d   C l a s s

It can be argued that those occupations which demand specific abilities or longer training have on the whole become more lucrative; while the commensurate wage for mechanically uniform activity, in which everyone can be quickly and easily trained, has fallen, and inevitably so.

—Karl Marx, *Economic and Philosophic Manuscripts*[1]

The U.S. workforce has exploded in the last half century, from 62 million workers in 1950 to 135 million in 2000.[2] Women have fueled this remarkable growth: in 1950, only thirty in every hundred workers were women,[3] but at century's end, this had grown to fifty in every hundred, and ninety-nine in every hundred women could expect to hold down a job at some point in their lives.[4] Some of these women are managers, physicians, executives, and attorneys, but most are not; most women still work in the same old jobs; in its list of the twenty leading occupations for women, the Department of Labor reports the following, in descending order: secretaries (almost three million); cashiers; managers and administrators; registered nurses; sales supervisors and proprietors; nursing aides, orderlies, and attendants; waitresses; sales workers; receptionists; accountants and auditors; machine operators; cooks; textile, apparel, and furnishing machine operators; janitors and cleaners; investigators and adjusters, excluding insurance; administrative support occupations; secondary school teachers; and, finally, hairdressers and cosmetologists.[5]

These jobs are not new; neither is the work of working-class women. They have always performed the dirtiest, heaviest, and least desirable domestic work and have eased the lives of middle-class women as long as there has been a middle class. But for centuries, their labor was hidden within households, and aroused little notice; no matter how backbreaking, it was invisible, "natural" women's work.

By moving working-class women into factories, the industrial revolution made their work visible and, for the first time, worthy of public attention. Only then was it exposed for what it was—hard, unforgiving labor. In fact, with men, women, and children newly crowded together in factories, all working-class work was now more visible, and its conditions so horrified Karl Marx and Friedrich Engels that they inspired a social movement that would change the world. Witnessing the degrading conditions of unbridled capitalism in England, the birthplace of the machine age, Marx wrote:

> Modern Industry has converted the little workshop of the patriarchal master into the great factory of the industrial capitalist. Masses of laborers, crowded into the factory, are organized like soldiers. As privates of the industrial army, they are placed under the command of a perfect hierarchy of officers and sergeants. Not only are they slaves of the bourgeois class, and of the bourgeois state; they are daily and hourly enslaved by the machine, by the overlooker, and, above all, by the individual bourgeois manufacturer himself.

Marx made an important observation, which applies as much today as it did in the nineteenth century:

> The less the skill and exertion of strength implied in manual labor, in other words, the more modern industry becomes developed, the more is the labor of men superseded by that of women. Differences of age and sex have no longer any distinctive social validity for the working class. All are instruments of labor, more or less expensive to use, according to their age and sex.[6]

In a sense, this substitution of cheap female labor for more expensive male labor can be seen again now, at the tail end of the process whose birth Marx witnessed, and we can learn much from this earlier period that is still relevant today. One important lesson is that women's work conditions have excited most reforming zeal when their work is highly visible, and when it is considered inappropriate to their "true" nature. When women worked alone or in small groups—as thousands do now, in convenience stores and small businesses—and when they were doing work that was "appropriate," it bothered no one, no matter how cruelly they were treated. Domestic workers, for example, were frequently mistreated by their employers, but, because this mistreatment was of individual women and it took place behind closed doors, it was easily ignored.

In the factories, however, working-class women's work was "unnatural," and the cruelty of their conditions was painfully obvious. In a widely publicized government report on women's working conditions and those of children—a report that Engels read and referred to in *The Condition of the Working Class in England*[7]—one observer described his reaction upon seeing, for the first time, women at work in a cotton mill:[8]

> Amongst other things I saw a cotton mill—a sight that froze my blood. The place was full of women, young, all of them, some large with child, and obliged to stand

twelve hours each day. Their hours are from five in the morning to seven in the evening, two hours of that being for rest, so that they stand twelve clear hours.... The young women were all pale, sallow, thin, yet generally fairly grown, all with bare feet—a strange sight to English eyes.

Women doing agricultural work aroused little interest until they were forced—en masse—into public view, working far from home as waged laborers. This happened when, as industrialization progressed, the poor were denied access to the common lands that had helped them subsist; now these lands were needed by sheep, which would provide their rich owners with valuable wool. No longer able to sustain themselves, poor families took to the roads in search of work. Commonly, women and their children worked in gangs as hired laborers, walking to distant farms to work for a wage. One gang worker, a Mrs. Stone, testified as follows to a government commission in 1843: "I went out gleaning this autumn for three weeks. I got up at two o'clock in the morning and got home at seven at night. My . . . three girls, aged 10, 15 and 18, went with me, . . . sometimes as far as seven miles off."[9] When they eked out a living tilling their rented plot, women were unnoticed; in gangs, working for a wage, they were unseemly.

Unnoticed, too, were the young working-class women who labored in the sculleries and waited on the tables of the aristocracy, but when those same young women earned wages in busy workshops, the reality of their conditions was undeniable. In a flurry of preparing young ladies for the London social season each year, working-class girls' fingers flew hour after hour; another reform-minded inquiry reported that young dressmaking apprentices worked longer hours than anyone. During the season, when the rich flocked back to the city after taking the waters in Bath, these young women worked fifteen hours a day, but in a pinch this would stretch to eighteen. When upper- and middle-class London enjoyed its balls, races, and afternoon teas, their young dressmakers would never get more than six, and sometimes as little as two, hours a day for rest and sleep.[10]

Most horrifying of all, was the sight of working-class women working in the mines, fueling the very engines of industrialization. Along with young children, they were employed to push or pull carriages full of coal along iron tram lines, from deep in the ground up steep inclines to the surface. At times, they were harnessed to the carriage by means of a girdle, which was "put on the naked waist to which a chain from the carriage is hooked and passed between the legs."[11] One married woman of thirty-seven described her experiences, saying she had pulled the carriage until "the skin was off me." The belt and chain were even more uncomfortable, she said, when women workers were "in the family way."[12]

The sight of women and children doing this work was horrifying to reformers who observed it. Especially horrifying was the sight of girls and young women aged between seven and twenty-one working in the heat naked to the waist. One reformer described his feelings upon reading a report on the mines. The part that most upset him, he said, was the description of how women were employed; he had listened to that part with "feelings of disgust, indignation and shame that in this enlightened country in the middle of the 19th-century such a savage state of things should be found to exist."[13]

The working-class realities they observed must, indeed, have shocked the nineteenth-century parliamentarians, for the middle-class ideal of womanhood then was one of "piety, purity, submissiveness and domesticity."[14] Industrial capitalism had created a growing and prosperous middle class that could afford maids for its wives, who were then released from drudgery to pursue what the historian Barbara Welter has dubbed the "cult of true womanhood." As Welter has noted, work was permitted for the truly womanly middle-class woman as long as it was religious work or the work of creating a domestic haven; women were naturally religious, it was thought, and religion did not entice them away from their proper sphere, the home. It was acceptable, a popular pamphlet reassured women, because they could labor at it "without the apprehension of detracting from the charms of [their] feminine delicacy."[15] The absence of purity in a woman was not only unfeminine, but unnatural; "without it, she was, in fact, no woman at all, but a member of some lower order." And to lose her virtue was to become a "fallen angel" unworthy of the company of her sex. As for submission, "true feminine genius is ever timid, doubtful and clingingly dependent."[16] Duly pious, pure, and submissive, the truly womanly woman was, above all else, domestic. A letter to the editor of a magazine for ladies suggested how she might best accomplish this: "A Woman never appears more truly in her sphere than when she divides her time between her domestic avocations and the culture of flowers."[17]

Such notions only add insult to injury, for working-class women have not only done the dirtiest, heaviest work, but, in doing so, they have forfeited their respectability—a quality that has always been defined by the middle class.

Well-intentioned middle-class reformers have long been out of touch with the realities of working-class life. In describing the battle that took place over the introduction of child labor laws and compulsory schooling, Viviana Zelizer[18] describes how reform efforts both in Britain and the United States met with bitter opposition—not only from puritans, who thought work was character building, but from members of the working class, whose economic security depended on the wages of every available family member, man, woman, or child. Zelizer reports that a cannery owner who tried to keep children out of his sheds was "besieged by angry women, one of whom bit his finger right through"[19] and notes that the battle over child labor laws was in part a class-based battle pitting middle-class reformers against working-class families and middle-class ideals of childhood against working-class economic realities.

The cleavage between middle-class ideals and working-class realities may not be so dramatic in the early twenty-first century as it was in the nineteenth, but it still exists; now, as then, "the ruling ideas are the ideas of the ruling class."[20] Now, however, these ruling ideas hold up as an ideal for all women to emulate—not the truly domestic woman, but the "career" woman who pursues paid work with a vengeance, makes it central to her sense of self, and climbs the career ladder. But what if there is no career ladder? What if the paid work is dead-end and boring? Only recently have middle-class scholars begun to acknowledge that, just as the experiences of working-class women may not be the same as their own, their goals, too, may well be quite different. As Elizabeth Fox-Genovese put it, "to deny the divisions among women by class and race is willfully to ignore the real challenge of feminist politics in our time."[21]

Meaning, Social Class, and the Life Course: Defining Concepts

The meaning of work and family, how it is shaped by social class, and how it is constructed over the course of a life are concepts that are basic to this book, but each of these three concepts—meaning, social class, and life course—is subject to multiple definitions. For this reason, I will introduce all three, give some theoretical background, and some explanation of how I will use them throughout the book. Later, I will specifically elaborate on the meaning of work.

Meaning: Subjective and Objective

The experiences of the women I spoke with were partly patterned and partly unique, and they had several different layers of meaning. They were all white, married mothers who shared the experiences of a particular historical period. But no two women had exactly the same history, the same personality, or the same immediate social, neighborhood, and family context; their personal biographies were unique.

Certain shared objective circumstances and life experiences encouraged particular patterned ways of viewing the world, but, on the other hand, similar objective events such as dropping out of school, giving birth, or finding work took on different subjective meanings for different women; these different circumstances, in turn, led to different consequences in women's lives. Laura and Phyllis, for example, both dropped out of school. For Laura, the meaning of this event was that she was "a loser," someone with limited intelligence who would achieve little in life; this belief had lasting consequences in her life. Phyllis, however, dropped out because she was pregnant; she believed this had nothing whatever to do with her intelligence, and her confidence in herself remained intact.

We begin to reconstruct actions as soon as they are complete, interpreting their meaning using a set of experiences and understandings that may not have been present when the action took place; when we reexamine our life story, we know what happened next, and to give the story continuity and meaning we may construct a new story line. As women recalled their past experiences, they interpreted them from a vantage point in the present, forty or more years later. For example, at the time, Phyllis believed she left school because she was pregnant: "I started school in September," she said, "and I found out that I was pregnant with [my daughter] and I quit. That was the excuse I needed." Now, she believed that leaving school was what she had wanted all along, and that becoming pregnant had been the means of achieving her goal. Liz also reinterpreted her past: "I didn't think so at the time," she said, "but the reason I became pregnant was to get away from home." Thus the two women became observers and meaning-makers of their own past actions, remembering them, interpreting them, and understanding them in new ways.

Sociologists vary in how they approach subjective and objective meaning. Some adopt an emic approach, in which understanding how the "actor" views the world and the meaning of her actions is the goal of research. Judith Rollins, for example, in her excellent study of domestic workers, described her approach as "based on the simple and fundamental assumption that those who have lived an experience know more about it than those who have not."[22] For sociologists with an emic orientation, understanding the meaning of events or actions is achieved when one understands how different protagonists interpret and make sense of them.

Other sociologists, often using quantitative methods, adopt an etic approach, in which understanding objective meaning is the primary research goal, and subjective meaning is not necessarily important. According to one of the founders of sociology, Max Weber, this "natural science" approach is most useful for studying large-scale statistical regularities such as death rates, crime rates, and occupational distributions. In most cases, however, meanings are qualitatively heterogeneous, and it is impossible to represent them with summary statistics such as averages.

Weber believed that neither an entirely subjectivist nor a "natural science" approach is sufficient to understanding the full meaning of actions. He gives the actor's point of view a special authority, but, along with Marx, he understood that we are subject to forces that are larger than ourselves, and of which we are usually unconscious:

> [C]onscious motives may well, even to the actor himself, conceal the various motives and repressions which constitute the real driving force of his action. Thus in such cases even subjectively honest self-analysis has only a relative value. Then it is the task of the sociologist to be aware of this motivational situation and to describe and analyze it, even though it has not actually been concretely part of the conscious intention of the actor.[23]

But how can we interpret the subjective meaning of an event that is outside our own experience? According to Weber, there are two kinds of understanding. The first is intellectual or "rational" understanding, which, in spite of its name, can be applied to ideas and actions, but also to "irrational" emotions.[24] For example, when we learn that Laura dropped out because she "felt like a loser," we can intellectually understand this connection because of the obvious and logical link between failing and wanting to leave school. The second, and more important, kind of understanding is what Weber calls "*verstehen*," which is sympathetic or explanatory understanding. With *verstehen*, we understand the meaning of an event for the actor by putting ourselves in her shoes, and understanding with our hearts as well as our minds. "For the verifiable accuracy of interpretation of the meaning of a phenomenon," Weber said, "it is a great help to be able to put one's self imaginatively in the place of the actor and thus sympathetically to participate in his experiences." To reach sympathetic understanding of Laura's dropping out we would draw on our own life experience to help us understand the events from her point of view; we might think back to times we failed in school, remember how it felt, and how we acted upon that feeling.

This kind of understanding is easier to attain if our own life experience is not too remote from the actor's. As Weber stated, "The more we ourselves are susceptible to them, the more readily can we imaginatively participate in such emotional reactions as anxiety, anger, ambition . . . and appetites of all sorts, and thereby understand the irrational conduct that grows out of them." By entering into an experience, we can understand actions that, from outside, appear irrational. For example, in terms of her future, dropping out of school may not have been Laura's best course of action, but in the context of her life at that time, her action had its own rationality and logic, which we can understand because we too are human actors with subjectivity and a shared repertoire of feelings, motives, and reactions. Weber recognized that our understanding may always be only partial; we may be able to grasp a meaning only from an intellectual perspective:

> Many ultimate ends or values toward which . . . human action may be oriented, often cannot be understood completely, though sometimes we are able to grasp them intellectually. The more radically they differ from our own ultimate values, however, the more difficult it is for us to make them understandable by imaginatively participating in them.[25]

Because our understanding depends at least in part on shared experience, *verstehen* can break down when the distance between the experience of the sociologist and her subject is too great.

Alfred Schutz, the phenomenologist, makes another distinction when he discusses the motivation for an act. He distinguishes between what he calls "in-order-to" motives that explain the action in terms of its intended goal, and "because" motives, which explain it in terms of past experience.[26] Liz, for example said she became pregnant at fourteen to get away from home. Now, observing her own action, she assigned to it both "in-order-to" and "because" motives. She became pregnant "in order to" get away from home—her intended goal—but she wanted to get away from home "because" her stepfather was sexually abusing her and her mother was too depressed to take her side. Liz was unusual for assigning both motives; more often, actors voice "in order to" motives, but not "because" motives. As social scientists, it is our job to try, through *verstehen*, to understand both "in-order-to" motives, as they are expressed to us, and also "because" motives, which are more elusive.

My approach to understanding meaning in this study is influenced by Weber and by Schutz. It assumes the importance of understanding from women's own points of view the meaning of work and family. And yet, as social actors, they—as we all—are subject to larger social forces that are not fully, or sometimes even partially, accessible to conscious thought. We are also influenced by experiences in our own personal biographies whose effects we may not realize. Thus the data in the book consist of the meanings women voiced and my attempts to understand those meanings in the context of their experiences and the larger social structure. Part of understanding meaning is attempting to understand motivation; by linking some of women's later orientations and experiences to earlier events in their lives, making connections the women themselves may not have made, I am, following Schutz, making my own guesses at "because" motivations, which may differ from the "in-order-to" motivations the women expressed. This interpretation is a dangerous business, and I do it with humility, understanding that observers of my own actions would no doubt arrive at an interpretation that is different from my own.

Social Class

Asked to name their own social status most Americans, reluctant to place themselves above (or below) others, lay claim to the middle ground. Confronted daily with evidence of vast wealth—the Bill Gateses, Donald Trumps, and Kennedys—most people acknowledge differences in riches, but balk at calling them class differences; the language of social class raises the specter of rigid European class boundaries and we like to think—with some justification—that our own barriers are less rigid, that any of us with enough good luck, talent, and hard work can make the leap from poor to rich. Bill Gates, after all, with his down-to-earth nerdiness, seems more like us than an English earl or a continental count.

To be sure, especially in the northeast and in the south, the most European parts of our country, there are hints of social class: the occasional mention of "old families" or "old money," with the understanding that "old" is better than "new," and the discreet reports of cotillions, country clubs, coming-out parties, prep schools, and even fox hunts. But these distinctions are hidden from view, and, in any case, seem, to most people, to be dated and merely quaint. The wealth we see on television, in magazines, and in newspapers often belongs to people who have made it on their own merits, and, though they may be smarter, luckier, or better looking than we are, they seem to be similar to us. That the wealthy should be similar to us is reassuring. It is also reassuring that the poor should be different; when necessary, we invent language to underscore their difference; labels such as "inner-city youth," "welfare moms," and "junkies" help us push poverty off to a safe distance. "Some people just can't make it," we sigh. "It's too bad, but that's the price we pay for the chance to get ahead."

If the average American has trouble accepting the reality of class, this cannot be said of sociologists, who spend a good part of their time thinking about how best to conceptualize and define it. Those following Marx's ideas emphasize ownership of the "means of production"; according to Marx's original thesis, there are two classes: owners and workers, capitalists and laborers. In the nineteenth century, when Marx wrote, these two classes occupied what were different and fundamentally opposed positions in the economy; rich capitalists owned the factories, workers labored for a wage. Now, however, workers may be Wall Street arbitragers and CEOs of multi-million-dollar public companies, and may be shareholders as well as workers; furthermore a vast "new" professional and managerial middle class has developed. It is no longer so clear who is working class and who is not. To accommodate these changes, different class theorists have drawn the line between classes in different places, emphasizing one distinction more than others: some draw a heavy line between professional/managerial workers and others,[27] some between a small ruling elite and others,[28] and some between those who exercise authority and those who do not.[29]

Other sociologists, beginning with Max Weber, take a broader view, conceptualizing inequality in terms of several dimensions. Weber assigns more importance to different patterns of consumption, prestige, honor, styles of life, and education. Indeed, in his view, differences in social honor are almost as important as economic differences.

Marxist class theorists see classes, not individuals, as actors in a larger struggle; classes are positions that act in certain ways regardless of who fills them. Most later theorists in this tradition, rejecting the early writings of Marx, have little interest in the social psychology of class—that is, in understanding how class is internalized and shapes how we see the world. Weberian status theorists, however, are interested in understanding individuals and ask questions such as the following: What is it that allows some people to climb the status ladder while others remain fixed? What is the relationship between parents' social status and that of their children? The two traditions are guided by different images of inequality; status theorists' image is one of more or less; individuals and groups have more or less status and income than others, and therefore have more or less ability to enter the market. Class theorists' image, on the other hand, is either-or; individuals and groups are either working class or ruling class, either owners of the means of production or workers, either exploited or exploiters, and the boundaries between these major class categories are sharply defined and discrete. When viewed as a continuum, not a dichotomy, as a finely graded hierarchy of rankings based on earnings, education, and occupational prestige, social inequality is often referred to as "socioeconomic status," not class. In the book, I use both terms interchangeably.

Both class and status theories have difficulty incorporating women—especially married women—into their framework. In Marxist theory, class is determined by position in the mode of production, so the productivity of women's household work has been at issue. Within status approaches, the central question is whether resources, however they are conceived—as honor or income—are equally shared, and to what extent a wife shares in her husband's occupational status.[30] Should women be considered as individuals for the purpose of understanding their class and status, or as members of families, especially wives. (In practice, if not in theory, wives' and husbands' statuses are strongly correlated.)

Pierre Bourdieu,[31] a contemporary sociologist whose ideas borrow from both Marx and Weber, has developed a conceptualization of class that not only assigns prestige an important place, but fully explores the subjective as well as the objective consequences of differences in class and status. Bourdieu views prestige as a form of symbolic "capital" and distinguishes between groups rich in symbolic capital and those rich in economic capital. He believes both forms of capital are important for shaping life experiences.

Bourdieu's analysis of symbolic capital is without peer. All status theorists consider differences in occupation and educational status to be important dimensions of social inequality, but Bourdieu takes an important extra step by recognizing differences within as well as between occupations and levels of education. A degree from Yale is not the same as a degree from the University of Baltimore, making partner in an elite New York law firm is not the same as making it in a small country law office, and teaching at Exeter is not the same as teaching at Eastwood High. Bourdieu understands that elite education teaches more than facts, figures, and finesse; it signals elite class membership and bestows an imprimatur that has both economic and symbolic value.

The Life Course: Change or Consistency

For Bourdieu, early socialization in the family is especially important for the acquisition of cultural capital, which along with "the manners and tastes resulting from good breeding"[32] includes "the art of conversation, musical culture or the sense of propriety, playing tennis or pronunciation."[33] In his view, the air of easy cultivation and grace that is intrinsic to cultural capital is available only to those who have inherited it from their families. The parvenu may have a scholastic knowledge of the arts, for example, but not the same self-confident, "natural," immediate aesthetic experience that is available to the person who was introduced early to "culture" (by culture, Bourdieu always means "high culture" or the culture of the dominant class). The aesthetic sense needed to appreciate "high culture" requires a certain basic knowledge and familiarity with cultural conventions that are learned only by children whose parents arrange for them to be learned. Thus according to Bourdieu, the family is the source of the necessary "means of appropriation" that enable one to decipher cultural codes; the family's cultural capital provides an environment in which appropriate tastes and other forms of symbolic capital are acquired, not through explicit teaching, but through gradual and imperceptible socialization.

By emphasizing early experience and socialization within the family, Bourdieu bucks the tide of much current social scientific thinking. Earlier "stage" theories of human development that emphasized the lasting effects of childhood experiences and socialization are now considered to be overly mechanistic and deterministic. More recent theories stress the possibilities for change and development over the course of a life. Challenges to more deterministic theories have come from several different quarters. First, objecting to portrayals of women as powerless victims, capable only of responding to the forces of capitalism and patriarchy, many feminist sociologists have begun to stress their capacity for independent action or "resistance." Second, reacting to portrayals of different groups—for example, poor black men or teenage mothers—as pathological and normless, sociologists have emphasized how individuals can subvert structural constraints and create their own systems of meaning and norms. Finally, with a large proportion of the population now living long and healthy lives, psychologists and sociologists have begun to study change and development in adulthood as well as in childhood.

Many social scientists have adopted a "life-course" framework to explore individual development and its interaction with a changing social and economic context; as C. Wright Mills put it over forty years ago, "we know that the individual lives, from one generation to the next, in some society; that he lives out a biography, and that he lives it out within some historical sequence. By the fact of his living he contributes, however minutely, to the shaping of this society and to the course of this history, even as he is made by society and by its historical push and shove."[34] In place of a one-sided deterministic of free-will emphasis, life-course approaches see the individual and her environment as "mutually constitutive,"[35] each responding to and shaping the other.

An overly deterministic view of development needed to be challenged, but the pendulum has swung too far. Now, the possibilities for change during an individual's life course are overstated, and structural constraints are understated; whether we like it or not, events outside our control play a large part in determining the contours of our lives. Wars, economic booms and busts, population explosions, migrations, and natural disasters and, more intimately, births, deaths, and divorces shape particular constellations of opportunities and obstacles that limit our choices throughout life. Gender, race, and social class constrain our choices in all spheres of life from birth to old age. Our parents' social class determines much of what we experience as children and how we come to see the larger world and our place in it. Children in working-class families live in working-class neighborhoods, attend working-class schools, play with working-class friends, and learn what is possible in the working-class world and what is not. By this means, the unattainable becomes undesirable, disappointment is avoided, and there are no hard feelings.

Parents do their best to equip us for the world as they know it by passing along their "stock of knowledge,"[36] which includes their understanding of their own and their children's place in the larger scheme of things. This stock of knowledge includes a commonsense understanding of the way things are and the way they should be, and consists of explicitly taught, formal knowledge that is imparted by social institutions—especially schools—and also tacitly understood, informal knowledge that is passed along incidentally in the normal course of everyday life. Our social class shapes what we take for granted as normal, and this includes different kinds of cultural capital for different classes. Thus, more middle-class than working-class children take SAT courses, attend college, travel to Europe, and learn to play a musical instrument because they can afford to, but also because their parents consider these activities to be right, natural, and necessary. Children in different classes, therefore, absorb much of this symbolic capital before they are old enough to make independent choices.

The social class origins of the women I interviewed for this study had shaped their childhoods and much of their later lives. With few exceptions, the daughters of working-class men worked in working-class jobs, were married to working-class husbands, and lived in working-class neighborhoods. Not a single daughter of an unskilled manual worker had attended college and about two in every three worked in unskilled, low-paid jobs. A handful of working-class daughters had moved into the middle class, entering professions and marrying professional men, but they were all daughters of foremen, self-employed men, or supervisors—men in the upper ranks of the working class. Conversely, every woman from solidly middle-class origins lived a solidly middle-class life, worked in a middle-class job, was married to a middle-class man, and lived in a middle-class neighborhood. As a group, these women enjoyed much higher family incomes than those earned by other women in the study, including two working-class daughters who had moved into upper-level managerial positions. Social class origins, therefore, had long-term consequences in women's lives.

From Theory to Practice: Defining Class in This Study

Deciding who was and who was not working-class for the purposes of the study on which this book was based was difficult. Should the line be drawn between supervisors and non-supervisors, manual and non-manual workers, elites and non-elites, owners and workers? Or is there no line, but a continuum of prestige? How to take account of social class over the life course? How to consider husbands' social class? And how to accommodate differences in lifestyle or prestige?

As it happened, the sample could be divided into two groups with very different access to both economic and symbolic capital: a minority who could be described as upper middle class and a majority who were working poor, working, or lower middle class. This split reflects Baltimore's demographic history: following the race riots in the 1960s, the middle class fled the city, leaving a handful of upper middle-class enclaves, a small number of lower-middle-class neighborhoods, and a large working-class area that has grown poorer in the intervening years. In most cases, the women's education was the best indicator of lifestyle differences between college-educated women and non-college-educated women. This was not because education in itself was so important but, as Bourdieu and others realized, education signaled differences in women's social class origins. Most of the college-educated women in the study lived in prestigious neighborhoods, were the daughters as well as the wives of middle-class men, and, along with middle-class taste in clothing, furnishings, and other lifestyle characteristics, their degree certified rather than created their social standing.

Because a college degree still permits access into the middle class, and because it marked off a definite lifestyle boundary between women, I treated it as the dividing line between the working and middle class. Unfortunately, as with any other artificial boundary, some loose ends were left and some important distinctions were obscured. One of these was the distinction between women with a teaching degree and women with other professional degrees. In terms of lifestyle, a teaching degree was worth less than other degrees; teachers (with the exception of Marie, who was from a middle-class background) had a similar style of life to secretaries and other office workers: they were married to men in similar occupations, lived in similar neighborhoods, and sent their children to local public schools. A second distinction lost was between women who dropped out of school when they were very young and women who dropped out later, closer to the end of high school. Women who dropped out in ninth or tenth grade or even earlier had often been in special education classes, and, compared with other women, they more often came from families troubled by alcoholism, violence, and mental illness. Compared with other women—even other dropouts—they were more often poor and more often rented houses or apartments that were lacking in amenities, small, unattractive, poorly furnished, and in bad neighborhoods. Although their life situations were often different from other women's, I have considered them to be working class, rather than underclass or poor working class.

In some cases, defining women's current social class was problematic; in others, it was their social class of origin. Mona and Rhonda, for example, presented a challenge when it came to describing their current class position. Both women were daughters of working-class men (manual workers), and both graduated from high school, then trained as beauticians. Later, however, they took slightly different paths. Both still worked as beauticians and were self-employed, but Rhonda's business was larger and more formally organized; she rented commercial space and employed a number of other women, a receptionist, a shampoo girl, and other hairdressers. Mona, on the other hand, employed no one and operated her business from the basement of her home. Rhonda was more affluent; she lived in a large, modern house in a new middle-class suburb. Mona had lived in the same working-class neighborhood all her life. But, although she was more affluent, Rhonda was not a member of the same status group as the women I considered to be middle class, her occupation was low in prestige, she lived in an area that was not particularly prestigious, and she lacked the cultural capital possessed by most of the middle-class women. For these reasons, with some misgivings, I considered both Rhonda and Mona to be working class.

Marie and Connie, both teachers, were another example. Marie, the daughter of a professor, was married to a successful businessman, lived in a prestigious suburb, and taught in a high-status private school. By contrast, Connie, the daughter of a factory foreman, was married to a computer operator who moonlighted as a coach, lived in a modest house in a middle-income neighborhood, and taught in an inner-city elementary school. Both women had degrees, so could be considered middle class. However, Marie's social origins (and her upper-middle-class marriage) gave her economic and social options that were not available to Connie. She had the cultural capital that made her attractive to a prestigious private school that offered generous job conditions and more autonomy than was available to Connie as a public school teacher, she lived in a prestigious neighborhood, and she had the resources to send her children to private schools.

Lillian was another exception. Lillian was the daughter of a foreman, had a fine arts degree but worked as a teacher's aide, a job she could have gotten with a high school diploma. Her husband had a medical degree but did not practice medicine. Instead, he scoured the countryside for antiques that he restored and resold for a very small income. With six children, the couple lived as close to a subsistence lifestyle as they could, but in a large house in a prestigious area. Because she had a degree (even though she had chosen not to use it professionally), I considered Lillian to be middle class as an adult, but working class in origin.

I decided on women's social class of origin using their fathers' occupations (working mothers were not yet the norm). This was relatively straightforward because most fathers were traditional blue-collar workers. But there were exceptions. Beth's father, for example, worked as a butcher for a grocery chain but then took a job managing a liquor store. Dawn's father was a mechanic who saved his money to buy a small farm, then a small grocery business. They lived on the farm, and Dawn's mother ran the business while her father continued to work as a mechanic. Both parents took some college courses over the years but never graduated. Pam's father was a dental technician who was trained under the GI Bill. He eventually established his own business, employed an assistant, and made dentures, servicing the dental needs of their small town. Pam's mother worked as a secretary for the government and completed a college degree in the evenings.

Pam's, Dawn's, and Beth's parents were not typically working class. On the other hand, they were not in the same social stratum as the families of women whose origins I considered to be middle class; none had worked in professional or managerial jobs, and although Pam's mother gained a degree after many years of studying part time, she was unable to translate it into a new profession. Finally, I decided to consider them working class.

Some women were socially mobile, so I need to explain how I refer to them throughout the book. For most women, it was unproblematic; most women who were working class in origin were working class as adults, and all women who were middle class in origin were middle class as adults.[37] In a handful of cases, however, "working-class daughters" became middle-class adults. In the text, I generally refer to these women in terms of their origin. When I statistically compare the women's jobs, however, these half-dozen socially mobile women are included with other middle-class women. (Leaving them in or out of the comparisons made no difference to the statistical results.) As we will see, the women who had been socially mobile had a qualitatively different life experience from other women.

Sampling and Interviewing

The women I chose for the study were mothers whose children were selected many years ago to take part in a study of the social, emotional, and educational development of students in the Baltimore school system. This larger study—the Beginning School Study—has been in the field since 1980 and as of this writing is in its twentieth year. Its original sampling was carefully designed to represent Baltimore city's elementary school population. In 1980, 800 children who were entering first grade in twenty city public schools were selected for study. A "two-stage random sampling procedure" was used to select the participants; schools were chosen according to the racial composition and socioeconomic status of their student body (mostly African American or mostly white, mostly blue collar or mostly white collar). Then, once the twenty schools had been selected, children were randomly sampled from them to obtain a sample that was representative by race and socioeconomic status.

Over the years, vigorous and successful efforts have been made to stay in touch with the original 800 families, and at the time I began my study, almost 700 were still participating. From this sample of 700, I selected women who were white, married or living with a partner, and who were working in paid employment for at least twenty hours a week. Using these criteria yielded a pool of ninety-three women; this ultimately shrank to eighty-one because two women preferred not to participate, seven had moved from the East Coast, and three were unable to schedule an interview. The sample is not strictly random, but its method of selection avoided some of the shortcomings of purposive or "snowball" sampling (where one study participant recommends another who recommends another and so on). The list of women who fit the profile for selection was exhaustive, and the only thing all the women had in common was that in 1980 they had sent a child to a Baltimore city public school. The sample that resulted was a good cross section; in terms of income and education, they were similar to white married women in their age group in Baltimore and the United States, and they worked in all but two of the Department of Labor's "twenty leading occupations for women." And the indirect mode of recruiting—through the experience of their children rather than some shared action or characteristic of the women themselves—meant that the study was able to reach women who are often missed because they are unable to read, for example, or because they have alcohol or other drug problems, or because they never volunteer for studies such as this.

The study focused on white women for two main reasons. First, race and ethnicity are such significant dimensions of difference among women that black and other minority women's experiences deserve study in their own right. Second, with the exception of a developing interest in cultural studies and women's studies, poor and working-class white women (and men) have spent several decades pushed into the background in both research and policy arenas. During this time, middle-class white women have had a clear and persistent public voice, and black and hispanic women have also begun to be heard. But still, the voices of poor and working-class whites are missing.

The sample was designed to explore similarities and differences in women's work and family experiences based on class. The women were similar on a number of important dimensions; they were the same race, roughly the same age, living in the same city and historical period, and sharing three major life roles—as parents, wives, and paid workers. Because other differences were minimized, the effects of social class are not obscured by other differences such as race, marital status, or age. And because women with a wide range of educational credentials and occupational skills participated, I could explore differences among working-class women as well as those between working- and middle-class women.

To help assure that questions were appropriate for women with widely different levels of formal education I pretested a preliminary version of the interview on nine women—three women who had dropped out of high school, three high school graduates, and three college graduates—and made several changes as a result. The final interviews included a wide range of questions—about equally weighted between closed- and open-ended—as well as extensive unstructured dialogue focusing on the women's family, school, and work experiences, as both children and adults. On average, the interviews lasted two and a half hours; they were tape-recorded and later transcribed. Most of the interviews took place in the women's homes, although six were held on the job, and three were in restaurants.

The Women

Of the eighty-one women in the final sample, the sixty-three who were of working-class origin take center stage in the book; the remaining eighteen women of middle-class origin appear only on occasion for purposes of illustration. I used the women's fathers' occupations to identify their social class of origin, and regarded women whose fathers worked in routine white-collar or blue-collar occupations as working class and women whose fathers worked in managerial-professional occupations as middle class. It is difficult to define the social class of families where both adults work, but relatively few of the women's mothers had consistently worked, and it remains unclear to what extent married women's employment affected family status in the 1950s and 1960s. It seemed best, therefore, to use women's fathers' occupations because they could be consistently applied to all the women except two, whose fathers' occupations were unknown. In these cases, I used the women's best guess.

There were wide differences in taste, affluence, and prestige between middle- and working-class women. Middle-class women lived in spacious privacy, their large houses separated from the street and from one another by shaded gardens or acres of well-clipped lawn. Interviews with them were private, uninterrupted by children or husbands, and held in hushed family rooms or kitchens where the only tangible evidence of other family members was a schedule on the refrigerator, photographs on the mantle, or the sound of a telephone being answered in another room. By contrast, most of the working-class women lived in modest houses in working- or lower-middle-class neighborhoods, the poorer among them in cramped quarters huddled together on narrow city streets or in barren apartment complexes tethered to the freeway. Their interviews took place in the hubbub of family life, with children—sometimes grandchildren—fighting, teasing, crying, and demanding attention, and husbands watching television nearby.

At work, too, middle-class women enjoyed more space and privacy, and could close doors and speak freely. This, no doubt, was the reason middle-class women were more likely to conduct their interviews at work. For working-class women, interviews at work were rarely an option.

With very few exceptions, these differences in how women lived and worked were more closely related to their social origins and to their husbands' occupations than to their own. Women of affluent middle-class origin invariably lived affluent middle-class lives, whereas the only women of working-class origin whose lifestyles were affluent middle class were the three women who worked in high-status managerial-professional occupations.

Because the women were selected on the basis of their children's age, not their own (they all had at least one child who had entered kindergarten in 1980), their ages varied between thirty-three and fifty-two, with an average age of forty-two. The more highly educated women were slightly older; on average, college graduates were almost forty-five, high school graduates were forty-one, and women who had less than a high school diploma were forty. Their average family size was between two and three children, but four working-class women and one middle-class woman had four or more children. Working-class women's families were slightly larger than middle-class women's, but the difference was small; they certainly did not conform to the stereotype of large working-class families; nine working-class women had only one child, and most women had three or fewer. Most of the women had only one or two children living at home, but six women had four resident children and one had six. Thirteen women had children under ten, three of whom were preschool age.

Thirty-four of the sixty-three working-class women were high school graduates. Among these thirty-four, seven had obtained their diploma via the GED (General Equivalency Diploma, an alternative high school diploma), five had trained in cosmetology after high school, and one had an associate's degree from a community college. Six women of working-class origin had completed at least a bachelor's degree, and three of them had graduate degrees. Among the middle-class women, eleven had a bachelor's degree, one had an associate's degree, and six had graduate degrees—one of these was an MBA, one a Ph.D.

Very few women were laborers, the male archetype of working-class work. Instead, they worked in traditionally female jobs as clerks, receptionists, secretaries, cashiers, teacher's aides, keypunch operators, food-service workers, bookkeepers, beauticians, housecleaners, and childcare providers. A few women worked in jobs that were not stereotypically female, such as assemblers, packers, or school bus drivers. One woman, Carolyn, worked as a "courtesy clerk," an occupation completely new to me (it refers to the person at the grocery store who bags groceries and returns "go-backs," those items we all furtively discard in the wrong place when we decide we don't want them after all). Three women worked in two jobs, and one woman had three jobs—as a paperhanger, a childcare worker, and the lead singer in a country music band. Seven women were self-employed; three were day-care providers, two were hairdressers, one was a co-owner of a burglar alarm business, and one was a housecleaner. Three of the six working-class women who had joined the middle class worked as teachers; three were in professional-managerial positions.

The middle-class women included teachers, a psychologist, a dietitian, a social worker, and a sales representative. Two middle-class women owned their own businesses; one of these was small scale, but the other was a large company employing several dozen professional staff. One woman was a research scientist.

Interpretation: Combining Qualitative and Quantitative Methods

Until recently, the division between quantitative and qualitative methods in the social sciences has been sharply drawn; in general, researchers used one approach and frowned on the other. Now, however, acknowledging that some phenomena lend themselves to "variable analysis," while others do not, researchers have begun to use both sets of techniques in the same studies. Together, the methods can promote a more complete understanding than either can on its own. By examining patterns, quantitative research highlights regularities and relationships; by examining concrete, heterogeneous experience, qualitative research highlights how those same relationships are experienced and interpreted by individual human actors.

For this study, it seemed clear that a quantitative approach, where variables are strictly defined ahead of time, could not capture how women think, act, and feel about their work and family lives. My own feelings about work and family were complicated and shifting, and I doubted they would fit into neat, mutually exclusive categories. Furthermore, as a graduate student working on surveys, I had come to appreciate that quantitative analysis often leaves out the most interesting data—for example, thoughts hastily scribbled in the margins of completed questionnaires or unusual cases (called "outliers") that are usually omitted. And the studies that I believed most successfully illuminate complex and ambivalent feelings about work, family, and social class—for example, *The Hidden Injuries of Class* and *Worlds of Pain*[38]—were rich in qualitative detail, not statistical analysis.

There are advantages, however, to quantifying data. Group comparisons are more compelling when statistics can be used to evaluate them; because the sample of women in this study was chosen to be as representative as possible, statistics would strengthen the claim that class differences were not peculiar to this particular group of women. Furthermore, by using questionnaire items that have been widely used to assess men's and middle-class women's experiences, I could assess how appropriate these items are for working-class women.

For these reasons, I used both qualitative and quantitative techniques. The women were selected to be as representative as possible, and in the interviews, I used predetermined questions (some developed for this study, and some borrowed from published surveys)[39] as well as discourse that was spontaneous or elicited by very general questions. My goal was that this combination of methods would reveal patterns of commonality and difference in the fabric of women's lives but at the same time would honor the integrity and uniqueness of each individual woman's experience.

Combining methods was sometimes frustrating, but ultimately illuminating. What should be done when, as sometimes happened, the two sources of data frankly disagreed—for example, when the woman whose questionnaire responses showed her to be very satisfied with her job, but who later told me she hated it? Or when the woman who scored the maximum possible score on a scale for "work commitment" later said she would quit her job in a heartbeat if she could? Finally, as I hope will become clear, I realized that these contradictions signaled real complexities and ambiguities in women's feelings that may have eluded the grasp of a single method.

Any interview—no matter what kind—can capture only how a woman is thinking and feeling at a fleeting moment in her life; formal questions tap into her opinions, unstructured discourse reflects what is on her mind, and a life history touches those events in her life that are foregrounded, all at that moment. How a woman responds today may be different from how she responds tomorrow, much less next week or next year—not because the question is "unreliable," but because the meaning of different events is constantly shifting as women construct and reconstruct, or, as Mary Catherine Bateson[40] describes it, compose their lives. Which response is "true"? The answer, of course, is "none" and "all," depending on which kind of truth we are interested in. Each response reflects a feeling, or the meaning of an event at the moment of the interview, but perhaps none mirror an ongoing, objective reality.

We describe our own feelings, actions, and beliefs and those of others from our own point of view, which is unique, and is available to no one else; similarly, others' descriptions of us and of themselves are from their point of view. Interpretation must take this into account. Thus when a woman says, "My husband approves of me working," does he really approve? Or is it just that she believes that he approves? In itself, this is important information because it gives us access to how a woman views ("constructs") her world, which may or may not be the same as how someone else would view it, or with "the truth." The following excerpt illustrates this. One of the interview questions asked women whether they agreed or disagreed that their husband would mind if they earned more money than he did. Martha, a home day-care provider, was emphatic. "I strongly disagree [that he would mind]," she said. She repeated this when I asked if her husband would mind if she had a higher-status job: "He's not like that." Later, when her husband, Alan, a carpenter, came home, I asked him how he would feel if Martha earned more money than he did, or had a higher-status job. "It would bother me a little," he said. "We know some people who have this kind of situation within the family, and ah, it might affect me slightly. We know for a fact that Karen and Tracy have a problem with that." Martha joined in, "He goes to school [and his wife says], 'I make the money and I make the decisions.'" Alan went on, "It depends on the individuals. I don't think it would bother me much that my wife earned more money, but if she were—like if I'm a carpenter and she's a doctor, type of thing, that might be a little difficult for me personally to deal with. There are other men who [it] wouldn't affect them at all. And it's funny because periodically we get into discussions about this kind of thing at work. Because I know several men that I work around whose wives make considerable more money than they do, and have some positions, and they seem perfectly happy and comfortable with it."

Martha blamed difficulties on the woman: "I think it has a lot to do with the woman's attitude toward it. I think [there's a problem] if she lords it over him, and says, 'I make more money than you do,' and keeps rubbing it in. If all the money went into a bank account and it's our money and it's for our benefit . . . and it's teamwork, I think that's what makes a difference." Alan gave an example of another friend: "Ritchie has been married three times and what he earns is his money and what she earns is her money, and she pays her bills and they pay certain bills that are joint. This is just the way he is." "That is not a marriage to me," said Martha. "It's not a partnership." Alan agreed: "It's taking advantage of a joint income tax deduction."

Martha's response to the question was "objectively" wrong: in fact, it would bother Alan quite a bit if she had higher status (or, more exactly, at that moment, he felt it would bother him). Taken alone as the literal truth—in spite of the most impressive statistics that might be brought to bear on it—her response would be misleading. In the context of the wider discussion, however, we reach an understanding of how Martha sees her world that might otherwise escape us. We learn that she believes a woman's attitude to be important in how her husband reacts to her work, and we can perhaps infer, too, that were she to be offered a higher-status job, she would make sure she didn't "lord it over" her husband the way their friend's wife lorded it over him. The contradiction between her own and her husband's responses raises questions about the responses of other women to this question: were women right when they said their husbands wouldn't mind if they had a higher-paid, higher-status job? Would their husbands even know how they would feel without having had the experience?

Two Worlds: Class Differences at Work and at Home

Although middle-class women appear in the book from time to time, its major emphasis is on working-class women. However, as part of the original project, I compared specific aspects of women's work and family experiences and found both commonalities and differences; I summarize some of these results here.

Both middle- and working-class women derived psychological as well as practical rewards from working.[41] Middle-class women were more likely to find their work fulfilling, but even women in unskilled jobs found that work added a different and satisfying dimension to their lives; it introduced them to new people and experiences and brought them independence, self-reliance, and a sense of achievement.

As expected, working-class women's objective experiences of work had little in common with those of middle-class women; but more surprising was the chasm in job experiences between high school graduates and women who had dropped out—this was especially true for women who worked in unskilled factory and service jobs. These women earned much less than other women, were eligible for fewer benefits, and had much less autonomy, control, and flexibility on the job; a 7:30 A.M. start meant 7:30 A.M., not 7:35 A.M., and time off was hard, if not impossible, to arrange. But most important of all, they were most often subjected to demeaning treatment—disdain even—by their supervisors, other workers, and customers. They had to struggle daily for respect.

Women who were dropouts felt their lack of credentials keenly (two had kept it a secret, even from their children). It pained and angered them when their employers and coworkers devalued their work experience and favored women with more education. Judy, for example, sometimes worked with college students: "I've come across some of them when you try to tell them something, you say, 'Hey look, this is an easy way to do it.' And they get nasty with you. I had one girl talk really nasty to me. And I said: 'Let me tell you something, hon, I have a son that's as old as you and he don't disrespect me. And I'm not going to stand here and let you disrespect me.'" And Laura was overlooked at work in favor of a younger, less experienced—but better educated—woman. "It's like, the one girl I work with," Laura complained, "she's only been with the company for a year! And she's the one that got all the designated recognition where I didn't! All because she's got a high school diploma. She's got a high school diploma and two years' college behind her. I still say that's what it is! And nobody's going to change my mind about it."

Because of their inflexible and sometimes appalling job conditions, work spilled over into family life differently for women such as Laura, even compared with other working-class women. Working-class women as a whole didn't approve of "bringing work home," but the women in unskilled jobs brought home an aching fatigue that, combined with lack of flexibility in their working hours, made it harder for them than for other women to juggle work and family responsibilities.

Feelings about work transcended class. A majority of both working- and middle-class women longed to do work that was finer, better, and more rewarding. According to the psychologist Erik Erickson,[42] the primary challenge of the middle years is to be "generative"; it's in this stage that we first think seriously about what we have achieved, and what we will leave behind for the next generation. This was true for many of the women in the study, both middle- and working-class. After the hectic years of bearing and raising children, they had time at last to pause and reflect on the larger meaning of their lives. As part of this process, many women were looking at work with fresh eyes, seeing it, often for the first time, as a possible source of personal fulfillment.

Regardless of their social class, many women longed to do work that would allow them to express their own particular talent or to pursue a personal interest—work in which they could express their deeper selves or make a difference in the world. They wished they were better equipped to find such work or even to know what it might be. Only a handful of women in the entire sample—and only one working-class daughter—could be said to have achieved success in this.

A small number of both middle- and working-class women said they would prefer to be full-time homemakers. These women were successful at work and quite enjoyed their jobs but felt they would be more fulfilled at home; when they evaluated paid work against unpaid work at home—in terms of where they were most needed, for example, or what they most enjoyed or were best at—work at home won out. Proportionately more working-class than middle-class women believed they would be more fulfilled either at home or doing volunteer work.

Regardless of their social class, most women worked what the sociologist Arlie Hochschild calls the "second shift" of housework.[43] On average, women put in almost two hours a day doing housework and childcare compared with their husbands' average of less than an hour. Only a handful of husbands (all working class) took an equal share in housework and childcare. And for a number of working-class women, housework and childcare was just the tip of the iceberg. The shorter generational cycling of working-class families had thrust some women into early grandparenthood, and several were caring full-time for their grandchildren. None of the middle-class women was a grandmother.[44]

A number of women were taking care of their own aging parents; here, too, social class made a difference. Because they more often lived near their parents and in-laws, and because they were unable to afford paid care, working-class women's caretaking was more hands-on. Maureen was a good example; because she and her husband couldn't afford to place her stepfather in a nursing home, they went to his house several times a week to bathe and dress him. Middle-class women's caretaking was more managerial; Eileen, for example, managed her parents' investments, and Denise, an account executive for a newspaper, supervised her parents' home care from a distance.

The worries that come with parenting adolescent children cut across class lines. Most women worried about their teenagers' behavior, but working-class women— forced to live in more threatening neighborhoods, to raise their children on smaller paychecks, and to send them to more troubled schools, worried more—and with good reason—about drugs and about their children's school progress.

These were just some of the similarities and differences I found, but they begin to show the diverging lives led by working-class and middle-class women. The pages ahead will shed more light on these similarities and differences, and also on important differences among working-class women. Chapter three begins with snapshots that illustrate the range of working-class women's jobs. Many of these were service jobs in what sociologists call the "secondary labor market," that sector of the labor market that lacks job protections and security. As we see in this chapter, these secondary labor market jobs provided welcome work opportunities for many women, especially those with few job skills and limited education. We see too, however, that jobs in this sector were poorly paid, usually inflexible, lacking in benefits, and often oppressive. The chapter explores at some length the unequal conditions women experienced at work, and their often surprising reactions to these conditions.

Chapter four uses case studies to illustrate the women's diverse experiences of work. Some women yearned for work that could become an important source of meaning in their lives, other women had found this meaning in their family work and would prefer not to do paid work at all, and others were content to have jobs that were enjoyable and interesting, but not a major source of meaning. The case studies show that work fulfillment was much more elusive than job satisfaction.

Chapter five explores the women's orientations to work, and its satisfactions and rewards. It shows that although their feelings about work were complex and often contradictory, most women derived important benefits from working. It shows, too, that because most working-class women worked *for* their families, they experienced little role conflict between work and family. Instead, however, because of inflexible job conditions and equally inflexible social institutions, they frequently faced practical conflicts.

A number of women were disappointed in work because their abilities were wasted. In chapter six, we learn one of the reasons for this: few women had worked consistently consistently enough to accumulate the skills and experience that would qualify them for more rewarding work.

Most women's workforce participation over the years had been dictated by their family caring work, and, as we learn in chapter seven, they were still doing this work. The chapter contrasts the caring work of working- and middle-class women, and points out that working-class women's caring work—both at home and at work—was more hands-on and physical than the caring work of middle-class women.

The fifties and sixties are often viewed as halcyon days, and they were for many families. However, many women were poor as children, and some had experienced poverty throughout their entire lives. Because this darker side of postwar family life is less well known, and because a number of women's well-being continued to be affected by poverty, chapter eight explores their experiences in some depth.

One of the consequences of childhood poverty was a heightened risk of dropping out of high school. Chapter nine looks at the relationship between poverty and dropping out, and it interprets women's subjective reasons for dropping out in the context of the difficult and painful school and home experiences that often accompanied poverty.

Chapter ten introduces the women who graduated from high school and the handful who went on to college and explores how their social class position as children had shaped their education and career choices. Far enough removed from poverty to make high school graduation possible, but not far enough to permit them to make "impractical" choices, they had learned to use common sense, and to give up ambitions that were "unrealistic." Unrealistic, that is, for working-class girls.

Chapter eleven, the final chapter, argues that education must be made more genuinely available to all women throughout their lives. But it also argues that improvements in education count for little unless job conditions are also improved and income inequality is reduced. Summing up, the chapter concludes that, in an anti–big-government era, the union movement offers working-class women their last, best hope for improving their work conditions and securing at least some measure of the economic justice they deserve.

Life on the
J o b

It's total patient care. Other than two or three things, we do everything the nurses do, [but] they're gonna start a nurse that was hired at eighteen dollars an hour; I'm making seven. . . . There's a big difference in the pay scale.

—Wanda

The really exhausting and the really repulsive labors instead of being better paid than others, are almost invariably paid the worst of all. . . . The more revolting the occupation, the more certain it is to receive the minimum of remuneration. . . . The hardships and the earnings, instead of being directly proportional, as in any just arrangements of society they would be, are gener-ally in an inverse ratio to one another.

—John Stuart Mill, *Principles of Political Economy*

Her job sure had its repulsive moments, Wanda thought; it was dirty work, and heavy. Not everyone would want to do it; she had been stuck with dirty needles, thrown up on, peed on, and worse. The hardest thing was cleaning up the dead bodies; it was scary at night when no one else was around, and it was really upsetting when the body was a child's. She was trained to handle sexual abuse cases, but training doesn't help much when you see a six-month-old baby come in, its poor, tiny body broken, blood-ied, and torn. She'd never get used to that.

Normal messes didn't bother her. The sight of a soiled bed or a soiled patient was still not one of her favorites, but at least now she could deal with it without wanting to throw up. And the lifting was no problem; she was strong, and could heft a 200-pound patient onto a gurney, push him around to X-ray, and heave him off again, no prob-lem. Besides, someone had to take care of this stuff.

What really bugged her were the nurses who looked down their noses at her. Just because she does the dirty work, they're better than she is? No way. As a matter of fact, there's only one or two things they can do that she can't, and then it's only the nurse in charge that stops her. Who do they think they are anyway?

Two Classes of Women Workers

During the last decades of the twentieth century, the provision of services stimulated remarkable growth in the U.S. labor force, to such an extent that at the beginning of the twenty-first century, jobs like Wanda's—service jobs—are what most people do, especially most women. Of the more than 70 million new jobs created between 1964 and 1999, 43 million went to women, and 30 million were in services—8 million, like Wanda's, in health services alone. In fact, jobs filled by women accounted for four in every five new jobs.[1]

The new service economy has been kind to women, but not equally kind to all women. Highly educated and skilled professional women who are trained to operate sophisticated computers, trade on the stock market, and practice law and medicine have done extremely well; one in every two graduates from medical and law schools are now women,[2] and women are awarded more than 50 percent of master's degrees.[3] Affluent and busy, pushed for time but not cash, these women workers and their families in turn generate the need for domestic and other support services: their meals must be cooked, their houses cleaned, and their children cared for; their aging bodies need careful maintenance and cosmetics, and their aging parents need in-home care.

The economy has been less kind to the millions of nonprofessional women, such as Wanda, who cater to these needs. They have jobs, but while the wages of women with college degrees have soared, theirs have declined: between 1973 and 1999, the average real hourly wage of workers with a college degree went up by 6 percent, and advanced-degree holders' wages rose even faster, by 13 percent. But over this same time period, wages outside the professional middle class declined: for workers with a high school diploma, they fell by 12 percent, and for workers with no diploma by a startling 26 percent.[4]

These changes have produced two classes of women workers: low-paid service providers like Wanda who do the cooking, cleaning, and caring-for-others work that has always fallen to working-class women, and well-paid professional women who have joined men in high-income professional and managerial jobs. And because low-earning women are usually married to low-earning men, and high-earning women to high-earning men, this split is even wider for families than for individuals; married professional and managerial workers bring home two high salaries to create mega-money marriages, while unskilled and semiskilled workers struggle to make ends meet.

Have these millions of new jobs reduced inequality in our society? Not at all. The yawning gap between rich and poor is wider now than ever. In a perfectly equal society, each fifth of the population would receive one-fifth of the income. In 1995, however, the lowest-paid one-fifth of male U.S. workers earned only 3.4 percent of the total male income, while the highest-paid fifth earned close to 50 percent, fourteen-and-a-half times as much. For women, the difference was even greater. That same year, the lowest-paid fifth of women earned only 3.1 percent of the total female earnings, while the highest-paid earned 47 percent—over fifteen times as much.[5]

Such extreme inequality in earnings is damning evidence of an unjust society, but the story of inequality doesn't end there. As Marx, John Stuart Mill, and other philosophers long ago pointed out, low-paid jobs are usually the worst jobs, so added to the injury of low pay is the insult of "repulsive" work. But are the new jobs really "repulsive"? We could be excused for being confused about this; on the one hand, we read that service jobs are low-paid and dead-end, but also that most of the new jobs are "overwhelmingly . . . good jobs." In any case, how can one tell what is a good job?

This question was explored in the late eighties by Christopher Jencks, Lauri Perlman, and Lee Rainwater,[6] who pointed out serious shortcomings in how sociologists, economists, and psychologists evaluate job quality. In most sociological studies, they observed, researchers use an occupation's prestige as the measure of a job's desirability, but this method has limited usefulness because it is based on occupations, not jobs. Using this method, which ignores differences in prestige, pay, and job conditions *within* occupations, researchers often find that men's and women's jobs are equal even though men earn more and, in most occupations—at least those they share with women—have more prestigious positions.

Economists overcome this problem by ranking jobs according to their pay, but this method also has limitations; for one thing, it assumes that pay is the only—or at least the most important—determinant of a good job. For some workers, Jencks and his colleagues argue, status and other job conditions might be subjectively more important than pay, and these are ignored when pay is the only criterion. Unlike economists, psychologists pay attention to people's subjective assessments of their jobs, judging them on the basis of how satisfying they are to the people who work in them. But because most workers rate their own jobs favorably, using workers' own assessments is also problematic. An example from my own study is that even though they earned only a quarter as much, women who worked as aides, janitors, or bus drivers in the school system were no less satisfied with their jobs than women who worked as teachers. Can we conclude, then, that their jobs are just as good? Similarly, women are often reported to be more satisfied with their jobs than men. Can we conclude that women's jobs are better than men's? Hardly.

To overcome these problems, Jencks and his colleagues decided to find out what job conditions were considered desirable by the *average* worker, not just workers in one occupation. To do this, they scoured the literature and identified forty-eight job conditions that are known to influence job satisfaction; these included pay and benefits, but also training and promotion opportunities, physical conditions such as whether the work is dirty or heavy, and other conditions such as having the freedom to choose one's hours. Having identified these job characteristics, they asked over a thousand men and women to rate their jobs in terms of their "goodness," and in terms of the extent to which they offered these forty-eight desirable job conditions. Having done this, they determined which of the forty-eight conditions were most strongly related to positive job ratings and then assigned weights to these conditions according to their average importance to *all* workers. Thus, they developed an index of job quality based on how a large number of workers in many different occupations ranked the importance of different job conditions.

Fourteen job characteristics strongly affected how workers evaluated their jobs. Listed in order of importance, these were earnings, educational requirements, number of hours worked, on-the-job training, clean work, weeks of vacation, setting one's own hours, freedom from close supervision, having a union contract, freedom from repetitive work, being a federal employee, being a state or local employee, position in the chain of command, and job security. Pay was the single most important characteristic affecting how jobs were rated, but non-monetary characteristics quickly outweighed salary. To illustrate, having clean work and being able to decide one's own hours, taken together, were more important than earnings, and the same was true for clean work and freedom from close supervision.

When they considered the non-monetary characteristics of jobs along with earnings, the authors found that inequalities based on gender, race, and class were heightened. Male workers in their study earned twice as much as females, but they also had twice as many non-monetary job benefits. (Women's jobs were inferior to men's on twelve of the fourteen measures in their index.) According to this method of evaluating job quality, therefore, men's jobs were not just twice as good as women's, as pay differences would suggest, but four times as good. Women would have needed to earn four times as much as they actually earned before their jobs could be considered as good as men's. The result for race was similar; pay differences between whites and non-whites accounted for only one-fifth of the difference in how blacks and whites rated their jobs.

Class inequality was also magnified. Researchers have long known that income and occupational status are largely "inherited"—in other words that the income and occupational status of children is disturbingly similar to that of their parents. But Jencks and his colleagues found that non-monetary aspects of jobs were even more strongly inherited than income: "Measures of monetary inequality therefore underestimate the overall degree of inequality of labor market outcomes," the authors concluded. "While all personal advantages confer non-monetary as well as monetary benefits, this seems to be particularly true for family background and schooling."

The upshot of their findings is that Marx and John Stuart Mill were both correct; low pay is just the tip of the iceberg of job inequality. As adults, working-class children fare worse in the labor market than children of higher-status parents, not just in terms of income and status but in terms of other conditions that workers value—for example, being able to do clean work, having freedom from close supervision, and having control over one's hours. Inequality, therefore, consists of differences in access to pay and what some sociologists call "social honor," but also to valued and rewarding conditions on the job.[7]

Researchers have found that as well as influencing job satisfaction, job conditions affect workers in other important ways, both positive and negative. For example, studies have shown that workers who do autonomous, complex, and challenging work develop their skills over time so that they become able to cope with more challenging, complex problems.[8] And countless studies show that stress on the job can not only impair health but shorten life; in particular, these studies consistently show the importance for health of being able to exercise control.[9]

Yet when research articles on work and job conditions tell us that certain job conditions—"autonomy," "challenge," and "variety," for example—are important, they rarely tell us how these conditions are actually and concretely experienced by women and men in the real world of the workplace, part of what Blumer calls the "empirical social world."[10] In the empirical social world, workers experience job conditions such as autonomy in relation to a particular boss or work process that makes particular demands in a particular context. To illustrate these particular, concrete experiences in the real social world of the workplace, we will turn now to some snapshots of women's daily lives on the job. For millions of women, a day's work still consists of office work: filing, typing, and bookkeeping.

Filing, Typing, Bookkeeping

Most of the women with a high school diploma worked in traditionally female pink- and white-collar office jobs as receptionists, secretaries, or clerks. Dorothy was one of these women: she described her job as a secretary and telephonist for a company that repaired heavy equipment:

> I'm on a switchboard with sixteen incoming lines. I open the board at eight o'clock. I answer those phones from eight to twelve. I go to lunch. I come back and I continue to answer them through that day. I do computer programming, data entry, billing, letters of all types, sizes and forms, dictation, transcribing off a transcriber. I also keep all the records and billing for a training class that is one day a week. . . . And from two o'clock on, I continue to answer the incoming lines. I do transcribing for the afternoon, stuff that's been left over from the morning. I do the correspondence and answer the mail that's come in that day. And I keep an evaluation chart for incoming telephone calls, for every department.

Rachael worked as a "collateral control specialist" for a bank; she was responsible for the paperwork associated with loans. "I release the documents for paid-in-full loans," she said, "or try to get the documents in for the collateral that we're holding. For example, if you get an installment loan and you're using your car as collateral, then I have to get the title work done and have a lien placed on that title." Checks often disappeared and had to be tracked down. "It might take me a couple of hours sometimes to find [a missing check]. The worst part is you may never find it. That's the worst part. I spent almost seven hours looking for one check, and we never did find it, which means it just got misplaced, or it was thrown away. Those things happen."

Jill was a secretary for an office furniture business that had recently been sold. "I do commissions," she said, "I do invoicing, I do all the ordering, I do ordering for supplies and I do all the typing for the salespeople. I'm the only one that types in that whole place. I answer the phones." Right now, she was learning to operate a computer system. "The thing's been sitting there for seven years. None of us have had computer experience, so we're learning; we have to learn on our own." She and her three coworkers had been told to put everything on the computer, including the salesmen's commissions. They had just assessed the results for the first month, and "nothing proved out for the whole month. Nothing! When we started this month, half the commissions were in the computer and half of them were handwritten. Well, the ones in the computer were all wrong so I had to go back and find all them jobs today. It was—it's been really like a crazy house in there all week. Nothing has proved out." It was chaotic but exciting, and "a real challenge."

Cooking, Cleaning, Caring

With the exception of a small number of high school graduates who worked in the school system as classroom aides or preschool teachers, the women who worked in these so-called unskilled jobs had not completed high school and were doing the same type of domestic labor—caring for children, sweeping, dusting, lifting, wiping, and cooking—that working-class women have always done. Doreen's job as a bakery assistant in a grocery chain-store is a good example of this new/old women's work: "[You] help them set up the racks to put in the oven, or go back to the freezer and pull up freight. You got to load the freezer up, lift all the boxes, take all the boxes from the big freezer in the back, bring them up to our freezer, and unload. I mean, you bust butt."

As was common in this kind of job, one of the most frustrating things about Doreen's job was her customers' thoughtlessness: "They'll come around the back! We have them that will walk right in through the bakery, hot racks and everything and touch you. 'Miss, miss,' [they'll say]. Instead of standing back and saying, 'Can you help me?' or 'Excuse me.'" What she liked most about her job, Doreen said with a laugh, was what she wouldn't get for doing the same work at home: her paycheck.

Sandra worked in the large elementary school opposite her house from three in the afternoon until eleven-thirty at night, five days a week. "The school is very large," she said. "I have an area, right now, I have twenty rooms that have to be cleaned absolutely every night. You get evaluated on that." The cleaning consisted of "dusting, scrubbing, windows, emptying trash. Anything that is out of order has to be put back for the next day." And then there was cleaning the chalkboards. "That's why my hands are so messed up," Sandra said, holding out her roughened red hands. "The chalk is real bad." The worst part of her job, though, was not cleaning the floors or even the chalkboards, but "when you've got different people working in the same building [and] different opinions clash." The best part was the paycheck, especially when she had overtime, which she "loved."

Wanda worked as a nurse's aide. She and the other aides were responsible for all the less glamorous aspects of patient care, for example, lifting patients, transferring them from bed to bath, cleaning up their messes, and wheeling them from one department to another. "It's total patient care," Wanda said. "We do a lot of body lifting. We do a lot of hands-on work with the patient. We're constantly hands-on." Isabel, another aide, found the work "hard and dangerous." She worked in a nursing home whose clientele included many patients with Alzheimer's disease: "Lifting patients. I've done gotten hurt already. You get some really nasty patients. There's nothing you can do about it. A lot of them don't even know they're on this earth. They clap their hands, and stomp their feet. They cuss you out."

Amanda cooked at her local community college. "I am a grill girl," she said. "I am behind the grill. I fix breakfast in the morning—all kinds, French toast, any kind of eggs you want. I start at five-thirty in the morning. I set up the line, get ready for the students and all. And then starting about seven-thirty, it's a madhouse." It was hot and hectic. "Being on your feet [is hard]," said Amanda, "and the heat! It gets really hot back there. There is an exhaust fan, but whoever built the building didn't put a big enough exhaust in there to get the heat out. And my boss got us a floor fan last summer but that just churns up the hot air. We sell pizza too, so we have a pizza oven. Two deep fryers, the toaster and the grill. That's a lot of heat there."

Wendy worked in a cleaning team for a building construction company. She and her team cleaned up new houses. As well as doing regular cleaning, they picked up spilled glue and paint, and removed paint cans, buckets, ladders and other equipment and debris left by the construction crews. Construction is one of the few industries that continues to thrive, but this was a mixed blessing as far as Wendy was concerned. When she had first started working, she could take her daughter to school and then meet her cleaning team at 8:45 for their first job. Now, she needed to leave home earlier and return later because her boss was bringing in more work. It was a long day and hard work: "I'm at my boss's house by seven. We leave her house about quarter after. We're on the job between quarter to eight and eight, depending on traffic. Most of the time it's three [of us], maybe four. And we go in and we start getting everything ready to clean, and we go upstairs and start. We complete the upstairs, then we do windows. We clean the bedrooms real good, and then we vacuum up, get the beds clean. Vacuum down the steps, all around. Then we take a break. And then we clean up. . . . They're all different sizes of houses so you don't know what time you're going to finish."

Wendy didn't mind the physical work; she said it was good exercise. What she did mind was having to deal with people who refused to pull their weight: "See, when we go out, we don't have the same people every day. Our boss changes, and they tell you to do more work, and you don't want to say nothing and you do it and get it out of the way. I try to say it in a nice way, because it's hard to have friction when you're working as a group."

Packing, Stacking, Assembling

Only seven women—six of them high school dropouts—worked in factories, but Harriet was the only one who was engaged in actually producing goods rather than packing them; her factory made windows, a byproduct of the booming construction industry. Her particular job was to operate a circular saw, cutting the pieces of metal— spacers—that fit between windowpanes. "I cut [the glass]," she explained, "[then] it goes to a lady. She builds it, and the next lady runs it through another machine. Then from there it's hung up, and then one piece of glass goes on the bottom, another piece of glass goes on the top." It was physically "very hard work."

Eliza operated a machine that put together packages of junk mail for distribution. "Don't let them hear me call it junk mail!" she said in mock horror, before describing her job:

> We have to keep [the] machine filled, and sort the mail. The machine has little hands to it, and they go in and they grab a piece of mail and pull it out onto the track. It comes on down. It's constantly moving. Back and forth. You could have it fast or slow. Last night I had mine medium. Because, I mean, this job was easy. Like I said, I had five pockets last night. I had the little sticker; it's about like this [a square about two inches by two inches], and you peel it off. It had a panda bear on it. That's what we do. We have to pull those, we have to sort them. They go by zips. They will either go into a bag—we have to rubber-band it if it goes in a bag—or they go in trays. And trays is what we've been doing a lot lately. We're trying to get rid of the bags. I'll be glad, because nobody likes the bags. The trays are so much easier. You have to rubber-band the bags, and these are not the best rubber bands in the world. My hands were so messed up. But I really enjoy it.
>
> There are times when I wish, I really wish, I could just stay home and collapse. I've fallen over there, messed up my knee. I've pulled muscles in my back. Muscle spasms. And the doctor chewed me out. I mean chewed me out good.

Standing all day was tiring and the pay wasn't great, but this was Eliza's first full-time job and she liked it. The only stressful thing about it was "putting up with certain people. There is one [coworker] I cannot stand."

Laura did data entry in a warehouse that distributed catering equipment to fast-food and carry-out restaurants. She said her job involved "answering the phone, taking orders, keying in the orders, getting the orders out of the system, and giving them to the guys in the warehouse to pull for the next-day delivery. We take the order down, we write it on paper, and after we've got the order and all from them, we'll go in and we'll key it into the system. Then, after about an hour or so of all of us girls keying in orders, we'll stop and we'll do a printout and we'll give it to the guy in shipping. And the guys will take that pick ticket and then pull the orders from that."

The hardest part of Laura's job was dealing with customers, both in person and by phone. "If somebody comes in and didn't call in an order, then we have to go in and take the order from them. And hope they know what they want! Because half the time they don't know what they want, and we have to come back in and spend time trying to figure out what they want by going through the inventory. . . . Or if a customer calls in and says they need a certain type of cup or plate and we don't stock it, then we have to say to them, 'Well, it's gonna take x amount of days, or a week, to order this in,' and we have to go over [and] talk to purchasing about it, get it ordered in, and make sure it gets in at a certain time so it can be delivered to them on time." There was "nothing" Laura liked about her job.

Terry worked on a line, assembling orders for shampoo, hair dye, and other products that were slated for beauty parlors and drugstores. She worked with six other women. Her job was to pick the items from the shelves and place them in the correct order on a roller near their box: "You just push a tooth that the box is in. And the paperwork has stickers on it. And you just look at the stickers that have the merchandise [written] on them and you just go to that section. Get however much you need and just put it in that order and push it all the way down the end. It goes down on the rollers until it goes right out front."

Terry said she liked the 7 A.M. to 4 P.M. shift best: "That way I'm home at a reasonable time. That way, we usually fix dinner at a certain time. Everybody's here. And if there's anything I need to do before dinner I can do it." She was permitted to be only six minutes late in a pay period before having her pay docked. Her job involved heavy lifting, which was tiring, but she said that over the years she had learned the correct way to lift. What Terry most liked about her job was the people she worked with. "There's six people there," she explained. "And the girls that check the orders, they're all the time coming down and getting merchandise that wasn't in the shelves the time the order went around. So you're not by yourself in the department. We have radios playing and [we're] laughing when something comes on the radio, you know, stuff like that." She couldn't think of anything about the job that she didn't like.

Sally worked as a school bus driver. "You have special training," she explained, "and you have to take the C.D.L. test. It's a driving test and a written test. It's for heavy vehicles, transporting kids—transporting children—brake endorsement, you have to know all the stuff about brakes and the different things." Her day was long: "I get up at five o'clock. I take the high school, I take the junior high school, and I take two elementaries, and sometimes three. Then I have a forty-five-minute break when I usually go get breakfast. Then I go and get my kindergarten. That's about a two-hour ride. Then I have another forty-five-minute break. So if I haven't eaten before then I eat then. My first break is about a quarter of ten. My second break is about one [P.M.]. There's nine or ten runs a day. I start work at a quarter of seven. I end at a quarter of five. That's if I don't have any sports trips. I don't work the summer and I do get paid [for the summer months]."

There were two things she especially liked about her job: "I like the people I work with, and I like working with kids." But the job had its frustrations: "It's changed. The kids have changed. Respect. There's no respect from any of them now. Society has just washed its hands. I got hit in the face with a rock last year by a kid. They took me off my bus, punished me. Nothing happened to the kid. Five other drivers had turned the same child in for throwing stuff at the windshield." What Sally liked least about her job was her supervisor: "He won't do his job so he takes it out on all of us. Nobody likes him."

Taking Cash, Serving Customers

Six women worked as cashiers or in customer service. Ruth worked for a pizza and sub store, where she took orders, filled in for the cook, and restocked the area in front of the counter. Cora worked at a local convenience store: "I work the three-to-eleven shift, sometimes six days a week. Every day there is something different. The boss leaves a worksheet of what she wants done on the shift. Like sometimes it will be clean the counters off, and wipe them down and stock the mustard and ketchup containers and do the windows inside and out. Do the floors." Ann was a cashier and customer service clerk at a local toy store. "I handle the service desk," she said. "That's where everybody hits when they walk in the door [and] they have a complaint or a question. Plus I ring customers at the same time. And answer the phone. I'm doing three things at one time. It's a little more involved than just ringing sales." Phyllis was a cashier on the checkout at a grocery chain, and had just taken a second job as a toll collector on the Bay bridge. Harriet worked evenings in customer service at Walmart (as well as at the glass factory I described earlier). What she liked least about her job were "irate customers. After the first of the month, there are very rude people," she said.

Carolyn was employed part time by a supermarket chain. After she had reshelved items first thing each morning, she wiped out all the cash registers; later in the day she did a variety of things: "I can be bagging or I can be outside putting groceries in a car. If I'm inside bagging, like if they need a price check, they'll call me and I'll go find the price for them. We do everything in the store."

These jobs do not fit neatly into the blue-collar and white-collar categories that have traditionally been used to describe men's work. They are not the blue-collar laboring jobs in the manufacturing economy that employed most of the women's fathers in factories and steel mills. Nor are most of them white-collar. Only three might qualify as white collar: Helen's job as an accountant, Sherry's as a bookkeeper, and Valerie's as a bank clerk. Nonetheless, many were manual jobs and relatively unskilled, such as aides, counter assistants at convenience stores, and assemblers. To capture their broad equivalence to blue-collar manual work, I group these jobs in the next section and call them "gray-collar" jobs. Similarly, I group office jobs, most of which were as secretaries, receptionists, or telephone operators, as "pink-collar"; like white-collar work, these jobs were clean and not manual, but most of them were jobs traditionally performed by women.

Job Conditions and Credentials: Gray-Collar Work and Pink-Collar Work

Some of what I learned about women's job conditions came as structured responses to specific survey-type questions,[11] some was stimulated by these questions but went beyond them as women elaborated, clarified, and extemporized, some came in response to a question about "a typical day at work," and some came spontaneously, in the context of quite different topics. The same was true of data on women's job satisfaction and on the job conditions related to it. The next chapter discusses the relationship between job conditions and satisfaction derived from the questionnaire data. In this chapter, I present only a brief summary of these data before turning to the qualitative data and the women's responses to two very simple, straightforward questions: What do you like most about your job? What do you like least? The women's responses to these open-ended questions and comments they made spontaneously have the advantage of being in their own words, and, as you will see in the next chapter, their own words—about their jobs, and what they liked and disliked—shed a different light on their survey responses.

Whatever the source of the data, it was clear that, on average, the women who lacked a high school diploma had by far the worst job conditions. Their average annual pay was only half that of women with a high school degree. They were also worse off when it came to eligibility for paid sick days, vacation days, and personal days, and to having work that was interesting, challenging, or autonomous. They most often had to do dirty, heavy work, and most often felt they had too much to do on the job and that they had to work too hard and too fast. They had to punch a clock, they had their pay docked if they were late, and they rarely had any say over the hours they worked.

High school graduates' job conditions were much better than those of dropouts, and when it came to a number of job conditions—notably autonomy—secretaries, who were high school graduates, were even better off than teachers. On average, a bachelor's degree brought a better job, but to get the best conditions, a professional degree was needed. The ten women in professional-managerial jobs earned over twice as much as teachers and four times as much as factory workers. They were equally advantaged in terms of non-monetary conditions.

What Did You Like Most? What Did You Like Least?

When asked what they liked most and least about their jobs, the women were remarkably consistent; most often, what they liked most was "the people" and what they liked least was "a person"—usually a supervisor. Whether or not the main activity on their job involved dealing with people—as it does in sales or customer service, for example—people mattered most. The women's answers to the following questions were critical for understanding how they experienced their jobs: Were they treated with respect and consideration by supervisors? With friendliness and warmth by coworkers? With courtesy by customers? Were they asked, not told, to do a job? Was their good work noticed, even complimented? Was their opinion asked? Were they trusted to work on their own?

Women were most satisfied with jobs in which they were respected. Being respected meant not being closely supervised as if one were a child, being acknowledged as a full participant in the workplace, and—although it seems quaint to say it—being treated with consideration and courtesy. They were least satisfied with jobs in which their supervisors were controlling, unappreciative, and lacking in respect.[12] Because of this, the least satisfied workers were those in factory jobs and unskilled service jobs outside the education sector.

The Gray-Collar Workplace: The Loss of Respect in the Pursuit of Profit

To compete in a global economy, companies have struggled to reshape themselves, squeezing as much profit as they can from the smallest possible number of permanent workers. Workers—especially working-class women workers—are increasingly employed on a part-time or temporary basis, not in permanent jobs. (Agencies that employ temporary workers are one of the fastest growing services.) The advantage of this practice for employers is obvious; they can avoid paying benefits and "carrying" workers during slow periods. The disadvantage for workers is equally obvious; they enjoy no benefits or job security. And, because their jobs lack permanence, they are denied long-term respectful, rewarding personal relationships at work.

The women with high school diplomas usually had permanent jobs but women without diplomas were often forced to work as temps, sometimes for companies that employed their own permanent workers; these women were second-class citizens whose supervisors were constrained by neither labor shortages nor by the personal bonds and loyalties that usually develop among people who work together over a lengthy period. One consequence was a harsh, tense, uncivil atmosphere in the workplace, in which supervisors exploded at workers and workers exploded at one another.

"Work faster," "Waste no time," "Work harder" were the watchwords, and supervisors neglected to say, "Good work. Thank you. I appreciate what you're doing." Laura described what it was like to have no recognition, and to feel disrespected:

> I never get told, "You've done a good job." You don't get no feedback. You just don't get it. And I know that out of the four of us there I know for a fact that I'm the top speed in keying in orders. I know I key in every bit of 250 orders myself a day. And it's like nobody gives you recognition. You need that to bring your self-esteem up.

Other women described being put down, and treated as less than adult. "It's just like you're really stupid," Phyllis said, explaining how humiliating this was:

> A lot of times, it just feels like I am, you know, in school. You know, like you don't know what you're supposed to do. We get W.I.C. vouchers for women, infants, and children, where they get milk and cheese and eggs and stuff. It used to be you just— well you had to check the date, make sure it was the right month, and make sure that they were getting the proper items, what's listed. And then you would just write in the amount. It couldn't go over the specified amount either, then you keyed it in. [The office staff] have to stamp these things before they send them back to the gov- ernment. Well, now, when you get a W.I.C. voucher, you have to ring the bell and wait for somebody to come down. It's just like you're really stupid, [like] you can't read the date.

This was not the first or only time Phyllis was treated like a dummy. She rolled her eyes as she told me about a test she needed to pass for her new job (collecting tolls on the bridge). "I filled out the application and I had to take a simple math test," she explained. "You need an eighth grade education. (In fact, you need a high school diploma for this job; Phyllis meant that the test was insultingly easy, at about an eighth grade level.) Then you had to take a hundred psychological questions, which were really stupid. They didn't even pertain to taking money from patrons. I mean, they were really stupid. [For example], if someone butts up in front of you in line, are you gonna say something? You know, things like that. I'm looking at this question and I know that I would say something if someone butts up in front of me, but I think, If I say yes, do they think I'm too aggressive? If I say no, am I too passive? You know, because you're dealing with the public."

Women in gray-collar jobs were bullied, and their rights were often ignored. "My supervisor . . . won't do his job," said Jill, "so he takes it out on all of us. Nobody likes him." Sonya was never certain when—even whether—she would be paid: "With my boss, it's hard too, because sometimes he'll pay me and sometimes he won't. It depends what kind of mood he's in."

In stores, warehouses, and product distribution centers, powerless workers seethed as hours were cut and shifts were switched around to eliminate idle time. Doreen explained what this was like at her store:

> We have a new boss, and he's just a jerk. He gets a bonus commission every time he saves payroll. And everybody in the place has lost anywhere from six to ten hours. Everybody. There's less work, there's less stuff done, you know, and it's hard. But he don't want to hear it. [He says], "You get it done! You get it done!" They say he's trying to get all the people disgusted [so they'll] quit. So he can get all part-timers in there, because it don't cost nothing to have part-timers in there. And, like, eighty percent of that store is full-time people that's been there for years. And most of them is married people that has families and stuff too. But they aren't going anywhere.

Impermanence, unpredictability, and insecurity often poisoned women's relationships, because it increased pressure, encouraged competition, and fueled hostility. "We just got over [an audit]," said Monica, a factory line leader, "and we didn't do too good. And people's tempers got short fuses." "They've got moods," said Carolyn of her coworkers. "Like sometimes they can be real nice to you and other times, it's just like they're a different person. They snap at you, or are real cranky and all. Or get smart with you. I just ignore them."

The Pink-Collar Workplace: Only High School Graduates Need Apply

Women with a high school diploma were spared the insecurities and indignities of gray-collar workplaces. Not forced to work in the "secondary labor market"—in gray-collar jobs that lacked security and benefits—they were able to find pink-collar "primary labor market" jobs. Only one woman with a high school diploma chose to work in a factory or as a counter saleswoman; mostly, high school graduates worked as secretaries, receptionists, or clerks—jobs in which the work was clean and pleasant, and in which they were treated with much more respect than gray-collar workers could command. Karen's job was a good example. She worked at Sears as a clerk in fine jewelry, where she had quite a bit of freedom to develop her own procedures and arrange her work day. "All the jewelry that comes in," she said. "I log that in. And keep a log of that. . . . I have to keep control of that, and [the saleslady] has to come down and pick it up, [and] sign it out. And she's gotta bring it back to me, and I have to sign it back in. Now if there's a box that goes up there and it's supposed to have, say, $50,000 worth of gold chains in it, and she picks it up and it's short, then the auditor comes in and he audits to find out what happened to it."

Karen acted as "banker" for several different departments in the store, including fine jewelry. She gave the sales staff change for large notes and made sure they had the correct amount of money in their registers. She explained how this worked: "All the cashiers upstairs can come to me if they need, say, twenty ones or something like that. So I make up a bank and I give them, say, twelve rolls of pennies, twelve rolls of quarters, 500 ones and all that. That way there's change for all the registers up there, and they don't have to run downstairs. There's three departments that'll get, say, a $600 bank and then that way [the others] can just go there for the change and break those rolls down." A lapse of concentration could mean the bank comes up short. Recently, for example, the one dollar bills started coming in rolls of one hundred instead of fifty. Because of this change, Karen's coworker had handed out twice as many rolls as she should have. "But then our bank was short. Our cash office was short. I kept saying, 'I know I didn't do that,'" Karen said, still shaken by the experience. "And [my coworker] said, 'I think I'm the one that did it.'"

The large amounts of money she dealt with and the possibility of making a mistake made Karen's job "scary." On the other hand, she was free to develop strategies that reduced the risk of error. "I always go in," she said, "and whatever money I'm taking from [the saleswomen] I add that up on the adding machine and [also] whatever money I give back, so that they can look at my paper and say, 'OK, she had $300 in, she gave $300 out.'"

Trudy worked as a secretary in the biology department of a large state university:

> Right now I'm involved in the admissions process. I process applications for the
> master's program. I make sure all the students' credentials are there, their letters and
> transcripts and GRE scores. I answer questions people have about the program. I
> write to people who write to the department asking about the program. I talk to
> people on the phone about it. I do the budget administration, process all of the
> stipend payroll forms for the students. Answer students' questions if they don't
> know about how to do something or what to do. I help prepare grants for funding.
> No day is ever the same as the one before.

Trudy had autonomy, and her boss, Dr. Smith, treated her with respect and consideration. To illustrate, some years earlier, when she complained that she was bored with working as a secretary, he gave her a job as a lab assistant. Then, after she had worked as a lab assistant for three or four years, he encouraged her to move on to administrative work. Her job was still boring at times—she had to do photocopying, typing, and "other mundane kinds of things"—but she enjoyed it very much.

Ethel, a prison warden's secretary, had autonomy, and she enjoyed knowing her boss valued her contribution:

> I kind of screen calls for him. [This morning] the phone rang and a lady wanted to
> talk to the assistant warden. But he was in a bad mood and he said, "Find out what
> she wants." But she didn't want to talk to me. An inmate's father had died, and she

wanted permission to come to the institution, and she had been told that she needed to speak to the warden. And she said, "I'd like to come now," and I said, "I don't think so, ma'am." It was kind of the problem of the morning. We always have something that's, "What are we going to do with this person?" He'll ask me, and I'll just tell him what I think.

Office workers were often able to work on their own, a luxury that most gray-collar workers could only dream about. "No one bothers you," said Rachael, a clerk. "As long as you know what to do, they're not over you." Sheila felt the same way. "Right now I like that I'm to myself," she said. "It's not like a lot of people telling me what to do. It's a place where the bosses are very lenient. If you have a problem, you can talk to them. It's not like anybody makes strict demands on you." And being her own boss was what Greta, a doctor's secretary, most liked about her job:

> Even though he's my boss, he's only there two hours out of the day. The rest of the time, I'm my own boss. Because he's in the hospital, or even when he's here, he's not really with me, because I have my own big office with a sliding door, and he's down the hall in his office. So we talk on the intercom, or I might walk down to his office, but I have my office here and he's there. So we don't work hand in hand.
>
> He don't know when I come in, when I really do come in. He's never there. He doesn't come in till ten. Like this morning I didn't get there until five after. I was listening to a song, and I stopped the car and the song didn't go off. I didn't want to miss it so, by the time I got in there, I was five minutes late, and I thought, "Oh well."

As well as being able to work on her own for much of the day, Greta was responsible for making decisions with real consequences:

> My day starts at nine o'clock in the morning. When I walk in, I have to get to the answering machine to take the messages off. Sometimes there'll be a lady on there, and she'll be talking for hours and hours. And she thinks that Dr. Anderson reads that tape recorder. He don't. I have to get off every itsy bit that's important then the tape is erased and that's when I tell him what I think is important. If it's not important, he don't want to know about it. So that's the tape. So after that, I start the Xerox and I start doing the billing from the day before so I have to get on the computer and do all the billing.
>
> I have to keep his schedule going, so he knows what he's doing from day to day. So he'll come and he'll go. I got an intercom system in my office, and he'll go, "Miss Greta, What's my schedule for today?" So I have to let him know what meetings he's going to, and I write it all down on a piece of paper, and I give it to him. He'll lay it on his desk, and I'll leave and it'll still be laying there. And he'll go to the hospital,

and I'll say to his wife, "I gave him that piece of paper, and he left it there. Why do I even write it?" But he'll look at it and he memorizes what is on there. And then he goes off to the hospital. And then if any doctors call while he's at the hospital, or patients call, I'm still scheduling for the next day. Doctors are calling. I've got to keep calling him on his beeper and, you know, making decisions for him.

It's a very tedious job, but you really have to know what you're doing. Because one foul-up, giving one wrong report of the wrong patient, you can end up really hurting somebody. By giving the wrong report. Because the doctor will call up and say, "Read off the report what I wrote on there." So you have to read off the chart what he wrote on there. I mean the doctor himself will call me and he'll say, "What did I write in my chart?" And I'll have to read his handwriting which is—half the time it's shorthand. It's his version—and I'm supposed to know what everything means. Patients come in and look at all that scribble and say, "What does it say?" [I say], "You came here today. He wants to see you in six months. You had a lab test. He put medication. He did a pregnancy test and he did a sonogram." It's all [on] that piece of paper. I know every code that he writes out.

Compared with many other women, Greta had an enviable amount of job autonomy; just being alone for most of the day was a freedom few women were given, and her relationship with her boss was friendly. But, by depending on her, he had encouraged between them a sense of personal connection that he manipulated; for example, he expected her to come in even when she was sick, because he "couldn't manage without her." In this, and other ways, women paid for the sense of connection at work that they so valued.

The Cost of Connection: Relationships at Work

According to the psychologist Jean Baker Miller, an early advocate of understanding women's psychology on its own terms, not men's, women's sense of self is "organized around being able to make and then to maintain affiliations and relationships."[13] Carol Gilligan, a Harvard psychologist, agrees; in her acclaimed book, *In a Different Voice*, she argues that "women perceive and construe social reality differently from men" and that "these differences center around experiences of attachment and separation."[14] To illustrate, she describes how female college students, telling stories in response to a picture of two women at work in a laboratory, associated competitive success with "danger." She concludes that "the danger women portray in their tales of achievement is a danger of isolation, a fear that in standing out or being set apart by success, they will be left alone." (For men, the danger is one of "intimacy or entrapment.") The view that women are essentially different from men is controversial,[15] but Gilligan's point is that women's concern for connectedness rather than separation should not be read—as it was by Freud and other psychologists—as evidence of their lack of maturity relative to men.

The quality of their relationships at work was important to the women in this study. As we have already seen, "the people" was their most common response when asked what they liked most about their jobs, and interpersonal problems were always a factor when they were dissatisfied. Unfortunately, "the people at work" were most important to the women who worked in the very jobs in which relationships were most problematic. In the rough and tumble of the gray-collar workplace, bad relationships were particularly noxious: the women in these jobs were most dependent on their supervisors' goodwill, and they were treated with disrespect more often than other women.[16] Most vulnerable to nastiness and conflict, the women in these jobs had the fewest options for dealing with them; they risked being fired if they argued with their bosses, and if other workers were hostile, they had no office to retreat to—often even the bathroom was out-of-bounds. And they were most likely to be working under the kind of up-close, in-your-face pressure that exacerbates tension.

Being able to withdraw was important to Loretta, a clerk. Here she was responding to a question about whether her work was mentally stressful:

> I think it's worse where I work. People let their personal lives entwine too much with their professional lives so I have a lot of problems, emotionally, trying to keep myself out on a limb, away from all of it. That's why I like where I am in my position, where I'm sitting, where people come and use the fax machine, in and out of the door, but I do try to keep myself out of their personal lives, because it can be very emotional. You know, someone else can change your attitude when they walk in the door because they have a bad attitude. It's like, "I can't handle this," I don't even hear it. It's just like, "Deal with it." I leave little notes on peoples' desks, like a serenity prayer, or I leave a note, or . . . I got that calendar by M. Scott Peck, "The Road Less Traveled," and I take little things about the difficulties of life and dealing with them, and I leave it on somebody's desk. One of the girls took it and threw it in the trash today, but she should have read it.
>
> I leave things on her desk. This one girl, she can be a really good friend, but she has a lot of emotional problems, and I like to leave little things on her desk about coping with life or something like that. She never says anything to me, but I know she understands. She usually calms down after that, too.

Had Loretta and her coworker been rubbing elbows on an assembly line and under constant pressure, these fairly minor irritations might easily have escalated into confrontations. (Notice that Loretta is not one to place connectedness above independence; she would prefer to leave emotions out of work, and she is not afraid to risk her relationship with her coworker by telling her to "get over it.")

No matter what their physical job conditions were like, women in gray-collar jobs were satisfied with them so long as they were on friendly terms with their bosses. But getting along with the boss was a fragile basis for job satisfaction; jobs were temporary, people were transient, and, too often, today's friend was tomorrow's tyrant.

Phyllis's experience is an example. Because she had liked her previous supervisor, she accepted that he needed to report her for not making her checkout quota:

> It used to be that you had to keep [your rating] at ninety or above. Before I had the surgery on my hands—because, you know, carpal tunnel can be really painful—my rating dropped down to eighty-nine. And my assistant manager at the time was really great. This guy was really great, and he was like, "I didn't want to put this down—I know about your hands, they know about your hands—but you know how it is." But it's always been above ninety or better. Even with two bad hands I feel like I'm a better cashier than most of them up there.

Phyllis's new supervisor was bossy and unapologetic about reporting her, so she intended to quit her job. She was enjoying the fact that he could no longer intimidate her; "I'm on his shit list," she said, "[but] I don't care."

Monica was on very friendly terms with her boss, and enjoyed knowing he valued her. He called her during our interview, and she showed me the $100 check and certificate she had earned for perfect attendance at work. She had no objection to the fact that eligibility for sick leave was left up to his discretion, even though workers in her factory were entitled to it:

> Well, we do [get sick days] but we're not allowed to take them because so many people, they misuse them. Like I took vacation yesterday and today, and we get personals. Next year we get two personals. If you are sick, now they have something called an incident. If you're out, say a week or so, that's just one incident. So most people, if they're sick, they have to take a vacation day. It's up to your supervisor. It's up to their discretion. I guess if they knew you were really sick, it might be OK. Each supervisor's different.

Laura used to enjoy her job, but now, with new owners, she hated it:

> They have no feelings at all. The company I worked for in the beginning did. Thompson's, it was a family-oriented company. This is too, Fuller is too, but not like Thompson's was. They didn't look at us as employees. They looked at us as family. And they were very, very easy to get along with. Very easy to get along with. This group—no way. Because the Thompsons, they had money all their life, but they don't treat you like they had money all their life. The Fullers have had money all of their lives, and believe me, they let you know they've had money all their lives, and they look down on us.

Jean's experience was similar to Laura's, but her position was even worse because, working as a housekeeper-cook at the local Catholic parish, she was alone, with no coworkers to support her. She described her job:

> The first thing I do when I go in is start lunch. It is for all the help. I have eleven people. Lunch consists of four kinds of lunch meat, three different kinds of bread, crackers and cheese, potato chips, and then the dessert. I clean up after lunch, then I go upstairs, clean the bedrooms, make the beds. It is five bedrooms. I come downstairs and clean the offices, then I go down to the basement, and they have a bathroom down there, a meeting room, money-counting room, laundry room—I clean [those]. While I'm cleaning [those], I throw in laundry. After I'm done that, I clean up the kitchen and start dinner. While dinner is cooking, I sit down and iron. [I] wait till they eat, clean off the table, put the stuff in the dishwasher, clean the kitchen, and walk out the door. I also do the grocery shopping.
>
> I have all the priests to take care of, and then they have visitors. Priests come in as visitors without notifying me. We get priests come in and stay for six months; you got to get up there and clean that room. If there are extra priests, there isn't no more money.

Jean's job was minimum wage, and there were no benefits, but, in spite of these drawbacks, she used to love her job. Recently, though, her old boss, the former priest, was transferred and her feelings changed:

> I loved him to death. This new one come and he was younger and it wasn't the same place. With the other one, he would say to me, "I'm not going to be here for dinner, Father O'Brien's not going to be here. When you're done your work, you can go." The new one comes in and he says, he says to me, "Your hours are eight hours a day." And I said, "Well, what do I do if you're not here, and nobody is here and my work's done?" He says, "Strip floors." And I said, "I wasn't hired to strip floors, Father," I said. "I do everything else. I'm not stripping floors. I'm not stripping floors." And I have to sit there, say if they went out at four o'clock, till six o'clock, working crossword puzzles when I have a family [at] home.

I asked Jean what she liked most about her job:

> Well, at first I liked being around the people. I liked everything at first. They didn't tell me what to cook, or how to cook it. Until the new one come. Then they wanted all this high-class stuff. Then they wanted all this lobster Newburg and crabs and . . . I said, "Look, I'm a cook. Fried chicken, I can give you." I said, "What the hell is lobster Newburg?" He says, "Get a cookbook." So I got a cookbook and I made it, I

made it. Shells, with crab imperial. I'd never made that before. And this was for
twenty-five people. I cooked things I'd never cooked before. I had to cook for
twenty-five people!

Jean's experience shows the cost of valuing connection, of depending on warm
personal relationships with supervisors in the absence of formal rights; unlike formal
rights, friendly bosses were disposable, and when supervisors left—as they all too
often did—a satisfying job could quickly turn sour. Like Phyllis, Jean was now so
unhappy she was about to quit.

The Velvet Glove: Connectedness in the Office

Women in gray-collar jobs were exposed to coercive control by supervisors; they were
told what to do, not asked, and their supervisors felt no need to couch their demands
in pleasant, polite language. Because their jobs required little or no training and lacked
union protection, these women were expendable, and they knew it. Office workers
were less vulnerable because they more often worked in permanent jobs with formal-
ized conditions and benefits, and they were harder to replace. For these reasons, the
iron hand of work discipline was softened by the velvet glove of charm.

Greta's relationship with Dr. Anderson is a good example. We saw that Greta had
more autonomy on her job than most other women; Dr. Anderson trusted her to run
his office for most of the day, and he wasn't right there looking over her shoulder. No
one could accuse him of failing to show her his appreciation:

He takes a lot of vacations. He's getting ready to go on a safari. He's going to Africa.
Every time he goes away, he brings me something back. He just came back from
India. Every country that he goes to he brings me something. I got stuff from
Hawaii; I got ashtrays from Fiji; I have jade from Japan; I have turquoise from Peru; I
have a silver and gold bracelet from some place over in South America he went. I got
a ring from India that he brought me back. He takes about four vacations a year. He
just got back from India. I got a pen—I walked into the office and he said, "Miss
Greta, how do you like this pen?" I said, "This pen is beautiful." He says, "It's yours."
And he just handed me the pen. He gave me this and he told me to write a check out
for my Christmas bonus. I get a week's pay for a Christmas present, and I get a day's
pay for my birthday.

Plus he's always buying me gifts. And [his wife], she went to Argentina, [and]
she brought me back a beautiful ashtray. It's a cow's hoof. I have a piece of jade that's
that big. I just got a bracelet too. And I got a beautiful necklace that he brought me
back. He's only given me one thing that has gold on it. It has a llama on it. He teases
me; he says if I'm there five years, he'll buy me a piece of gold.

But if Dr. Anderson called and Greta was not at her desk, she was obliged to explain why:

It's a very demanding job. It's a full commitment. You have to give up a lot for this type of job. When I say a lot, I get lunch hour but I don't get lunch hour. I eat my lunch at my desk because I can't leave the office because somebody might call. I can't go outside for a half an hour and sit outside unless I change my hours. . . . One day I was talking in [another secretary's] office, but when you sneak out of your office you don't hear the phone. It might ring, and it might be the doctor and you're not there, and then the first thing is, "Where were you?" You might have gone to the bathroom. Well, sometimes he'll ask me, "Where were you?" And I'll say—our little saying is, "Taking care of business." And he knows "taking care of business" is that I had to go to the ladies' room. Because the phone just constantly rings, and you can't jump off the toilet and run to the telephone.

And he made certain she would never take time off:

You'd have to tell him [I'm entitled to personal leave]. He's funny. Like when [my husband's] father died, he got very bent out of shape over that. I've been there three years. I'm entitled to five sick days, [but] in three years I have taken one full sick day. That means not going in all day long. I got three phone calls that day, from him. [While I was] laying in bed, he called me, "Miss Greta, I can't find this, I can't find that." I said, "Well, I'll be in tomorrow [even] if I'm dying because you can't find nothing without me. Don't call me no more today, and I'll try to get well, and I'll be back." It's not worth staying home because he could call me.

Just as surely as the most dictatorial factory boss, Dr. Anderson secured Greta's compliance. She complained about how unreasonable he was, but she did it with a tolerant chuckle. Like difficult children, she and other office workers knew, difficult bosses such as Dr. Anderson needed to be tolerated and "handled"; as Jill, another office worker, said, "You have to laugh, or you'd cry."

Jill told me about her boss who, much to her delight, had just sold his company; she still had to work with him, but he no longer had the power to make her life miserable: "He goes off in fits once in a while. We just have to ignore him. We do [ignore him] and I think that's half his problem now, because we're not coddling him anymore. . . . And he throws temper tantrums. He's spoiled—he's a sixty-two-year-old spoiled person. We even went to his wife one time. Elsie did, right after she started there. She said [to his wife], 'You got to talk to him, because he gets us crying.'"

Greta and Jill had learned how to humor their bosses. Part mistress, part mother, part maid, they jollied them out of bad moods, ignored their tempers, and protected them from life's frustrations. "You find doctors with their ups and downs," Greta said. "But you just have to know how to get along with [them]. If you get along with them, fine. I mean you can make your job easy or you can make it hard."

Being the Boss: Who Needs It?

Most women were reluctant to become supervisors, because supervising denied them the easy companionship and emotional support of other women. Polly, for example, the director of a nursery school, said she disliked "dealing with the staff when there's problems. Telling them when they've done something wrong, that sort of thing. When I have to stop being their friend and be their boss, I don't like that. Just being a teacher relieved me of some of the boss type details. I liked that."

In part, too, the problem with supervising was that few women exercised genuine authority;[17] instead, they occupied a lonely, ambiguous position, neither ordinary workers nor management, but something in between. Judy, a packer, had learned this the hard way:

> I didn't want to do line leading because you have to tell people, and I'm not going to stand there and tell a bunch of adults. . . . Like I could say, "OK, remember girls, four eyeliners in a box." OK, and then I have to tell them to look for foreign matter, and I have to tell them to make sure the blister isn't pliable. So when [the line-leading] position came up, I didn't sign up for it, but [instead, the supervisor] put me in for quality control. All I do is go around and pull samples, [and] make sure every pallet [that] goes out has a sample box in it. So that I like, because I don't have to tell nobody. . . . Let me put it to you this way: I am not—I can't stand up in front of a bunch of people. It's like, "Aghhh, I can't do this!" I just get this really eerie feeling. So what I do is, I'll look at one person. You know, evidently I must feel comfortable with this one person. And all I have to say is, "Now look, someone must be packing wrong." And before you know it, you got three or four people yelling and screaming at you, "Well, it wasn't me!" And it wasn't like I said, "You packed it wrong."

Monica's experience as a line leader was similar: "Around Christmastime we had one girl that was upset because she hadn't done her Christmas shopping, and it was the last three days until Christmas, and she got upset. Her and I haven't talked for a long time because I asked her to help me do some work, and she didn't. Instead of just saying, 'I don't have enough time,' she got in a huffy mood. They don't mind doing it for [the boss], but for me [they mind]. [A coworker] actually told me that I have no life, so I should not expect her not to have a life." Judy and Monica were both front-line supervisors who lacked the status of management and had to face the open resentment of their coworkers without the protection of real power. By becoming supervisors, they gained little, but lost the warm and friendly relationships with coworkers that mattered so much.

Dorothy's situation was a little different, yet it illustrates the same tension felt by other women who had one foot in each camp. As an executive secretary, she had known that her previous employer was facing foreclosure but was forbidden to tell the women she supervised. Knowing they would soon lose their jobs, she had to maintain the pretense that all was well. She was still upset about it several months later:

> It's hard to bring a fine line between friendship and supervision. It's an art. It's an absolute art, one which I never achieved. I mean, when I knew that business was going to close, I knew exactly who was going to be losing their job, and when. And I had a lot of very confidential information, and I carried that around with me for a year. About my friends, and, you know, people that had their jobs there thirty years and . . . were like two years away from retirement. And I carried that around a long time. That was very hard for me, and I never want to ever be put in that position again. That was just too much stress, I don't want it. So when I left [that job], I deliberately went for something downscale. I knew I'd take a terrible salary cut. I knew that going in. But I knew it was also worth it. For the peace of mind, and less stress. The stress is a killer. It's a killer.

Women who worked as customer service clerks were in an ambiguous position too, on the front line and forced to mediate between the store management and customers who felt free to abuse them. "We have had things thrown at us," Ann said. "I was called a bitch one day, because a man bought a bicycle and the inner tube went flat. And we did not have an inner tube in the store to give him, so they said he could go anyplace else, and spend any amount of money he had to on it, and bring us the receipt, and we'd pay him. He called me a bitch! I refused to serve him when he came back in with the receipt. I thought, 'Why me? I had nothing to do with it.' I had only related what my boss told me to tell him." When the customer walked away, Ann thought to herself, "What a jerk! You should hear us when you leave."[18]

Daughters whose fathers were entrepreneurs or supervisors were more often supervisors,[19] and they more often felt comfortable in that role. Dawn, for example, the daughter of a small business owner, was in a managerial position:

> Today I was in a hospital where we are taking over. [I] was going in and assessing the capabilities of the existing dietitian, and [asking], "Do we offer her a position, or do we not?" Assessing their policies and procedures: "What do they have, what needs to go in place?" I make recommendations, and in this case we had to hire a dietitian. I do have input into whether or not someone is performing well. If I feel strongly that they are not performing their responsibilities, I would have some impact on that.

And Pam was not intimidated by being a manager:

> I am a manager. I manage a branch of a library and I manage four other branches with it. That's an offline kind of management, so I spend a lot of time, probably ninety percent of my time, dealing with either the public or customers or patrons or the staff who I'm directly involved in supervising. I do a lot of checking schedules. If staff are in the building, or if we have somebody call in sick, or if we have a problem any time during the day with, "Hey I have to go to the doctor," I do that kind of staffing concern.

Eileen, the daughter of upper-middle-class parents, was the only woman in the sample who seemed to relish authority; she said she had always liked being in charge:

> That's a personality characteristic. I remember as a little child going into my father's business, and I loved sitting at the desk. Playing office was important to me. I don't know why it appealed to me, but I remember sitting at the desk with all the pencils and papers. [That] was definitely a role that I could relate to and like.
>
> I was also a competitive swimmer and I liked competition. I liked to win. Being encouraged to win and to be a competitor was not something that was a typical experience . . . but I had done that and done that very successfully, and I liked that. I really did like to compete. My parents encouraged that a great deal. In fact, these would almost be my mother's key words, "Whatever you're going to do, do it well, and be the best."

Regardless of class, very few women in the entire sample sought or particularly enjoyed positions of authority. Alice, for example, a middle-class daughter who worked as a marine biologist in charge of a large lab, was just as uncomfortable with authority as were most working-class women. "I'm in tears every couple of weeks," she said, "over something horrible that's happening where I just can't believe that somebody said something, or my technicians are at each other's throats or something. I mean it really gets to me. . . . It's some of the personal interaction, you know, somebody's saying something like, 'Oh, my God, how could you say that?' . . . I had a woman in my lab who drove me crazy for years. Oh, God! I finally had to fire her. And it was so hard. I thought it was the hardest thing I ever had to do. I hate being the boss. I really don't like being the boss."

Being Boss in a Workforce of One: Home Day Care

Being a boss over other workers was unappealing, but being one's own boss was a different matter.[20] Marlene, Martha, and Cindy had chosen an increasingly common way to be their own boss by setting up as home day-care providers. Marlene originally started her own day-care business so she could care for her children at home. By now, though, her autonomy and the respect she could command in her job were more important than its convenience.

Marlene had quit school in eleventh grade because she was pregnant, but she was not sorry; an independent person, she was just as happy to get out and get on with her life. She worked in a factory until her baby was born, then as a cashier in a drugstore. After about a year in the drugstore, she got married, and six months later she was expecting a second child. As the mother of two young children, it made no sense for her to pay for day care while she worked—besides, she worried about her children's safety when she wasn't there—so she passed her GED test and became a certified home day-care provider. She was still running the day-care center with six children in her care each weekday. Her own two children were now in their teens, but she had adopted a younger niece and nephew whose mother—her sister—was in prison, convicted of murder. She described a typical day on the job:

> The first [child] is supposed to be here at six-thirty. That child is eight. Then the rest of the kids come in, then we do breakfast. Then three of them go to school. Then the other three that stay here just play all day. Ben is one, Sean is two, and Connor is four. We do lunch, then it's nap time, then it's snack time. Stacy [Marlene's daughter] comes home. She'll read to them or do a craft with them. She gets home at three. Then the other three come in after school. They do their homework and have a snack. All of [the day-care kids] are out of here by five o'clock.

Marlene had no trouble completing the GED and various other correspondence courses, because she could do the work on her own terms. "Everything I know," she said, "I'm self-taught. I taught myself how to use a computer. I do everything on my own. We have two computers. I took an accounting course. I'm taking a child psychology course right now. A lot of these courses are home-study courses so you can do it at your own pace when you have time. I took a tax course. I have to learn on my own pace. I hate to be forced to learn stuff." She relished being her own boss, and made sure her clients respected her rights:

> The worst thing about this job is some of the parents' attitudes. It's like they're trying to tell me what they want, and that's not how this works. I am not their employee. It is a profession. They're trying to treat you like a teenager instead of treating you as, "This is your job." When they call me a babysitter I say, "I'm not a babysitter: I don't sit on your kids." And another thing I tell them is, "I pay taxes just as well as you do." They more or less think it's a freeload job, I guess. I sent memos out and told them, "If your child is not picked up by five o'clock, it automatically starts overtime, and there's no exception, because that's personal time for me and my family." I won't

work without a contract. I sue them and everything. Everything's legal.

I don't help with homework. If [the children] have a problem, they have to take it home to their parents. I mean their parents have to do something! . . . I get sick days. I call them [if I am sick], and they get someone else, and I still get paid. Five days a year sick days, five personal days. It's all in my contract. We do our own contracts. I have lawyers, accountants. The state gives us a guideline, but we put on our contracts what we want. And either they sign them or they go somewhere else. I also get one week's paid vacation. . . .

I got to the point where I tell [parents] if they don't like it, they can take their children [and] put an ad in the paper. I'm in one profession that's always going to be needed as long as there's jobs. . . . [The state] can come any time they want, but usually they only come if a report is fined against you. They can't dictate what I do.

Did she like what she was doing? Marlene laughed out loud: "I have my good days and my bad days, like everyone else, but I'd rather do this than work for someone. . . . I'm doing something I want to do. I always said I'd have my own business and I do. . . . I'm very satisfied with my job."

For Marlene, respect was more important than having friendly relationships at work and she carefully distanced herself from her clients. She made it very clear that her role was not that of a parent: "I have some parents now that think they can drop their kids off any time they want. I'm supposed to go get the kids from school when they're sick. And it's the same laws here as it is in school. They're not allowed here. I told the school, 'It's a registered home, call the parents.'" For Cindy and Martha, however, warm, friendly relationships with clients were an important added benefit of home day care, and where Marlene was careful to cultivate a professional, businesslike relationship, and to keep her work self and her home self separate, Cindy and Martha blurred the lines between their work and home roles. Cindy acted much like a mother to her day-care children, and their mothers became her friends:

I have two boys from seven-thirty to eight-thirty in the morning. Their mom's a teacher. She teaches in Baltimore County. And then I have a girl and three other boys after school from three-thirty to about six. Their ages range from seven to eleven. They're all elementary school children, but no babies. You know, they're easy. And really, three of the boys are my little boy's age, they're in his second grade, so they play wonderfully together. He loves them being here. There's no resentment about other children. On the weekends, he's really lonely.

They come at seven-thirty. They usually watch a cartoon. I fix them breakfast. Usually a hot breakfast—they eat here. That must be great for their mothers. Well, we've all become friends because I've been watching the children for several years, so it's appreciated. They have breakfast, we go to the bus about 8:30, they get on the school bus. Different [children come in the afternoon]. Different ones. Their dad picks them up at three, and they go home. Then, the children, the little ones, come home at three-thirty and play for a half an hour, they have a snack, do their homework, and then they play until their parents come. They always do their homework though. Every day they do their homework here, which their mothers are also grateful for. They don't have to contend with that when they get home. And I really find that when they all sit down together to do it, they help each other—they work together at it—so that's good for them. They all sit around the table here. I clear it off.

Martha's approach was similar. Amy, one of her day-care children, usually came first thing in the morning, then Vanessa, her son's daughter.

Amy will usually have breakfast with me, then Vanessa comes. They will have breakfast usually. And then the kids will sit down and watch TV. And then Lauren comes in about, between eight-thirty and nine o'clock. Sometimes she wants a bottle, sometimes she doesn't. She lays in her crib. Later, I'll put her in her infant seat in the living room so she can watch the kids. . . . They're not allowed to watch any regular TV. No cartoons. I don't like any of that stuff. They have to watch something either educational or at least clean. No bad commercials in it. And then, they'll do that, and I clean up the kitchen. And then depending if I crochet or not, I'll sit down in the living room and crochet, or . . . Suzanne [Amy's mother] brought a big plastic car the other day and that was a blast.

Martha had developed friendships with some of her day-care mothers:

Amy's mother used to always come and have lunch with her, which is really nice. She's become a good friend. So when she comes, I fix lunch for the rest of them. . . . And then sometimes Katy's mother comes. And then after lunch, Suzanne always took all the toddlers out to the backyard for play . . . while I ate lunch. And then at one o'clock, she went home and I put the kids down for a nap. They all go down for a nap, babies, kids everyone. So then I sit, and I can read, or I sew. I can do what I want to do . . . put away the clothes, load the dishes, whatever. And that gives me time to change gears and then they wake up about—Amy sometimes slept until about four o'clock, when her mother came home. And Katy usually takes about an hour-and-a-half or a two-hour nap. Lauren also needs her nap. One day it's in the morning, and another it's in the afternoon. I don't know why she does that. But if she's not taking a nap, she's a real good baby. She'll just sit and play and look around. They are both really good. Katy is the pleasantest kid I've ever seen in my life.

I've had lots of day-care babies. Amy I've had the longest. I've had her since the time she was six weeks. And now she's two and a half. She has really outgrown this situation, and so she needs to be like coloring, and stuff like that, but I can't have coloring and stuff like that when the little ones are around, because they want to color too, and I don't want my walls colored. . . .

Being friends with her clients worked out well for Cindy in part because she cared for fewer children than Marlene and Martha and her arrangements were informal. It was more problematic for Martha because she was a licensed day-care provider supervised by the state. Obviously still upset and angry, she described an incident with a mother that eventually involved the authorities:

[This mother] was a real superwoman, "I'm going to do it all, and I'm going to be perfect at all of it." And she drove me crazy. . . . She asked me if I was using [her daughter's] wipes. And I said, "I just use whatever wipes. . . . I just take them out of the box." "Well," she said, "we use this at home, and if it's good enough for us . . . but if you prefer another brand, then I'll certainly get them, but I'd prefer you use her wipes." And I'm like [Martha rolls her eyes]. And I said, "Well, if she has a messy diaper, it sometimes takes two or three, and they're not heavy enough." I said, "Mine are heavier." And she said, "Well, she couldn't have any dirty diapers for you. She has them at home." So then I stopped telling her anything. But she got upset at that. So she called my worker. And she told him that I sent her home in the same diapers that she came in. And that baby got changed the most! She was the one who, if you were in the middle of changing her diaper and she wet it again, she wanted off! You couldn't leave a wet diaper on her. And [the mother] told him, her [baby's] butt was bleeding. And I said, "If her butt's bleeding, it's because she's constipated because she insists on keeping her on that iron formula." And she was constipated. And she told him that I was uncommunicative with her. And I told him, I said, "I cannot talk to her?" And no matter what I said to her, she turned it around. And it was like, a direct attack on her. My other mothers just take it or leave it. She took it as a direct attack on her motherhood. She was perfect and she knew it, and I couldn't tell her anything.

It blew my mind that it turned out like that. And it ruined my self-confidence. I mean, I'll bet you it took about six weeks to recover from that because I just felt so bad. And she called my worker, was it twice? And he came out every time. If they get a complaint, they have to come out. And she just—I didn't know how long she was going to keep it up. So I told him, when she first came, [the baby] was three-months-old, and she was a really heavy baby, and she couldn't keep up her head, and [the mother] would pick her up by her arms, and her head would drop back. It'd drive me crazy . . . to see her head drop back. So [my daughter] said, "You hold that baby's head. You're supposed to hold her head." So when she went to the door, [my daughter] said, "Now don't forget to hold her head!" And she got really [mad]. She said,

"You're trying to tell me how to raise my child." And that's when I realized that it wasn't going to work out any more. I told her. When she came that morning, I had it written on a piece of paper. I said, "I think you need to find other day care," and she said, "I've already started." She said, "In fact, I'm not leaving her here today either." And she picked up and waltzed out. It just blew my mind.

The interaction between Martha and this mother underlines the tensions inherent in the relationship between day-care providers and the mothers whose children they care for. Differences in childcare practices are one source of tension.[21] Another is differences in beliefs about whether mothers of young children should work; often day-care providers are women who have chosen day care because they believe mothers of young children should stay at home, yet the mothers whose children they care for work. Martha believed that mothers should stay home if they could afford to, and she criticized her "problem" mother for working when she didn't "have" to: "She didn't want to stay home," Martha said. "She was like a career [woman]. She was a yuppie. I don't know what she was."

Marlene was right when she said the day-care profession would always be in demand; there are almost half-a-million family day-care providers and family day care is rated by the Bureau of Labor as a "growth occupation." Working for themselves was the surest way for women to have autonomy on the job—a big plus—and, as Marlene found, it was also a way to win respect. But day-care providers pay a heavy price; it is difficult to draw clear boundaries between work and home, and they have to work long hours for low wages. Marlene, for example, worked almost sixty hours a week taking care of the six children in her charge, but her net income was less than $12,000. This is typical for home day-care providers and explains why most are married women; a recent report from the Center for the Child Care Workforce reports that the median hourly wages for family day-care providers are only $4.82 (compared with $7.38 an hour for parking lot attendants, and $12.39 for animal trainers). Not surprisingly, the childcare workforce across the country has turnover rates between thirty and forty percent; the report notes that "this 98 percent female workforce . . . suffers a higher concentration of poverty level jobs than almost any other occupation in the United States."[22]

Different Worlds, Different Words: Social Class and Survey Research

Survey research has an air of scientific authority that interviews lack; for example, researchers "administer" an "instrument" (a questionnaire), which is "standardized," with carefully "constructed" "items" (questions) that are designed to be neutral and objective. But this authority and technical language can mask the fact that different classes, races, genders, and ethnicities live in very different worlds, in which the same words can have very different meanings. This problem is recognized when it comes to cross-cultural research, where linguistic differences are obvious, but it is no less real in research that is conducted in a single language.

Some examples from the interviews illustrate these linguistic traps: When I asked them if their parents lived nearby, middle-class women often said yes, even if their parents lived in Washington, D.C., or Philadelphia, both cities at least an hour from Baltimore. On the other hand, when I asked them the same question, working-class women often said no when their parents lived in another Baltimore neighborhood or in an adjoining county. "Near" and "far" were measured by life experience, not an odometer. Working-class women had very often lived in the same neighborhood—even on the same block—as their parents and other extended family members for their entire lives; it was not unusual for three generations of the same family to live on one street. And, as we will see later, many women had lived for much of their lives with no access to a car. In this context, especially in a city with inadequate public transport, a few miles was far. For middle-class women, on the other hand, accustomed to far-flung families and travel by air as well as by road, fifty or even several hundred miles was nothing.

Living in neighborhoods with others whose life experiences were similar, both working- and middle-class women had come to share assumptions that needed no articulation. For working-class women, one of these assumptions was that women of their kind did not graduate from college. When I asked how far they went in school, high school graduates almost always said, "I graduated," assuming that I would understand them to mean, "I graduated from high school," not from college. But when I asked middle-class women the same question, they invariably said they had "graduated from college," and they usually specified their degree—bachelor's, master's, or Ph.D.—and often their major field of study. Similarly, when I asked middle-class women how often they had to do work that was dirty, several women laughed nervously because they were confused about what I meant. Was it a joke? Working-class women, on the other hand, knew instantly: for them, dirty work was not a joke but an everyday reality.[23]

None of the working-class women complained about clocking on or signing a time card, but Kate, the only middle-class woman who was ever forced to use a time clock, described it as demeaning. (Kate was briefly required to clock on when the publisher she worked for tried to institute a time management system.) And women in unskilled jobs that involved heavy lifting were no more likely to describe their jobs as physically demanding than were professional women, even though by any objective standard, unskilled jobs were physically much more demanding. And finally, although they earned only a fourth as much as the professional women I interviewed, the women in unskilled jobs were no less satisfied with their pay.[24] As we will see later, many working-class women had grown up in families that were poor or short of money, and many had also been poor as adults; this was especially true for the women in unskilled jobs. By and large, the lowest-paid women had the lowest expectations: they came from the poorest families and they were married to the lowest-paid husbands whose jobs, in many cases, were little better than their own.[25] Thus their survey responses reflected subjective judgments that, in turn, reflected very different life experiences.

The survey responses failed to catch qualitative differences in women's experience. To illustrate: in response to a question on how stressful their jobs were, Phyllis, a cashier, and Kate, the editor, gave identical responses; both agreed that their jobs were stressful. Their narratives, however, made clear that the kind of stress they experienced, and its effect on them, was very different. For Phyllis, "Seventy percent of [the stress] is mental stress. Because everything's timed, see, on that computer. And they can pull up [my work] for a week. They can see how long it took [me] to wait on each customer." Mental stress was also an issue for Kate, who knew she could do an excellent job, but was slow:

> I like to give it more time than it should take, and they do ask for how many pages we do. . . . We have to account for every quarter hour of our time, or each tenth of an hour, and record it all, and it takes a long time just to remember what you were doing. And so I know that they are judging by quantity as well as quality. On evaluations, they go into all that in detail. I feel very confident, and at the same time stressed, because I feel like I can't tell them how much time it takes me. I take things home to finish them up.

The essential difference between Kate's experience and Phyllis's was that Kate was able to control her level of stress by taking work home and finishing it up on her own time. And because she also found her work exciting and interesting, she experienced "a good kind of stress":[26]

> It's challenging all the time. No two articles are the same. I'm always working hard to pull something out of my brain or find something in a reference book. It's very challenging, but I like that. Usually I have an idea that I've either encountered something before and have some idea that I—at least I know that there's something somewhere in a library or somewhere in a reference where I can find material. Or if I have to totally give up, and I don't want to query the author, I just make a decision. And I like doing that too. Sometimes I have to say—the only way I can do it is to just cut through and do it a certain way. And I do that too. It's a good kind of stress.

Their survey responses also masked differences in working- and middle-class women's experiences of autonomy at work. The specific questions were able to pick up social class differences in the *amount* of autonomy the women experienced, but not qualitative differences in its nature, which were obvious when they talked about their jobs in their own words. Very few working-class women had true autonomy—the freedom many professionals have to define when and how they do their work, even what they do. Greta and some of the other office workers enjoyed a kind of pseudo-autonomy that consisted of being less closely supervised than they might have been, but this was light-years away from being their own boss.[27] Pam, a librarian, perhaps best illustrates the difference between the genuine autonomy she enjoyed on her job and the pseudo-autonomy that was the best available to most working-class women: "I like the autonomy of choosing what I do," said Pam. "I can make my day what I want it to be. And that's a powerful thing." Pam and other professional women had freedom to choose how to do their work and structure their day. Most working-class women, on the other hand, when they had freedom, had only freedom from intrusive, heavy-handed supervision.[28]

The words that describe job conditions—"challenging," "pressured," "interesting," for example—are not neutral signifiers of an objective reality. Women in unskilled jobs occupied a distinctive work world with distinctive conditions; they had not just a little less autonomy, but a lot less, not just a little less pay, but a lot less. And many of these same women had also occupied a distinctive world outside the workplace, a world in which money was scarce, conditions were hard, and jobs offered few rewards. They were offered a miniscule fraction of the monetary and non-monetary rewards available to middle-class women, but by the time they had entered the workplace, this was what they had learned to expect.

In the days of a manufacturing economy, the split between manual and non-manual labor was often used as a quick indicator of men's social class; and, within manual work, a secondary division into skilled and unskilled labor was common. There was a gulf between manual and non-manual work, a lesser one between skilled and unskilled. Skilled manual workers usually had a trade qualification or extensive job experience that enabled them to do highly skilled work; a high school diploma was usually not necessary because training was conducted on the job. A similar gulf existed here between gray-collar and pink-collar jobs. In fact, in terms of job conditions, the gap between pink- and gray-collar working-class work was wider than the gap between pink-collar work and low-status professional work. In terms of job conditions, then a high school diploma was an important credential, because it brought freedom from gray-collar work.

In the chapter that follows, I will explore the implications of these differences in job conditions for women's job satisfaction and for the meaning of work in their lives. As might be expected, the women in jobs with the worst conditions were the least satisfied with their jobs, but we will see that differences in satisfaction were relatively minor considering differences in the job conditions women experienced. We will see that some women were satisfied with their jobs, but disappointed in work, but we will see, too, that regardless of whether they were disappointed, most women still found important meanings in work. I turn now to an exploration of the complex linkages between the orientations women bring to the job, their experiences on the job, and the meanings they found in work.

Can't Get No
Satisfaction

I don't mind what I'm doing now. It's satisfying. It's cleaning other people's homes. I can make my own hours, and I can be home when my son gets home. I like the fact that I can make my own hours. And I do a good job cleaning, and they're always satisfied. It just leads up to more jobs. And I like to do it. I don't have a problem with cleaning. I can come home from cleaning someone else's house and come right in and do my laundry and stuff. No problem.

—Cheryl

I'm satisfied with my job per se. Take "job" and put it in quotes. But I'm not so satisfied with where I am in life, do you understand? I mean I . . . should have gone on to college. Everything was open to me. All I had to do was do it. And [I could have] had a profession now—be a professional now, not just a working person. But overall, taking the job per se, I'm pleased with it.

—Ann

A Job Is Just a Job

Most of the conceptual categories that are used to describe feelings about work were developed over decades of research into men's work. This research has privileged middle-class men's experience, and it embodies middle-class values and assumptions about how workers *should* feel about work. According to these assumptions, workers should be personally invested in work, committed to it, make it central to their identity, and find it intrinsically meaningful. Regardless of its quality, work should be engraved with a special significance. Adopting the same assumptions, many students of women's work have tried to fit women's feelings and the meanings they derive from work into the same neat categories. In one, the "good" category, are intrinsic motivations, commitment to work, identification with work, career motivation, and a "work" (not "domestic" or "family" orientation).[1] Women whose feelings and experiences conform are considered to be less "traditional." But women's feelings about work refuse to fit tidily into categories borrowed from men.[2] Most of the women I interviewed were committed to work—in the sense that they would prefer to work rather than not, and valued the rewards they derived from it—but commitment did not mean they placed work at the center of their being. Many women were committed both to work and to family, and they valued both extrinsic and intrinsic rewards.[3] The meanings of work for women—and their orientations to work—demand their own vocabulary, one that describes an untidy reality, and avoids narrow assumptions. The historian H. F. Moorhouse puts it well:

> Most analyses assume that the dominant values of capitalist society present some work ethic to its members. But students of the meanings of work need to be alive to a diversity of dominant sources representing different messages about work. They need to be aware that while dominant values will provide a good deal of input, albeit in a more complex and contradictory fashion than is often suggested, other sources exist with their own institutional supports which will mix and mediate with dominant views. Class, gender and ethnic cultures will make complex inputs, as will quite precise occupational ideologies formed in varying workplaces which will have both formal and informal expressions. The meanings of work are unlikely to be neat and simple or form some uncomplicated "ethic" but are rather likely to be jumbled and variegated, so that any individual has a whole range of types and levels of meanings on which to draw.[4]

Some women were satisfied with their jobs and with the rewards of work, but others were left with the feeling that something was missing in their lives. Some were looking for another outlet for the physical and emotional energies they had previously devoted to their families. Others only now recognized what might have been, and regretted their lack of opportunity earlier in life. Some of these women were becoming aware for the first time that work was a potential area for deeper rewards; as Lisa, who was now attending nursing school said, "I used to look on it as a chore." For most of these women, their job was satisfying, but their experience of work was disappointing.

These two experiences of work, simple satisfaction and disappointed satisfaction, were qualitatively quite different. In this chapter, I introduce women with both experiences of work as points of reference, so that when, in the following chapters, I explore these experiences more fully and abstractly, they will have human faces. I have chosen Sheila, Rosalie, Sandra, and Mona to illustrate the experience of women whose satisfaction was unequivocal and straightforward. These women were pleased that neither their jobs nor their families made heavy demands on their time or emotional energy, and that, at last, they could easily manage the demands of both.

Sheila and Rosalie both worked in offices in jobs they enjoyed, and felt drawn neither to more demanding work nor to a heavier involvement at home. Sheila had only one child, and although she had to cope with a mentally ill mother who was in an institution, she had these demands under control, at least for now. Rosalie had two children, one in the Marines and one in high school, who were both doing well. Before she returned to work, she had been bored at home. Mona operated a beauty salon in the basement of her home, which allowed her to balance work and family with minimum stress; she could weave them together, flicking a duster around the house or dashing out to the store between seeing clients who were also her neighbors. Sandra worked as a janitor, and although she didn't particularly enjoy cleaning chalkboards and some of the other duties of her job, she was content with its convenience, the modest demands it made on her, and the freedom from close supervision and relatively generous financial rewards it offered.

Like a number of others in the study, these four women were satisfied with their jobs and with their work experience; they were content with jobs that offered reasonable autonomy, flexibility, and convenience, and that were not stressful or too demanding. Sandra, for instance, had tried running her business full-time, but it was too time consuming and demanded too much attention: "I was in home interiors and gifts for years and that takes . . . the whole time you're awake. If you're awake, you're working, so you try to go to sleep so you don't work." For these women, work was a significant—if not a central—life interest; it enhanced, but did not define, their lives.

Sheila

A dainty, youthful woman with a sweet and ready smile, Sheila talked to me in her enormous country kitchen, which was designed, she later told me, by John, her husband of nineteen years. All his life he had dreamed of a house with a huge kitchen. It was still early morning when I arrived, and Sheila had the day off work, but she was already carefully and skillfully made up, her thick mascara, violet eyeliner, and pearly pink lipstick evidence of the effort she made to present a well-groomed face to the world. As we sat sipping coffee in front of the open fire that was the kitchen's centerpiece, she told me her history.

Sheila's housepainter father and mother were "low income," so, even as a high school student, she held down two jobs, one in the school office during study periods, and one in a five-and-dime store on evenings and weekends. At first, she had hoped to become a teacher, but when she discovered that she would need a college degree, she gave up that idea, and switched to cosmetology; then when she later discovered that she would still have to go to school, even for cosmetology, she decided to work full-time at the five-and-dime store. Where would she get the money for more schooling?

Sheila married her first husband, a coworker at the five-and-dime, when she was nineteen, and they divorced four years later. After Sheila had worked at the five-and-dime for several years, the store closed, but she soon found another job in a department store, and she worked there until just before the birth of her only daughter, five years later. She stayed home with her daughter for about six weeks, returned to work briefly, then stayed home for a year or so, working as a babysitter from time to time. When her daughter was two, Sheila returned to the department store as a cashier and service-desk attendant; she remained there until they too closed, and then moved on to Kmart as a cashier.

Sheila worked at Kmart for about five years and quit only because she and John came into a little money and decided to move to the country. In the country, she worked for several months housecleaning with another woman, then went out on her own, persuaded by John that she would make more money that way. But she didn't especially like cleaning, nor did she like working on her own, so after a year, she found another job as a switchboard operator and receptionist for an insurance company. She was still in this job, and enjoyed it, even though it was "very, very busy, very hectic":

> Sometimes I say, "Man, I've gotta come up for air." It's like people always calling, you know, about either accident claims or else their homeowners' insurance or auto insurance. A lot of times people call and they don't know who they want. So you're trying to get this out of them [who their agent is] so you know who to connect them with. And meanwhile, you've got to ask them to hold because you've got other lines right there. Most times I'll say, "Do you happen to know who your agent is?" and they'll say, "No." Or else they'll say, "Can you hold a minute?" And then I'll have to ask them to hold because I have four lines. Sometimes they don't [know who their agent is] or they say, "It's at home and I'm at work." Then we have people who handle, like, a couple of units, so we give it to them. We don't have a computer out there, and lots of times they don't realize that they're just talking to a switchboard. You know, they'll go into their long story about their accident, you know, and I'll say, "Excuse me. This is a switchboard."

Sheila's workplace was congenial, and her job conditions were fairly good: she had a morning and afternoon break and forty-five minutes off for lunch. Best of all, there were "not a lot of people telling [her] what to do," and her bosses were "very lenient." "If you have a problem, you can talk to them, and nobody makes strict demands on you." Her bosses' tolerance was important to her, because at times she had to ask for time off; whenever her daughter needed to go to an appointment, it was Sheila's job to take her—John had pointed out that it made more sense for Sheila to do it because he earned more money and worked further away—and, on occasion, she had to ask for time off to deal with her mother.

Sheila's mother suffered from paranoid schizophrenia, which was not always controlled by medication. Some years earlier, reluctant to place her mother in a nursing home, Sheila had tried to care for her at home, but it hadn't worked out. "It got really hectic," she said, "with everyone having to leave [for work and school] at the same time. I would give her her medication and her breakfast and fix her lunch in the morning, then [my daughter] would come home from school and give her her bath and medicine. One day [my daughter] called me at work and said the ice cream had melted all over the cabinet, because Mom had gotten it out and put it in the cabinet."

It took Sheila several months to find a suitable nursing facility for her mother, but then her mother was evicted because she was aggressive and kept absconding. Sheila had to take more time off work to find another home; eventually she was successful, and, at least for now, the new placement seemed to be working out—"Touch wood," she said.

Even so, it was a constant worry; periodically, Sheila received urgent calls from the nursing home staff, asking her to talk to her mother and calm her down. On occasion, she had to go to the home, and once or twice the police called when they found her mother wandering the streets. In spite of these difficulties, though, Sheila found caring for her mother rewarding. She visited her every Sunday, and at least one evening a week. The previous Sunday was typical; she had taken her daughter and her daughter's boyfriend to visit her mother in the nursing home for about an hour, dropped them at the skating rink at seven, returned to the nursing home, sat with her mother again until a quarter of ten, then picked up the young people at the rink and drove them home. Sheila said she felt much better after these visits, and would like to be able to spend more time with her mother.

Sheila much preferred working in an office to cleaning. She liked to dress well and wear makeup, but it made no sense to dress up when she was a cleaner, and after a while, she had become fed up with wearing jeans and old clothes all the time. She knew that if she didn't work at all, she would soon give up caring how she looked; she would have more time—a definite plus—but she would lose her motivation to "keep up with herself." Working in an office, on the other hand, motivated her to take care with her appearance. "You meet people," she said, "and you keep yourself better." Sheila considered her life to be much better than her mother's. Working, she was out and about with other people and she got to drive a car; her mother had done neither of these things.

Rosalie

Rosalie, a petite woman with brown curly hair, was neatly dressed in a turtleneck, denim skirt, and comfortable flats. Her small, suburban house was cozy and welcoming, brimful with family photographs, mementos, and an impressive porcelain doll collection. Rosalie's husband was home watching television—I later learned that he was a former shipwright with the Coast Guard and was on permanent disability following a serious accident at work.

A high school graduate, Rosalie was the daughter of a steelworker. As a young girl, she had wanted to be a nurse, but following kidney surgery as a teenager, her doctor told her she should avoid heavy lifting; she chose cosmetology because her mother advised her to make sure she had "something to fall back on." After high school, she tried working as a cosmetologist, but hated it, and after a few months found a clerical job with the government. She worked as a clerk with the government until she had her first child several years later. She then quit her job and stayed at home for thirteen years, until her second son started high school and she decided that it was time to go back to work. "I went to work for boredom," she said. She was now working for the government once more, again as a clerk. Her duties were to sort the mail each day, enter incoming letters into a computer, and verify the hours on employees' time cards. The job was not closely supervised, and she liked that "as long as you know what to do, they're not over you."

Rosalie's husband had opposed her taking a job, and when she first started working, he complained that he was lonely at home all day. But he adjusted, and when a promotion opportunity came up, he encouraged her to apply for it. Without his encouragement, Rosalie said she would not have applied for the job because she lacked self-confidence. As it was, she applied, was successful, and found the job to be well within her capacity.

Rosalie sometimes felt pulled in two directions trying to keep her husband and son happy, but she still considered herself better off than her mother because her mother "had no interest outside the home." She was happy with her life, which was "all right."

Sandra

A beautiful, gentle woman whose long, blue-black hair and chiseled cheekbones hinted at her Native-American ancestry, Sandra lived in a picture-perfect, small white house in the suburbs. As we talked in her sunny kitchen around eight-thirty in the morning, a pair of cardinals busied themselves at the birdfeeder just outside our window, and children playing in the schoolyard opposite screamed with delight.

Sandra left school at fourteen, in eighth grade, but completely unable to read. No one knew why. "I had so many testings at the hospital downtown," she said. "We had everything done to see what was wrong. Back then they just did not understand what it was. Then they considered you just plain stupid."

After leaving school, she worked as a waitress for a year or so, then got married and quit because she wanted to start a family right away. Nine years later, after eight miscarriages, she finally gave birth to her daughter, Carmen, "a very sickly child," whose health problems continued throughout her childhood. "She had a kidney problem," Sandra explained, "she had a severe ear problem, she had very sensitive skin. She had to have no soap; the stuff we had to buy was $10 a bar. It was called non-soap. She had to use prescription washing powder . . . and she stayed sick all the time. Every month she was in the hospital."

Sandra's husband had helped her cope with her reading disability. "My husband had a great big beautiful sign made," she said, "with Carmen's name, the way it was spelled, so that if anybody came in, I could spell her name. It was always hung up in the front room. It's up in the bedroom now, but it's beautiful the way he had it made." She later showed me the sign, which was carved in golden oak, with Carmen's name painted in large, clear, white letters.

Even with her husband's help, caring for a frail child was hard: "He always tried to make everything easy for me, but at times I ran into problems that were just impossible. I had to bring someone in from the neighborhood if she had to have a particular medicine that had to be measured. They had to read it. So that made it kind of hard. But she was always taken care of, always. I always figured out a way that she would get it just right."

About a year after her daughter's birth, Sandra took a factory job, but she didn't enjoy it and so, after three years, she started selling gifts from home. She then established Sandra's Creations Plus, a flower-arranging business she ran part-time from home. She also took a job as a janitor in the school opposite her house, working from 3 P.M. to 11 P.M. each day. She still worked in this job, and still did some flower arranging part-time.

Sandra liked her paycheck, and the fact that she could often boost it by working overtime. She had used some of the extra overtime money to build a tiny house for her daughter in the block next door, a miniature of her own house. "I like being independent," she said, a bit guiltily. "And, I know it's horrible to say, but I like being away from home. . . . I just don't like being home all the time."

One of five siblings, Sandra took the lead in caring for her parents. "I'm like their mother," she said. "If there's problems, I'm there." She felt neither better nor worse off than her mother had been at her stage of life, but she would like her daughter's life to be different. "I'd love for her to get everything out of life," she said. "Whatever's there, grab for it."

Mona

A very pretty woman, her red hair fashioned in a French braid and tied with a tiny black bow, Mona flipped the sign on her basement salon door from "OPEN" to "CLOSED" when I arrived, wordlessly communicating one of the advantages of being her own boss. Her hairdressing salon, A Cut Above, was just a block or two from the university in a neighborhood that houses the children and grandchildren of Kentucky coal-miners who, many years earlier, had come to Baltimore seeking jobs in the steel mills. The jobs were gone, but the families had stayed; except for a few students and young professionals, most of the residents, like Mona, had lived there all their lives.

As a child, Mona had wanted to be a nurse, and chose cosmetology only because she found out in high school that her math and vocabulary scores were "too low" for nursing school. With hindsight, however, she felt everything had turned out for the best. After she graduated from high school, she had worked in a neighborhood beauty salon for five years, and was married and had two children, a boy and a girl. She then opened her own salon at home. She liked that she didn't have to rush, and it was convenient; when she had some free time between clients, she could close the door and rest or do housework. She enjoyed talking with her clients, most of whom were elderly regulars, and she knew she provided them with a useful service, not only by agreeing to style their hair in the old-fashioned styles they liked, but also by listening to them. "I'm their priest," she said, "their psychiatrist, their doctor." Looking back on her decision, she said that unless you were ambitious—which she wasn't—it was not a job in which you made a lot of money, but it was "very comforting."

Four years earlier, when her husband's florist business went bankrupt, Mona had been afraid she might have to close the salon and take a regular job, because the business didn't bring in enough money to support a family. She could breathe easier now because her husband earned good money working close to sixty hours a week as a messenger service manager.

Her husband liked her working, but he complained that she had no time to be with him on Saturdays, his day off: "Because he's off, I should be off, because he's home, I should be home," Mona said, amused. He liked her to be around because she gave him advice, "like Hillary [Clinton]." Mona's life, she felt, was much better than her mother's had been. "My husband doesn't drink," she said. "That's the basic thing that [my mother] had a problem with." She would like her daughter to be more independent than she had been—and, she said, she already was.

So-Called Satisfaction: When a Job Is Not Enough

The women in the study had entered adolescence just as female roles were beginning to change, so they were caught between the past and the future, between a fast-fading family-centered model of adult female development and a new model, not at all clearly defined, in which work would occupy a more dominant place. Their paths would follow a zigzagging, stop-and-start, meandering course between family and work, and would require them to negotiate a path between the two, making compromises in both. A major concern for them now that they are well into their life journey is coming to terms with these compromises and dealing with the disappointments that have inevitably followed. For many women, a central disappointment has been their failure to find deep satisfaction in work.

In later chapters of the book, I will explore more fully how gender and class had limited working-class women's choices and shaped their work compromises. For now, however, I will introduce some of the women who felt regretful and disappointed—satisfied with their jobs, but not with their work. Ann regretted her decision not to graduate high school and go on to acquire a profession, Helen had accomplished her career goal but didn't feel "fulfilled inside," and Pam wondered what other paths she might have taken. All three women felt restless and discontented as they second-guessed their past. Terry and Jill, though less regretful, would prefer not to do paid work; they believed they would find more fulfillment in family and leisure activities at home.

Ann

A trim, athletic woman dressed in jeans and a purple sweater, her curly hair pulled loosely into a ponytail with a beaded scrunchy, Ann met me at the door of her row house. Her city neighborhood, one of several that were settled earlier in the century by German immigrants, has clung to its air of solid respectability; like all the others in the street, Ann's house was faced with form-stone, mass-produced, gray, cementlike slabs that cloak and conceal the original handmade red brick of houses throughout working-class Baltimore. Like Ann's, all the houses on her street were entered directly from the sidewalk via white marble steps, kept scrubbed and shining by residents. As she led me down a long passageway to the large, open kitchen at its end, I could see that the interior of Ann's house was just as neat, spotless, and carefully maintained as its facade. This, I decided, was a woman who was not only highly efficient and energetic, but who kept her house clean for her own sake, not for her neighbors'.

Ann seemed keyed up at first, and as we talked, I realized that she was the kind of person who found it difficult to sit when there was work to be done. And there was always work to be done—floors to be scrubbed, meals to be cooked, woodwork to be painted. When I complimented her on her well-organized, tidy kitchen, for example, she protested and pointed out a few barely visible scratches and marks on the paintwork. I learned that the source of this perfectionism was her foreman father, who was a strict, unbending parent:

> When I was growing up, my father ruled. It was, "Ask your father." That was it. He was such a disciplined man: you got up and you went to work. This is what you did. You work, and you go to school if you have the opportunity. You get the best grades you can. Never could I bring home a B. They had to be A's, and even [with] an A, he would want to know why I didn't get an A plus. You did the very best you could. He demanded this. You had responsibilities. You did your responsibilities in the house and to yourself, and that was just how it was. So I guess it was inbred in me. It was inbred in me. I had no other choice. . . . I didn't go out until my jobs were done, and they had best be done in those days. . . . This is just how I am today.

Even now she was forty-nine, Ann still dreaded her father's disapproval: "I still feel I have to be perfect around my father. I still feel that. I still feel that. I still do. It will never go away. If he says, 'That's wrong,' I never fight the issue. I say, 'You're right, Dad.' I still do what I was going to do, but I say, 'You're right.' I have too much respect for my father to disagree."

Unlike many of the women I talked to, Ann had enjoyed a financially secure childhood; her parents could afford to keep her in high school, and they had encouraged her to graduate. But eager to get out from under her father's yoke, she had insisted on going to a two-year business school instead of a regular high school for ninth and tenth grade:

> I went to business school, which was only like a two-year course. That was it, you only went for two years, you graduated, and you went to work. It was a Catholic school. It was ninth and tenth grade, and that was it. They had several [schools like that].... I loved school. Oh yes, this was a big thing. I regret that, not following and going to the four years of high school. I should have gone to a regular high school. That was a big contention between my father and I, that I was going to a business school. He wanted those four years of a Catholic high school. This was a big thing between us. I don't even know how I won that one. It was the only one I ever won. I was just too anxious to get on with life.

At sixteen, she took a job in the office of a furniture store, and worked steadily until she became pregnant with her third child. Her sister-in-law, who lived near the store, had taken care of the first two, and was willing to continue, but it was "getting to be too much," Ann said. "We only had one car. And we lived all the way out in [the suburbs], and I had to go all the way into South Baltimore to work, and it was too much, transporting the two children, and then I think I got pregnant with the third, so I just stopped working." As soon as her youngest child was a year old, she took a job working nights in a local toy store, while her husband watched the children.

Ann was still working at the toy store, for the last ten years on its service desk. She quite liked the job, not least because the women she worked with were like a family and had supported her through the many ups and downs of raising six children: "I mean I'll go in there and they'll say 'What is wrong? Are the kids OK? What happened?' So it's nice when you can go to work and feel that. And I can call up and say, 'This happened the other day,' and say, 'Look, I'm supposed to be at work tomorrow, but I've got a doctor's appointment for [my son], and I have to take him.'"

Over the years, Ann had always put her family first. She had "loved the whole thing. I'd do it again if I could. I loved the labor. I loved the delivery. It was just a totally satisfying situation." Now, however, her enjoyment was fading; five of her six grown children were living at home, two of them with their own children, and she was tired. "They're all home but two," she said. "I say to my husband, 'Do you realize we're no further than we were because now we have the two-year-old ... we are no further than we were fourteen years ago. We're still ... wiping up the same spills, wiping the same fingerprints off the walls.'" She felt she'd seen it all: "You go through so much with six [kids]. We've had just a little bit of everything. We've had teenage pregnancy. We've had drugs. We've had so much. If another one does do it, you think, 'OK, we've lived through it before, we'll handle this.'"

As she approached fifty, Ann found herself examining her life and second-guessing her choices: "Actually, this thing has just hit me within the past three years. I haven't felt this way until the past three years. And now I'm reflecting back onto this. Because I have no babies and I think I'm getting bored. And I guess, with me it's just an inborn thing; I feel that I should be giving this care that I gave to these babies now to people that need it. Now I don't have that. Now I think, 'If I would have gone to high school, and if I would have done this.' But this is the way it worked out." Attributing her feelings to menopause, she felt fed up, frustrated, and bored:

> I went on [hormones] because my emotional stability went downhill really bad. So I went on them for that. I had that blood test, and my hormones [were] really out of balance. In the past year, I could have just taken my clothes, gotten myself an apartment, and just lived there, you know. That's it, don't anybody bother talking to me, and I won't talk to you—just leave me alone. Now I fight it. Now when somebody drops something and spills it, I say to myself, "Don't yell, don't yell at this mess." They'll either commit me or it'll balance out, one or the other. When you start going through menopause, your female hormones stop producing but your male hormones continue to. The same thing happens to men. That's why you hear women say, "He's getting mellower." We get more aggressive. One day I'll rule the roost here. It's the same with my mother. She doesn't say anymore, "Ask your father." He's saying, "Oh I don't know, I'll ask your mother."

Ann's job was familiar and she liked the people she worked with. It allowed her to manage a domestic life that included four resident children and two grandchildren as well as her husband. But, although she liked the job well enough, she wished she had a profession, not just a job: "I'm satisfied with my job per se," she said. "Take job and put it in quotes. But I'm not so satisfied with where I am in life, do you understand? I mean I should have gone to the regular high school. I should have gone on to college. Everything was open to me. All I had to do was do it. And have a profession now. To be a professional now, not just a working person. But overall, taking the job per se, I'm pleased with it." If she didn't work, she said, "I wouldn't feel I was contributing, at this point. I would lose a lot of independence. . . . Independence seems to be getting very important to me."

Helen

From her childhood in a family that was both very poor and very unhappy, followed by an early pregnancy and a youthful marriage, Helen had steadily worked her way up the career ladder. For nine long years, she had raised her children, studied part time for an associate's degree in accounting, and worked full time, usually in two jobs: full time in her accounting job in a large public hospital and part-time at a different hospital as a computer operator. At last, with her degree in hand, she was eligible for a promotion she felt she had always deserved:

> [Now] I can move up to a senior accountant. I mean, really, the promotion that I've gotten, it has not really changed my job. I mean I've been in the department, I've done the jobs many times before, it's just that it's going to be more my responsibility. I felt I should have had this promotion before now, but it was always brought up to me that I didn't have the piece of paper that I need. I just thought it was very unfair if a person had the ability to do the job—but it didn't come about until I had the degree. So it doesn't really make any difference.

But, something was still missing. Should she try a different job? Go back to school?

> Well, I know I want to go back to school. I don't know if I'm going to pursue another degree. I'm planning . . . this summer I'm going to take a real estate course. At this point, it took me ten years to get my AA [degree], it's going to take me another ten years to get my B.S. So, I mean at this point I want to take something I want. You know, when you're going in a degree program, you have to take all these courses. I'm on a break this time, 'cause I went straight through last year, summer school and all, just to finish up. So I'm taking a break.

Helen knew she had a good job—for an accountant:

> I think [what I like is] the interaction with the different departments, that I'm not just sitting there doing the reports. Accounting jobs are very boring. It's a job you would get bored in very quickly, but this part of my job makes it very interesting because you get that interaction with outside departments.

She had worked hard for the prize of her job, but now that she had won, she wasn't so sure she wanted it. "I don't want to really stay in this job," she said. "I don't want to move to management level, especially not in the field I'm in."

Helen had chosen to work as an accounting clerk because she was good in math, but along the way, she had discovered computers:

> I'd like to go back to school for computers. If I go back for my degree, a B.S., it will be for computers because I like doing systems design, going in to set something up.

And I'm a more organized person. That's why I do so well in computers, because it's logic, step by step. And you can't get to the next step unless the last one's correct. That's why I don't see myself going into management.

If the opportunity opens up, I'll be there. I've been also asked to take a full-time position in the lab at the other hospital I work in, but I turned it down because it is a management position. It was managing a computer. But I don't really want to get into that because I feel it will hinder my goals of going back to school and stuff. You have to be on call; it's a lot of responsibility. Right now, I'm not at the point I need the money. It would have been more money, but it would have been more time.

She was still searching for a balance between work and family that would allow her to be fulfilled, but her search was sabotaged by her husband's attitude:

I wanted to go to school when [my husband] was at school, but he said, "How can you do that?" I mean, he has changed now, but that's the way he was. And it was like, I just feel I was cheated. Because he would say, "You don't need this. You don't need that." And I found that I had a lot of marital problems when I did go back to school because I think that he felt that I was gaining too much independence.

In part because of lack of support from her husband, she had taken a large pay cut—$400 a month—and transferred out of a job that was challenging, but demanding. She had also dropped her computer course:

I really hated leaving the job, [but] it was getting . . . I was really in poor health. I had to have surgery on my gums. I went down to like 110 pounds. And so I asked for a transfer within the hospital, which I had to take a demotion and a lower-paying grade . . . paying salary. But healthwise I felt better, but I didn't feel fulfilled inside. I was still in school and that's why I left because I couldn't, you know, I couldn't . . . I dropped out because I . . . I was . . . I was going for computers . . . computer science, and I was in . . . I was taking Cobol2, and I dropped the course because I missed a week of school because of work, and it was impossible to keep up.

It was just that it was differences between my husband and I, and I didn't feel that sense of security there.

Originally, Helen hadn't planned on a career; she had intended to leave work when she had saved enough money for her first house. She stayed at work for two main reasons. First, she "started excelling in the lab, and getting promotions and taking on more responsibility, on the outside, outside the home. . . . I liked working with the computer, and it just came natural to me." Second, her marriage was disappointing, and she "didn't have that security there." She had scaled back at work, and although she still worked in both jobs, it was at a fairly low-level that didn't require her to work shifts and be on call.

Helen was all dressed up with nowhere to go; she was driven by a strong desire to find personal fulfillment in work, but she wasn't sure what that work should be. She described her job in accounting as "less boring" than it might be—hardly a ringing endorsement—and although she enjoyed exercising her analytic skills doing computer work, it was by no means clear that she had made a commitment to that line of work. She had pursued her courses for "sensible" reasons, but now, she said, she would like a rest, and then she would like to do something she *wanted* to do, as against something she felt she *ought* to do. She summed up what was missing for other women who were satisfied with their jobs, but disappointed in work; they were doing what they ought to, not what they wanted to, and they were satisfied with their jobs because they felt they ought to be, not because they really were. At least not with the kind of satisfaction that would make them feel, as Helen put it, "fulfilled inside."

Pam

Pam, a vital, athletic woman with a clear complexion and glossy dark brown curls, met me at the door of her spacious suburban ranch house dressed in loafers, chinos, and a bright white polo shirt, clutching the collar of her eager yellow lab. She shared the house with her husband and their two sons, who were all at a football game. This was a rare treat, she said, because since her husband's business had failed two years earlier, hers had become the sole family income; ball games were now a luxury, not the every-home-game treat they used to be.

Pam worked as a library manager. She liked her job—it was interesting and well paid—but she didn't love it. Asked if her feelings about work had changed, she replied like a fun-loving person who had mended her ways, not like a woman who loved her work. "Over the years," she said, "I have definitely become a better worker. When I first started working, I felt like I was a little unfocused and I don't think I was a model employee. Through the years, I really have improved my behavior. In other words, I don't take sick leave just to play for a day. I show up to work on time. I meet all my deadlines. I can't say that in my twenties I really fulfilled that."

She was a "model employee," but she would have doubts about taking her job if she had to choose again: "Because now women are doing lots of different things. I always think, if I took another path, would I be something else today? I've stayed in this path, and I certainly have advanced, and it's working well for me. But if I'd just taken another path, what else would I be doing?" If she didn't need the money she earned? "I would not work at all," Pam said. "I would do other creative things like traveling. I would keep busy, but I would not . . . there's a nine-to-five grind . . . that's why we want retirement . . . so no, I would not work. If I were independently wealthy, I would not work."

As a young mother at home, Pam had missed working "a great deal, an enormous amount," and had felt "very lonely and isolated":

I've always laughed with a friend—gee, if we had married doctors or Indian chiefs or somebody like that—if we had married really successful financial men, would we have taken the same road? At that time, when we were really tired of working, which you tend to get, we said, "Wouldn't it be nice to stay home?" However, when I stayed home with [my son] those early years, I could hardly stand it. Now they've come up with—I should have formed a mother's group back then. I remember feeling really lonely, and I had another friend, and we were both staying home together, and when our husbands came home, we would sometimes jump in the car and take drives, because I just felt like I'd been in the house all day.

Even now, she was dealing with guilt about whether she should have worked for most of her children's lives, or worked part-time:

[I have] the guilt of the working mother. There's a new type of [part-time] job in libraries now. If that had been offered to me when [my son] was just born, I might have taken it and might still be doing it because it offers lots of time with your children and family and then a certain amount of work time. There are times I feel I should be doing more homework with them. [But] it's only when I'm tired and really stressed out that I really think about it.

Throughout the interview, Pam's ambivalence toward work continued to steal into the conversation. "I have to work," she said, "I don't have a choice, but I still think it makes my happiness too." She was "satisfied" with her job because, as jobs go, it was excellent; after all, she had a great deal of autonomy, and her salary supported her entire family. But something was missing—off the job as well as on. She wished she had traveled when she was younger and "gotten that out of [her] system." And that she had gotten more out of college: "I kind of have the feeling now that I wish I could go back to school again. That I wasted some energy. That I wasted some classes. I needed to broaden myself in other directions."

Pam had fallen victim to the technological changes that have redefined the librarian's work, and her success had moved her away from hands-on contact with books and into administration and supervision. She was the sole breadwinner at a time of life when she had expected more ease and affluence; she had hoped to travel, for example, or return to school, but these options, which would have been possible except for her husband's unemployment, were now out of reach. She was trapped by seniority, a relatively high income, and breadwinning responsibilities in a job that was not fulfilling.

Jill

"If money wasn't an issue, I would stay home," Jill said. "I would be a housewife. I miss that. I don't cook too much anymore." We were talking in the spotless kitchen of Jill's house, lulled by the hum of the dishwasher in the background. Jill lived in the same neighborhood she had lived in as a child, but it was hardly recognizable; twenty years earlier, families had lived side by side, their children playing ball on the narrow streets, and their doors left wide open. Now, every second house was boarded up and forlorn, garbage was strewn on the street, and open-air drug markets frightened parents, and forced them to keep their children safely inside. But, as if to make up for the menacing streets outside, Jill herself was warm and welcoming, and the small, inner-city row house she shared with her husband and two teenage children was cozy and cheerful.

Jill and Dennis, her husband, were high school sweethearts who got married just after graduation. After fifteen years as a full-time housewife and mother, she had started working in her first job only about a year before our interview "for financial reasons." Her job was somewhat stressful; she was the only person in the entire business (a furniture store) who typed, and she had just been asked to computerize all the store accounts. On top of that, her boss was difficult and demanding. In spite of these difficulties, however, and in spite of her stated preference for being a housewife, Jill liked her job and felt that working had made her a "stronger person." "I was so young [when I married], and I depended on my husband. [Now] I'm more confident that I can do things. I think it made me independent."

It was clear that Jill was a central figure in her extended family, and had been for many years. When her children were still toddlers, she had moved her own family into her parents' house to care for her dying mother, and on two occasions, she had taken in her nephew and niece: first when her sister and brother-in-law went through a bitter divorce, and later when her sister was hospitalized for drug and alcohol addiction. Her extended family all lived in the neighborhood—her nephew on the same street, her sister-in-law one street over, her father three blocks away, her sister across the alley, and her parents-in-law just around the corner. As we sat talking, as if to demonstrate Jill's importance to her family, her nephew opened the front door without knocking, strolled into the kitchen, took down a teapot, deposited something in it, then left—with only a quick and casual "Hi." After he left, she explained, "That's one of my sister's kids, and they're closer to me than they are to their mother. This one doesn't get along with the stepfather. . . . I hold his money. He gets paid on Friday, and by Sunday he'd be broke. So Friday he brings his extra money in and puts it in the teapot, and then he comes and gets it when he needs it."

Jill enjoyed working, but she also valued her role in her extended family, and it felt out of control; she cared about keeping her house clean and orderly and was upset that she had too little time to maintain her high standards. Because of this overload, she found herself liking her job less: "Since I'm getting a little older, it's harder to do things around here. . . . And depression! I get the depression. [The doctor] just gave me medication. I said that now that I've got that [premature menopause] straightened out, I want something for the depression. Because it's really been getting bad. Just like, for a day or two, Dennis can look at me, and he'll say [to the kids], 'Don't talk to your mother.' [Laughing] Because it's just like, you know, I can sit there and start crying. And that's ridiculous!"

But it wasn't so ridiculous. Jill had created a circle of care and safety for her own children and her sister's—but this was work, and it took emotional energy and time. Take, for example, her daughter Jennifer's marching band practice:

> Sometimes you really have to juggle your schedule around her. She practices on Monday, Tuesdays, and Thursdays now. She practices out at Seven Hills. . . . I leave here say quarter after six and I get home about eight-thirty, three nights a week. Sometimes with her, it's all day in the summer. We often have to leave here at six-thirty. I've been at it for seven years.

Dennis shouldered his share; he came home at three o'clock in the afternoon (unless he was working overtime), cooked dinner, and threw in a load of laundry. Jill rushed in from the office at five, gulped down a quick meal, and was out the door again by six-fifteen for the drive to Jennifer's practice. If Dennis had to work overtime, dinner was leftovers, and the laundry stayed soiled.

They were a close family. Jill valued her marriage and boasted that she and Dennis were one of only two couples from their high school class who were still married. She enjoyed their life together as a family; she, Dennis, and the two kids spent hours doing complicated jigsaws, and they "talk[ed] about everything." She monitored where the children were, whom they were with, and what they were doing, and at the same time she and Dennis made home a place they wanted to be. "We have, knock on wood, really nice kids," she said.

A perfectionist with a demanding, stressful job, high domestic standards, and a deep concern to maintain a safe, happy family life, Jill was struggling to "do it all," and she was feeling the strain. Her immediate family had stayed safe, her kids were growing up to be well-adjusted, likeable people, and she and Dennis were still married—and happily so. For now at least, who could blame her if she felt that her work at home was more important—and more rewarding—than her work on the job?

Terry

Terry lived with her husband, Tony, their two children, and her son from a previous marriage in an old and comfortably cluttered clapboard house, its enclosed veranda littered with muddied boots and discarded work clothes, its dining room dwarfed by a huge cage that housed a family of pet rabbits. Papers, tools, pet food, craft materials, a sewing machine, and the odds and ends of a busy family life vied for space on every available surface.

Beginning at fifteen when she dropped out of school, Terry had worked for the major part of her adult life mostly as a waitress and factory worker; at present, she worked sixty hours each week as a part-time waitress and a full-time cosmetics packer. She liked both jobs, and she also liked the paychecks she brought home; they made a huge difference to her family's quality of life, and had allowed her to provide pleasures for her children they would otherwise have been denied.

At first, Terry spoke so fast and so softly she was hard to hear, but as the interview progressed, she relaxed. She was a high-energy person who liked to keep busy, and she seemed unaccustomed to sitting still—much less talking—for more than two hours. (She later said that both her sons had been diagnosed as hyperactive.) It was hard to find out how much she liked or disliked different jobs, as though liking were beside the point. Had she liked that job? "Yes." Quite a bit? "Yes, it was OK." What about being a short-order cook? Did she like that? "Yeah, I like mostly anything. I'm not too partic-ular." What did she like least about her present job? "I've been there so long, it's hard to know." She liked her job, but when I asked if she'd work if she didn't have to, she said, "No—I'd do my crafts." Later, the importance of these crafts became obvious.

Terry had worked for most of the eighteen years she and Tony had been together and she said that during this time they had always tried to share all their responsibili-ties equally. When their daughter was a baby, Tony had worked nights and cared for the baby during the day; later, when Tony was laid off for two years with an injury, Terry had worked three jobs to support the family:

> We reversed roles. He took care of the house, and I worked. He did a lot, believe me. He can cook, he cleans, he takes care of the kids. He did everything—laundry, mop. If it wasn't for him, I'd be up the creek. He does a lot of stuff for me. We're so lucky we can't get over it. He cooks. He does the major cooking. Thanksgiving, I don't cook. He cooks. Christmas, he cooks. It's always been that way.

Tony had recently built new kitchen cabinets, relined all the walls in their old house, laid hardwood floors, and put bedrooms in the basement and attic. "He's done all that," Terry said. "He's a real handyman." Her face lit up when she talked about these home projects, and she was eager to show off some of her own—cheerful, ruffled cur-tains at the kitchen window; golden loaves of bread, preserved and arranged in baskets along the top of the kitchen cabinets; and families of toy bears, dressed up in gingham and lace. "See the teddy bears up there?" Terry asked. "I buy the lace [and] the teddy bear separate. I sew the clothes. They're all hand-sewed, and then I hot-glue them onto the teddy bear. I'm very satisfied with my crafts."

Self-Actualization or Flow: Loving What You Do

Musicians must make music, artists must paint, poets must write, if they are to
be ultimately at peace with themselves. What humans can be, they must be.
They must be true to their own nature.   —Abraham Maslow[6]

In the 1950s, Abraham Maslow, the psychiatrist, developed a theory of human motivation that challenged the Freudian idea that "higher" forms of human behavior such
as creative work represent sublimations of more basic needs. Maslow's theory saw
"higher" behaviors as needs in their own right—in his view the need for respect is as
real as the need for food. Like Freud, he believed that basic needs are important—not
because all other needs are conversions of them, but because they must be satisfied
first before one's attention can be given to less basic needs. "A person who is lacking
food, safety, love, and esteem would most probably hunger for food more strongly
than for anything else."[7] To one who is hungry, "consciousness is almost completely
preempted by hunger," and talents or abilities that are not useful for satisfying hunger
lie dormant. In this, he agreed with Marx, that before all else comes survival.

Thus Maslow saw physiological needs—such as the need for food and sex—as the
most basic level in a hierarchy of needs; those needs must be satisfied before attention
can be paid to the next higher level. Once basic physiological needs such as hunger are
satisfied, the need for safety, security, and freedom from fear emerges. When safety is
no longer a concern, the need for a sense of belonging, and of being loved comes to the
fore. When the need for a sense of belonging is satisfied, the need for "self-respect or
self-esteem, and for the esteem of others" becomes dominant—this includes the need
or desire for independence, freedom, recognition, dignity, or appreciation. Finally,
when these other needs are gratified, there arises a desire for what Maslow called self-
actualization; often "a new discontent and restlessness will soon develop, unless the
individual is doing what he or she individually, is fitted for."[8]

Similar to this concept is "flow," described by another psychologist, Mihaly
Csiksentmihaly, as optimal experience, a kind of peak experience that is completely
absorbing. Flow is activity in which we lose ourselves; it consumes us and is intrinsically rewarding. Its key element is that it is an end to itself. Csiksentmihaly coins the
term "autoletic" to describe this kind of activity, from two Greek words, *auto* meaning
self, and *telos* meaning goal: "It refers to a self-contained activity, one that is done not
with the expectation of some future benefit, but simply because the doing itself is a
reward."[9] Both work and leisure activities can be autoletic when they are highly rewarding in and of themselves. Csiksentmihaly, too, is at one with Marx; autoletic work,
which is performed for its own sake, is the opposite of Marx's alienated work, which is
performed purely as a means to an end.

According to Maslow, discontent and restlessness arise when basic needs are satisfied, but self-actualization needs are not. It was this discontent and restlessness that women who were satisfied with their jobs, but not fulfilled by their work. Helen, Pam, and Ann, all three of whom were financially secure and satisfied with their jobs, were examples. Helen and Ann had achieved success in their professions and had earned recognition and respect, yet neither woman was doing the work for which she was "uniquely fitted." Neither knew what that work might be, exactly, but they both knew that it was missing. Ann, too, was restless; when her children were young, caring for them was self-actualizing—she "loved the whole thing," but this was no longer true. Both Terry and Jill had activities outside paid work in which they attained "flow," or self-actualization: Terry's crafts and home improvements offered this level of reward, as did some—not all—of Jill's home activities, especially her hobbies.

One difference between self-actualizing—or flow-producing, non-alienating— activities and others is whether they make us feel enriched, not diminished. As Csiksentmihaly put it:

> So much of what we ordinarily do has no value in itself, and we do it only because we have to do it, or because we expect some future benefit from it. Many people feel that the time they spend at work is essentially wasted—they are alienated from it, and the psychic energy invested in the job does nothing to strengthen their self. . . . [In contrast] flow lifts the course of life to a different level. Alienation gives way to involvement, enjoyment replaces boredom, helplessness turns to a feeling of control, and psychic energy works to reinforce the sense of self, instead of being lost in the service of external goals. When experience is intrinsically rewarding life is justified in the present, instead of being held hostage to a hypothetical future gain."[10]

Most of the women in the study had some activity they loved to do—sports, knitting, crochet, other crafts, and home decorating were just some—and these activities required hard work. But only one working-class woman, Cindy, was paid for her self-actualizing, flow producing, unalienated work. In a later chapter, I will discuss more fully why this was so, but for now I will simply introduce Cindy, and her experience of "flow."

Cindy

Cindy had three jobs. She ran a day-care center from her house, worked part time as a painter and paperhanger, and sang at night in a country band. When I complimented her on her skill as a paperhanger—judged on the basis of the perfectly matched patterns on her dining room walls—she said she was careful. "I've learned, over the years, a lot of things. I use a level. I'm very conscious about leveling everything so that the corners don't have the patterns going in different ways. I'm very conscious about it. In fact, that's one of the reasons I want to redo this room.

I'm not happy with the way I did this room. It's not—you don't walk right in and see it, but I sit in here and [see flaws.] I'm hard on myself."

Cindy was careful and competent when she painted and papered, and she also took good care of the children in her day-care center:

> They come at seven-thirty. They usually watch a cartoon, I fix them breakfast. Usually a hot breakfast—they eat here. I've been watching the children for several years, so it's appreciated. They have breakfast. We go to the bus about eight-thirty. They get on the school bus. Different children, little ones, come at three-thirty and play for a half an hour. They have a snack, do their homework, and then they play until their parents come. They always do their homework though. Every day, they do their homework here, which their mothers are also grateful for. They don't have to contend with that when they get home. And I really find that when they all sit down together to do it, they help each other, they work together at it, so that's good for them. They all sit around the table here. I clear it off. . . . Because there are six of them, the money's not bad, and I really only have them for a few hours, so it really works out a lot better.

Both her "day" jobs gave Cindy the flexibility to care for her children and also to help her mother, her "best buddy":

> I have my days open. My schedule is flexible and with my mother's health problems— she's on home dialysis, so she has a lot of doctor's appointments. She sees a cardiologist . . . and a urologist, and a nephrologist, and she still sees her oncologist. You know, they don't prepare you for aging parents and how demanding it is. But she relies on me a lot, so that the wallpaper hanging and things like that, it gives me a lot of freedom to say, "Well, I can't do it Friday, but I'll do it on Thursday." So I'm pretty flexible.

Cindy talked about her two day jobs the way other women who were job, not work, satisfied talked about theirs: their jobs were "flexible," they paid "quite well," they were "better than" some of the other jobs they had tried. She began to describe her part-time job as a performer in the same ho-hum way—it was "profitable," and "flexible":

> We play top forty and oldies and country. We do clubs and dances and bull roasts. Things like that, occasionally a wedding. It's been profitable. My husband and I are in it together; it's a six-piece band, and we run the band, so we get a double cut of the profit because of both of us being involved. And I handle the bookings and the agency work. Again, it's been pretty good because we are flexible. You know, if we have a commitment for a weekend and we can't work, we don't have to answer to another employer. You know, we just don't take a booking for that weekend.

But as she went on, her tone and her words changed—this work was *fun*, it was *wonderful*, it was *great*, it was something she would *have to*—not *want to*—stop doing, something that would mean a lot to her, even were she not paid:

I'm the lead singer. My husband and I both front the band. We just got a new sax player, a black guy. He can really play, and he's got a wonderful voice, so he's gonna be the third front person. It's really great. . . . When we look back and we are too old, and we have to stop doing it, we'll look back with some great memories. We've made very close attachments with the other members of the band, and we've had a lot of terrible jobs, and we've had a lot of wonderful jobs. We all have our little fantasies. You watch someone on TV, singing, or hear a record. . . . Well, there's a few hours a week when I get to sing a song, and somebody will come up to me afterward and say, "That was great, you sounded so good," and I think, "I was a star! For an hour they thought I was a star." It kind of helps you, especially [because] I don't dress up and go to work every day, I don't go out to lunches to nice restaurants [but] then I get dressed up on the weekend, fix my hair—it's not always like this—fix my hair and put on a little makeup and you know, it's kinda that alter ego.

If I didn't have to think about money at all, I'd still be involved with music. But I write music, and I would spend a lot more time writing and trying to promote my music. Of course there's no money in it unless you meet the right person who says, "Your stuff's great." But it's very time-consuming to write and record. . . . I've entered it in contests and I've had copyrights on all the songs. I've really not sent it out to individual record companies. I guess I could. I always thought before I reached that point I'd rather rerecord them with some more instrumentation. Most of it's a drum machine and a guitar and me, and overdubbing my voice with har-monies. But I like my songs, so I always felt like they were worth something, but again . . . there's a tremendous amount of competition. [Would she consider sending her material to Emmy Lou Harris?] Ah, that would have been one of my picks, Emmy Lou. Yeah, in fact a couple of songs I've written I've thought, "She could do a great job with these." I thought about giving a tape to Maura O'Connell, but I felt it wasn't good enough. If I didn't have to earn an extra income, I'd devote a lot of time to that.

Work with the band builds my self-esteem. I realize the older I get, the fewer years I'm gonna be able to do it, because it is physically taxing. So it's more precious to me now, you know. It's not like a job where you can't wait to retire. You hope you can hold out another year.

Like most of the women, who were helping to pay the bills, not doing what they loved to do, Cindy refused to be considered a victim. She was pragmatic, and stressed that she had made her choices consciously:

I was an—I don't want to use the word—obsessive mother. When my children were babies, I felt like I never wanted to leave them. I never wanted to leave them with a sitter. If something was going to go wrong, they needed me there. And really, the kind of personality that I was, it would have been very difficult to go out and leave them eight hours a day. I don't think I could have left them in day care. It would have had to be a relative. And there was nobody available. But I just felt like nobody could be their mother the way I was. So I felt very strongly about being there.

And then there was also the guilt. I felt, "I need to contribute some money to the house. I just can't stay home with these children, and not feel like I'm being productive in some way." So then I started taking other children in. I felt like—I wasn't paying taxes on the money. It was under the table. I didn't have the expenses of going to work, and I was there with the kids. I took care of the house. Instead of going out and getting a job and paying someone to do the renovating, I did all the painting, I did all the wallpapering, I did, you know, all the housecleaning, and the things that a lot of people have to pay someone to help out with.

I don't have a stereotypical attitude that women that stay home aren't smart enough to go get a job. There are women who volunteer at the elementary school who are intelligent women who all feel that their children are better off. [Do I feel I must apologize for staying home?] If I didn't have the band, I think I would. The band builds my self-esteem. We all need someone to pat us on the back and say, "You're doing a good job."

Shakespeare, William Blake, and countless other creative artists have been forced to pursue their work and their paid jobs separately, leading a "double life."[11] Cindy had an extra, and complicating, layer: she wanted to be the person who took care of her children and her mother. But Cindy showed what was missing from most women's experience of work: her music was a passion, and performing was "fun." When she was singing, she was living to the full, and living in the present; she was not hostage to an uncertain future. She could pursue her passion only part of the time, but, during that time, she knew she was a star. As she said—and who could disagree—"there's a lot to be said for loving what you do."

What Work
M e a n s

I didn't like things when I didn't work. If something needed to be done and we were short of money, we couldn't do nothing, because there was no money there. I like to work, I feel that I'm doing my part.

—Doreen

I think [working] made me more independent. I think it makes you a stronger person. You know, because I was so young, and I depended on my husband. [Now] I am more confident that I can do things.

—Jill

The stick of starvation has always prodded men and women to work, but American culture has also offered two ideological carrots, both of which working-class women might be excused for mistrusting. The first, exemplified by the myth of Horatio Alger, offers the promise: Work hard and you will get ahead. This ideology has particular appeal in a nation of voluntary immigrants, many of whom came to this country to "get ahead." The second, exemplified by the Protestant work ethic, offers the promise: Work hard and you will earn riches, which are a sign of God's grace. According to this ethic, which has its roots in America's Puritan past, work is a moral imperative—every Christian has a duty to find and follow his or her calling. "There should be some special employment by which our usefulness in our neighborhood may be distinguished," said Cotton Mather. "There should . . . be some special and settled business, wherein we . . . should be helpful to other men."[1] In the nineteenth-century, this ethic fueled the capitalist fire:

> The central premise of the work ethic was that work was the core of moral life. Work made men useful in a world of economic scarcity. It staved off the doubts and temptations that preyed on idleness, it opened the way to deserved wealth and status, it allowed one to put the impress of mind and skill on the material world.[2]

For many years, sociologists and industrial psychologists have operated under the assumptions of a third ideology, which was articulated over thirty years ago in a classic study by Kornhauser, who stated:

> Work not only serves to produce goods and services; it also performs essential psychological functions. It operates as a great stabilizing, integrating, ego-satisfying central influence in the pattern of each person's life. If the job fails to fulfill these needs of the personality, it is problematic whether men can find adequate substitutes to provide a sense of significance and achievement, purpose and justification for their lives.[3]

The first two ideologies see work as a stern taskmaster; whether we enjoy it or not is immaterial—in fact, we may be more worthy if we endure work we dislike. The third sees work as a "central life interest"; we should embrace it with open arms, making it not only a central part of what we do, but of who we are.

Different in content, and originating in three different historical contexts, all three ideologies hold up an ideal of how workers should experience work. But there is a problem. All three ideologies assume an experience of work that is middle-class and male, not working-class or female. Working hard makes very different demands and offers very different rewards to working- and middle- class workers, and "getting ahead" leads to very different destinations. Yet the influence of these two work-hard-for-just-rewards ideologies is so pervasive and powerful that most people, when asked what they would do if they won the lottery, say they would continue to work—even though, in fact, most people do not.

The third ideology—the "work-is-the-purpose-of-life" ideology—is also predicated on middle-class experience, ignoring the reality of most people's lives.If identity is to be defined by paid work, where does that leave the women and men whose work is scrubbing toilets, flipping hamburgers, or polishing floors? The expectation that work should be central devalues other sources of identity and pride that are important for many people—for example, religion, hobbies, and family.[4]

The conceptual waters of research into work are muddied by the often unacknowledged assumptions of one or more of these ideologies, all of which proclaim that paid work is the most worthy domain in which to invest one's best efforts, and one's essential self; the following assumptions are common: strong involvement in one's paid work is good, a pragmatic, instrumental orientation to it is bad; valuing intrinsic characteristics of the job is good, valuing extrinsic characteristics is bad; commitment to paid work is good, commitment to leisure activities is bad; making work central to one's identity is good, not identifying with work is bad. But the ideology that everyone "should" not only work, but work hard, make work a central part of their lives, and look to the workplace as a major source of identity ignores unequal job opportunities and uneven job rewards.

Marx's ideology of work differs from the first three by emphasizing what *work*—not *workers*—should be like; his yardstick measures the quality of jobs and the nature of the work they offer. Marx and Engels contrasted the grueling, mind-deadening labor and misery they saw around them in nineteenth-century England with the creative work of a craftsman or the self-sustaining work of a peasant, and concluded that the changes wrought by capitalism were devastating to the human spirit. Instead of performing work whose purpose was clear and whose value was obvious, workers under capitalism performed work with little intrinsic value, which produced a product they neither needed, wanted, nor could use; their work became no more than a means to an end. As hired labor, workers had no chance to exercise the creativity that distinguishes humans from animals; instead, alienated from their work, they were also alienated from their true human selves.

The appeal of Marx's ideology is obvious; it's hard to argue with the basic notion that freely chosen and intrinsically interesting work is better and more human in every way than work that is performed solely for the purpose of earning a living. But although the essential point of Marx's analysis still rings true, work is no longer the cruel, harsh enslavement he observed in the dark, Satanic mills of England, and his stark depiction of the miseries of wage slavery no longer quite fits an early-twenty-first-century reality. Because it paints all work under capitalism with the same black brush, Marx's analysis obscures the differences in quality among different kinds of waged work and also obscures the fact that even if it is performed as a means to an end, work for wages can offer real rewards—increased competence, confidence, and independence, to name only three, and real satisfaction.

Job Satisfaction

Perhaps because it is in the interests of both management and labor that workers should enjoy work, job satisfaction and its determinants are widely researched, and studies addressing questions such as how to reduce "employee turnover," increase "organizational commitment," and "decrease absenteeism" jostle for space on library shelves with more humanistic studies of workers' job conditions and the effects of those conditions on satisfaction, health, and well-being. Regardless of its motivation, this voluminous body of research comes up with remarkably consistent results. First, and most striking, is that regardless of their race, age, gender, education, and the work they do, and in spite of wide differences in their job conditions, most workers seem to be at least moderately satisfied with their jobs.[5] To illustrate, 16 percent of respondents to the 1998 General Social Survey, an annual survey of around 15,000 adults in the United States, said they were "completely satisfied" with their jobs, 33 percent were "very satisfied," and only 3 percent were "very" or "completely" dissatisfied.

Furthermore, 17 percent of women but only 15 percent of men were "completely" satisfied with their jobs, and 34 percent of women but only 31 percent of males were
"very" satisfied.[6] Many researchers have been puzzled by findings such as these, which
demonstrate few differences between groups and high overall levels of job satisfaction.
Why, they wonder, are most workers so satisfied?

Values, Orientations, and Expectations: Gender and Class Differences?

Some sociologists have suggested that gender and class differences in values or "orientations" may explain workers' high and relatively invariant levels of job satisfaction.[7]
Gender differences have been reported; one researcher found that complex work was
more satisfying for women, authority was more satisfying to men,[8] while a number of
others have concluded that women value pay and promotions less than men, and
interpersonal relationships more. Surveys sometimes find that women are less "committed" to work than men.[9] Until recently, the most widely held view was that women
invest less than men in their jobs because they have been socialized from an early age
to consider work as secondary to marriage and family. In addition, because they bear
a larger share than men of the responsibility for families, they have less time and
energy to devote to work outside the home.[10] This view has been challenged, however,
by research that suggests that women's lower involvement with work or commitment
to work is the result of their objective experience of jobs that offer fewer rewards. One
study found, for example, that women's job involvement was even greater than men's
when they worked in jobs with similar levels of job autonomy.[11] Both these views
would lead us to expect a low level of work commitment among working-class women
like those in this study; as women, they presumably were socialized to consider work
less important than family, and as women who are working class, their jobs were more
likely to lack autonomy and other characteristics that foster commitment.

Women are also said to be more "instrumental" than men in their orientation to
work—that is, to value job conditions such as convenience, companionship, and flexibility that are extrinsic to the nature of the work itself. Men, on the other hand, are
said to value intrinsic characteristics. Because an instrumental orientation has also
been attributed to working-class workers, the working-class women in the present
study might be expected to be instrumental in their orientation to work, content with
work that is convenient and offers companionship, whatever its nature, and its intrinsic interest. However, other studies have found that women value both companionship
and the intrinsic interest of what they do. The nature of working-class women's orientations then are still an open question.[12]

An alternative explanation for relatively small group differences in job satisfaction is that different groups have higher or lower standards for evaluating job conditions. Women may care just as much as men—and working-class workers may care
just as much as middle-class workers—about conditions such as autonomy, opportu-

nities for promotion, and challenging work, but they may have a different threshold for satisfaction. Satisfaction thresholds would vary if women and working-class men had lower expectations than middle-class men. This explanation is consistent with psychological theories of "relative deprivation," which state that when deciding what they are entitled to, and therefore what they are satisfied with, people use as a basis of comparison—or "reference group"—others who are like themselves in certain key ways. Thus they compare their own work conditions with those of coworkers', and are satisfied as long as they are on a par with others like themselves. Or, women might have work values similar to men's but lower expectations about what they are entitled to because they compare themselves with other working women, or with housewives, not with men.[13] Moreover, to feel dissatisfied, what is missing must seem attainable; if women and working-class workers feel that certain rewards such as high pay are beyond their reach, they will lower their sights.

Women's Job Satisfaction and Work Orientations

The survey and interview data shed some light on the question of women's job satisfaction and its relation to their orientations and expectations. In the remainder of this chapter, I will first focus on what the survey data tell us about job satisfaction, and then I will move on to the more complex story of *work* satisfaction, which is told by a combination of interview and survey data. Putting these pieces together, I will describe different relationships with work, which will be the subject of case studies in the chapter that follows. I will conclude the current chapter by reporting what women found to be the main benefits of working.

I used the following questions, various combinations of which are commonly seen in the literature, to assess women's job satisfaction:

1. All in all, how satisfied would you say you are with your job? (Not at all satisfied, Not too satisfied, Somewhat satisfied, Very satisfied)
2. If a good friend of yours told you that she was interested in working in a job like yours, would you strongly recommend your job, have doubts about recommending it, or would you strongly advise against it?
3. Knowing what you know now, if you had to decide all over again, would you definitely take the same job, have second thoughts, or would you definitely decide not to take it?
4. How much do you enjoy your job (on a scale from one to seven, where one is "not at all" and seven is "very much")?

The questions formed a scale on which women could be assigned a score.[14] The most common score on the scale was the maximum possible one, which meant that women were "very" satisfied with their jobs, enjoyed them as much as possible, would "strongly" recommend them to a friend, and would "definitely" take them again. There were class differences—according to the scale, on average, working-class women without a high school diploma were least satisfied with their jobs, and working-class women as a whole were less satisfied than middle-class women—but these differences were not as large as might be expected based on differences in women's job conditions. In part, this was because working-class women's job satisfaction differed widely according to their type of employment. Working-class women who were self-employed or who worked in the school system—as school bus drivers, aides, or janitors—were much more highly satisfied with their jobs than women who worked in gray-collar factory or service jobs; indeed, women who worked in schools in a non-professional capacity were more satisfied with their jobs than teachers.

Job satisfaction was more closely linked to job quality than to class-based differences in work attitudes. Compared with middle-class women working-class women were less satisfied with their jobs because they had worse jobs. When they had good jobs, such as jobs in the school system, they were equally—and sometimes more—satisfied. The findings also suggest that working-class women's lower expectations—based on their life experiences—made them more tolerant of poor job conditions and more appreciative of good conditions. Teachers had higher expectations than women in non-professional jobs; they expected to be treated as professionals, and were disappointed when they were not. Working-class women who were employed as school aides and other semi- or unskilled workers in the school system were gratified to have jobs with intrinsic meaning and some autonomy.

Both the survey and interview data addressed the question of whether working- and middle-class women find different job conditions satisfying. In their interviews, working-class women emphasized the importance of autonomy—and respect more generally—in the workplace. Middle-class women emphasized autonomy and challenge. Survey questions asked about the presence in the workplace of challenge, job pressure, and what I take to be two indicators of respect: autonomy and recognition. Both sets of data showed that, for working-class women, not feeling pressured, but feeling autonomous and acknowledged were the job conditions most strongly related to job satisfaction. Most satisfied were women like Greta and Margaret, whose bosses supervised them only loosely and let them know they were appreciated. For middle-class women, having autonomy and being recognized were important, but by far the most important job condition—at least the one most strongly related to their job satisfaction scale score—was having challenging work. Challenging work was positively (but less strongly) related to job satisfaction scores for working-class women with a high school diploma, but not for women without a diploma.

These survey findings on job satisfaction suggest that regardless of their social class, women wanted work that gave them autonomy and recognition; for working-class women, who were often denied both, these conditions were most important, and not being pressured to work too hard or too fast came close behind. For middle-class women, challenging work was most important for job satisfaction, with autonomy and recognition next in importance. The main difference between working- and middle-class women, therefore, was in the importance of challenging work.

What do these differences mean? Why was challenging work more important for office workers and professional women than for women working in unskilled jobs? The answer is plain to see: for women working in gray-collar unskilled jobs, challenging work too often meant pressure and pressure in gray-collar jobs was altogether different from pressure in professional or secretarial jobs. It was not "I must finish this paper by July 27 if I want to get it published," but was "Get it done now—or else."

This is not to say that working-class women in gray-collar jobs wanted dull, boring work; in fact, they preferred work that was not boring. Harriet, for example, said she liked that her job in a window factory was "not boring" and that it kept her busy, and she preferred her evening job at Walmart because, she said, "I like doing the math," and "I like meeting different people." Put differently, one might say that she preferred her Walmart job because it offered more challenge without the do-it-now-or-else pressures of the assembly line. Monica also disliked being bored, and enjoyed her job as a line leader in a warehouse "because I'm not sitting in one space. It's not boring. There's always something different happening." Similarly, Carolyn preferred her supermarket job to the only other job she'd had, packing tomatoes, which was "boring"; and Ethel thought she'd be "more bored" in a bank:

> Yeah I enjoy my work. It's busy. I keep busy. It's always something to do. And it's different. It keeps my interest. I feel like I'm not stagnated because it's constant motion. Things are going on, and it keeps you interested. I think I'd be more bored in a bank. I'm not real locked into [one kind of work]. I think when I worked for the attorneys, that was more boring. You can get a brief, and they say, "Type this," and you take all 149 pages and type. The things that I type are interesting. It's a mini series.

So, working-class women were delighted to have challenging work if pressure was not part of the package—but for most gray-collar workers, challenging work meant punishing pressure.[15]

Involvements, Commitments, and Central Life Interests: Does Class Matter?

I asked the women a number of questions about their "involvement in work," their "work commitment," their pursuit of "personal fulfillment" in work, and the importance of work to their identity. These questions explored whether, as sometimes claimed, working-class women are relatively satisfied with their jobs because they are less committed to work and less involved in it, or because work is not as important to

them as a source of identity or personal fulfillment. What were the women's "orientations" to work, and did a different orientation cause working-class women to differ
from middle-class women in the job conditions they found satisfying?

First, job involvement. By far the strongest difference in job involvement was
between working-class women with and without a high school diploma; there was
little difference between working-class women with a diploma and women with a college degree. Only 19 percent of the women without a diploma described themselves as
"strongly involved" with their jobs, compared with 48 percent of women with a
diploma and 54 percent of women with a degree. Second, the importance of work for
identity; high school graduates were *most* likely to say that work was "very important"
for their identity; 43 percent of working-class women with a diploma said this, compared with 32 percent of women with a degree, and 24 percent of women without a
diploma.[16] In terms of what is often termed "work centrality," therefore, the important
dividing line was not between middle- and working-class women, but between working-class women with a diploma, and those without—not coincidentally, this was the
same dividing line that most strongly separated "good" from "bad" jobs.

As for "work commitment"—measured by "the lottery question," which asks
respondents whether they would continue working even if they won the lottery—
middle-class women more often said they would continue working, but the difference
between working- and middle-class women was not large; on the whole, three in four
women said they would remain at work (71 percent of working-class women [with or
without a diploma] and 85 percent of women with a degree). So no matter what their
social class background and educational attainment, at least seven in every ten women
were "committed" enough to work to believe they would continue to work even if they
didn't need the money.[17]

Thus, working-class women with no high school diploma were as committed to
work as women with a diploma, but fewer of them had been able to find jobs that were
involving and satisfying.[18] And their lack of involvement was not the result of a failure
to seek personal fulfillment in work; remarkably, given their economic status and the
nature of their work, they were just as likely as women with a high school diploma to
agree that "the main reason" they worked was for personal fulfilment—over 50 percent of working-class women, with or without a high school diploma, agreed with this
statement compared with 77 percent of middle-class women.

Both the interview and survey data suggested that, regardless of social class, some
women were "instrumental" in their orientation in the sense that they didn't want
their job to be their "central life interest." Although many were involved in their jobs
and satisfied with them, these women did not look to work for intrinsic meaning, and
were quite happy with their jobs so long as they were paid a fair wage for a fair day's
work. Most of the women with this orientation enjoyed, or even depended on, work's
benefits—social contact with coworkers, income, a broader life experience, and a sense

of accomplishment—but work was an enjoyable activity, not a source of identity. Phyllis, for example, when asked how, if at all, she would feel differently about herself if she didn't work, replied, "[I] wouldn't [feel different]! It took me a long time to get to feel the way I do about myself. It took me a long time." And Lillian, a social worker who had chosen to work as a teacher's aide, had a similar perspective: "I don't think I would [feel different]. [Work is] not important at all. It should be, but I gotta say it isn't, or I wouldn't be doing what I'm doing." Women such as Phyllis and Lillian could meet their need for personal fulfillment in activities outside work. For them—around 40 percent of the working-class women and 20 percent of the middle-class women in the study—it was fine to have a job that was "just a job."

For over half the women (around 60 percent of working-class women and 80 percent of middle-class women), however, a job that was "just a job" was not enough; they wanted fulfilling, meaningful work. According to their responses to the lottery question, most of these "meaning-seekers" were "committed" to work—that is, they said they would continue to work even if they won the lottery. Other women said they would quit work if they won the lottery, but went on to say they would volunteer in their children's classrooms or do hobbies, crafts, or other activities they found rewarding.[19] How women responded to this question was class related; working-class women were less likely to believe they could be paid for doing activities that were now hobbies, interests, or work they had done as volunteers, and therefore they were more likely to believe they would have to quit work to do what they loved to do.

The determinants of job satisfaction depended on women's orientation to work as well as their social class. Regardless of class, women who sought personal fulfillment and intrinsic meaning in work needed autonomy and recognition to be satisfied—more so than women who were content with "just a job." And although most "meaning-seekers" were satisfied with their jobs, as we will see in the next section, they were more likely to be dissatisfied with their work; as Ann put it, they were satisfied with their jobs "*per se*," but not fulfilled by work. There were class differences among "meaning-seekers" in whether they had found personal fulfillment in work; fewer working-class women who sought fulfillment had been able to find it. The special satisfaction that comes from being paid to do intrinsically rewarding work—much less work you love—was thus another life condition most working-class women were denied.

Work Satisfaction

The job satisfaction scale yielded a single score that represented fairly well women's satisfaction with their jobs, but it failed to capture how they felt about work. Yet very different kinds of satisfaction with work were obvious in the interviews, when the women talked freely about their job experiences, and also in their responses to the questions on job satisfaction. Some women responded to the questions politely and positively, but minimally, while others expanded on their feelings at length, lighting up with pleasure as they explained what they liked about their job. Other women contradicted themselves sometimes, like Brenda, expressing conflicting feelings within the same sentence as they struggled to find the right words. "Much as I say I don't like my job," said Brenda, "I do like it."

These contradictions often expressed a real conflict between the women's enjoyment of some parts of their job (very often their personal relationships) and their disappointment with its content (its intrinsic characteristics). This was the case for Brenda, who said she both liked and did not like her job:

> It's comfortable, it's home. . . . It's a family, in the sense that I know all the employees in the mall, and I know everybody that walks through the hall, and the people that work upstairs. So you know, you talk to all these people that you see. I see the same faces and it's nice. That part of it, it's like going to a workplace where I know lots of people. Even though I only employ three people, I see people all day long that I know [and they say], "How you doing, how's things?" and you get to talk to some people, and you know their kids and they know yours, and that type of thing. You might not know their names but you know them.

Brenda sold flowers in a mall, a business she had not really chosen; she had taken over the business when her husband moved on to something better. She worked part-time, and also volunteered at a school for handicapped children one day a week, which was work she found more gratifying (it was what she would do if she didn't have to think about money at all). She was disenchanted with business. "It's not rewarding," she said, "financially or psychologically. . . . Even if it was a business that made a lot of money, it would not be rewarding. Business is not very rewarding to me." In spite of these reservations about the work she was doing, Brenda considered herself to be moderately satisfied with her job.

Although not apparent from their scores on the job satisfaction scale, differences in women's work satisfaction showed up in how they responded to the individual questions that made up the scale. Responses to the question that simply asked how satisfied they were—All in all, how satisfied are you with your job?—indicated a high level of job satisfaction; altogether 92 percent of women without a high school diploma, 91 percent of women with a diploma, and 97 percent of women with a degree said they were either "very" or "somewhat" satisfied. Responses to the second question, however, which asked whether they would have taken their jobs if they had known what they were like, suggested a lower level of satisfaction; 80 percent of professional women and high school graduates but only 60 percent of high school dropouts said they would take the same job. And in response to the question on whether they would advise a friend to take their job, 25 percent of high school dropouts said they would "strongly advise" a friend *against* taking their job, compared with only 10 percent of high school graduates and none of the women with a college degree.

These responses strongly suggested a fairly widespread ambivalence about work, which was not revealed by the job satisfaction scale scores. Liz's responses were an example; Liz said she was "very satisfied" with her job, but on the other hand, she would not recommend it to her friend. "If you put it all together," she said, "it's a horrible job. Who wants to sit in one spot for eight hours and not do anything? I mean you're not using your brain. You're not using your hands. You're just existing. You're like a bump on a log. OK, I don't mind being a bump on a log, but I don't see too many other people wanting to be a bump." Liz was "satisfied" with her job because it accommodated her circumstances at that time. Her son was struggling with a crack cocaine addiction, and she was worried sick every day—would she get a call to say he had been found dead on the street, or in jail? The job was right for her, "all things considered." But why would a friend who didn't have to deal with her problems take such a job?

The lottery question also addressed work satisfaction. As well as asking women if they would continue working if they won the lottery, I asked them if they would remain in their present jobs, and also what they would do if they quit work. Very few women said they would quit working altogether, but fewer than half the working-class women—33 percent of women without a high school diploma, and 45 percent of high school graduates—and 69 percent of the women with a degree said they would continue to work in their present jobs. Thus almost seven in ten middle-class women, but fewer than four in ten working-class women, though "satisfied" with their jobs, were not satisfied enough to believe they would remain in them given a choice. Class differences were strong, therefore, in the extent to which women were truly satisfied with the work experience their jobs provided; working-class women were less satisfied with work than middle-class women, and working-class women without a high school diploma were least satisfied of all.

Only about one in three women, therefore, were so satisfied they believed they would stay in their jobs; and most of these women were those who had modest expectations of work and were contented with a job that was "just a job." Similarly, only a handful of women had high expectations of work that were being met, and only one of these women was passionate about her work. Only a handful of women were downright dissatisfied. Most of the remaining women, about two thirds of the sample, many of them women who sought personal fulfillment from work, had reservations; theirs was a kind of regretful acceptance, a feeling that their jobs were about as satisfying as could be expected, but their work was not as rewarding as they would like; they were satisfied with their jobs, but not with their entire work experience. They had evaluated where they were in life, what they had to offer on the job market—in terms of educational qualifications, work experience, and availability—and what the job market had to offer them, and had decided that, all things considered, they were satisfied.

In Marx's terms, these women were satisfied with their jobs, but alienated from work. Marx calls work that is not chosen for its own sake but out of necessity "alienated" labor. "Labor is . . . not voluntary but forced, . . . not the satisfaction of a need but a mere means to satisfy needs outside itself. Its alien character is clearly demonstrated by the fact that as soon as no physical or other compulsion exists, it is shunned like the plague." For Marx, the ideal form of work is work that is undertaken for its own sake, its particular form freely chosen by individuals as the very work that matches their unique interests, abilities, and talents. Alienated workers remain at their jobs, but only because they must.

It took very little to job-satisfy women—basically, all they required was to be treated with respect. It took more, however, to work-satisfy them. Women who were not work-satisfied said they would choose different work—"something creative," "something that helped people," or "something with children"—if they were freed from financial need. Jill, for example, said she would "buy houses, maybe gear up toward having a shelter for homeless people, something like that. I would want to do something charitable. I think people with money should do that. I think they have a responsibility to do that." Amanda would volunteer at a hospital or a nursing home. Phyllis would "probably be a little bit more involved with the schools and stuff. So I'd know what's going on. If I didn't have to work, I wouldn't work." Polly would start her own school. "I would still work," she said. "I would have my own business. I'd like to run my own day care." Dawn would grow plants: "I think I would like to have an herb garden. And a shrub farm perhaps . . . someplace, maybe over on the eastern shore, somewhat secluded, about twenty-five acres or so, at a nice easy pace. It would still be work, but it would be at a different pace, and sort of working with nature, I guess, and you could do as much or as little as you wanted. If you won the lottery." To borrow the words of Connie, the satisfaction these women found in their present jobs was not the kind of satisfaction that comes from "loving your job the way a scientist does," it was the kind that comes from making the most of what one has. Only one working-class woman, Cindy, loved her work in that special "like a scientist" way.

In the following chapters, I will introduce case studies of women who experienced these different kinds of work satisfaction. First, however, I will describe some of the rewards of working. Regardless of their orientation to work or their satisfaction with it, most women derived both monetary and non-monetary benefits from work. Fortunately, these benefits were available even when personal fulfillment was not.

The Monetary and Non-monetary Benefits of Working: Family First, Self Second

I asked the women to choose from a list the "three most important things about working" and then counted the number of times each alternative was chosen. For women as a whole—both middle- and working-class—"the feeling of achievement" (58 percent), "helping to pay the family's bills" (56 percent), and "making a contribution to others" (37 percent) were chosen most often. Working-class women most often selected "helping to pay the family's bills"; 71 percent of working-class women chose this alternative, and there was little difference between women without a high school diploma (67 percent) and those with a diploma (74 percent). Differences arose in what the women chose next most often; the second-most common choice among women without a high school diploma was "having one's own money" (50 percent), while for women with a diploma "the feeling of achievement" ranked second. "Not having to ask one's husband for money" (33 percent) ranked third along with "the feeling of achievement" among women without a diploma, while "making a contribution to others" (39 percent) ranked third among women with a diploma. (Middle-class women chose the following: "the feeling of achievement" [85 percent], "helping to pay the family's bills" [45 percent], "making a contribution to others," and "having others recognize one's abilities [both 37 percent]).

The three questions on financial rewards—"having one's own money," "not having to ask one's husband for money" and "helping to pay the family's bills"—dominated the choices of working-class women without a diploma. This was not surprising. Virtually all the women without a diploma were married to men who themselves had not finished high school and worked in unskilled, low-paid jobs; the family incomes of these women were often barely above poverty level, and some were sole breadwinners. High school graduates, on the other hand, were usually married to men who were also high school graduates and worked in better-paying jobs. But for all the working-class women, helping to pay their family's bills was the main benefit of working; the issue for them was not work *or* family, it was work *for* family. As Ann put it, "A job is a job, that's all that is. That's a job. I can get that other places. This family I will never get again."

One in three women said that without their earnings, their family would be deprived of basics such as food. But whether for essentials or "extras" (items such as vacations that middle-class families take for granted), women's earnings made an enormous difference to their lives and those of their families. Monica and Phyllis were typical. "I've only been working [full-time] a little over five years," Monica said, "and I make almost as much as [my husband] does, and he's been working fifteen years. So I've doubled our money. My husband still every once and a while brings up the fact that I was out of work for two months, and it made our bills back up." Phyllis: "People think because [my husband] works at G.M. and I work at Southern Foods, they think we're rolling in the dough. Well the money's good at G.M., when he works, but he was laid off two weeks in July, for model changeover. One year they went out on strike for a month. Three years ago, he got laid off in December and didn't go back till May. So,

I mean, the money's good but it's good *when* you work." Phyllis's husband agreed: "We couldn't survive without her income."

Speaking of her children, Doreen said, "I work so they can have." Terry worked two jobs; her primary job, as a factory worker, was for basics, her secondary job, as a waitress, was "just my extra money. For the kids, and for us to go to see the beach. . . . The kids love it because they get to go and see new things. I was able to take my vacation and take them to Ocean City for a week. They really enjoyed that. . . . I take them to places like that. They love it! We go to the ocean, and we go hiking. We go on picnics, stuff like that. . . . You know, things that I want to have extra for the kids. So that my full-time check can go in for the household. That way if I want something for the kids, I'm not neglecting the bills or the groceries, things like that. Because me and my husband, we try to share everything. That way we're not neglecting anything, you know. So that the kids get it pretty good." Before she worked, "when it came time to do things with the children, we just didn't have the finances."

Working to better their families' standard of living was most women's main reason for working, but rewards for themselves were an unexpected bonus. Having their own earnings gave them permission to buy what *they* wanted, and what *they* believed their families needed and often, the first thing they bought was a car. In a city with woefully inadequate public transportation, owning a car made a huge practical and psychological difference in women's lives. Two of the women who were most dissatisfied with their jobs were stuck in them, in part, because they had no car; Laura's husband owned a car, but she depended on her sister-in-law for a ride to work each day, and neither Ruth nor her husband owned a car. A car brought independence. Terry, for example, described herself as an "outdoor person," and said her husband was averse to crowds, the beach, and the boardwalk; without her own car, neither she nor her children would have been able to go to Ocean City. And Judy enjoyed having her own money, but also being able to get up and go whenever *she* chose:

OK, you've gotta understand. Before, when I wasn't working, I'd say to my husband, "Well, leave me some money because I have to [whatever]." Now I don't have to say that. So it's given me a sense of independence. You know what I mean? It's like, it's the same as I never drove and I was twenty-five years old. And I said, "If one of my children would get sick, I'd have to depend on my mother-in-law or my father-in-law." So then finally I made my mind up and said, "I'm gonna go get my licence." And finally I did. So that gave me a sense of independence. So now if I want to go, I just pick up my keys. I go out, I get in my vehicle, and I go. And I don't have to call anybody or ask anybody.

Independence tasted especially sweet for Doreen. Doreen's husband, Dave, complained when she spent money on her nieces and nephews even though he had caused

Doreen to lose her house when he used the mortgage money to buy drugs. Now that she was working, Doreen had the consolation of knowing she would never again end up on the street. She had described her boss as a "real jerk," and complained that she had to "bust butt," but she said she was satisfied with her job:

> That's my job. I wanted the job, I got the job. And now I got the responsibility. I mean, I'm there until they get rid of me. . . . See I respect my job. I have never missed a day's work but one day in two years and I've been late three times in the last three months. Somebody keeps turning my circuit breaker off in the house, and my alarm doesn't go off. But I do not mess with my job. I go to work and I come home from work. Dave's completely different. He will take off any time he's ready. . . . My pay-check, it's guaranteed it's coming into the house.

Doreen's paycheck meant she could thumb her nose at Dave and spend money on her sisters and their children, if she wanted to, and because she could now pay the mortgage herself, and she knew that her family would always have a roof over their heads. Would she feel differently about herself if she didn't work? "That's a hard question. I didn't like things when I didn't work. If something needed to be done and we were short of money, we couldn't do nothing, because there was no money there. I like to work. I feel that I'm doing my part."

Independence was a major benefit of working for many women. "I think [working] made me more independent," Jill said. "I think it makes you a stronger person. You know, because I was so young, and I depended on my husband. [Now] I am more confident that I can do things." "If I didn't work, I wouldn't feel independent," said Dorothy. "I wouldn't feel like I was my own person. I wouldn't feel anything!" And Carolyn said:

> I would like for [my daughter] to have a better job. And be a little bit more independent than what I am. I mean, I'm independent but not as much as I should be. I count on my husband a lot for a lot of things. I don't take care of any bills. I don't write checks out for nothing. He takes care of all that, the gas and electric, you know, all of that. If I had to write a check out, or something would happen to him, I wouldn't know the first thing about how to do it. I've been thinking about that lately, and I've talked to him, and he's gonna have my name put on the checking account too. And he's gonna teach me how to do that. Because I've been thinking about that lately too. Thinking what if something should happen to him? I don't know the first thing about how to do nothing like that. Because he's always been there to do it, you know.

Citing statistics that show higher divorce rates among working women, some social commentators bemoan this increased female independence, fearing it will spell the end of marriage. There was no evidence of this among the women I spoke with. In fact, the effect of working was quite the opposite; by sharing the burden of breadwinning, most women strengthened their marriages, as well as themselves. Sue, for instance, worked for the telephone company as a maintenance supervisor, and her husband, who had lost his job as a highly paid factory foreman, now worked nights as a security guard:

> He worked for a major company for twenty-some years. They went under. And then he went to work for another company, and he worked there for three years, and they closed down. He was off about four months. We were at a point in our life where we were financially secure, our children were older, we didn't have babies to take care of. And I have a relatively good job, so he didn't need to get a job making $50,000 a year to supplement our income. My job made a lot of difference.
>
> [He] likes it that we're at a point in our life where he doesn't have to go out and make $50,000 a year for our family to survive. He can depend on me. . . . [His job] is not stressful. But it was before. His one and only job before was very stressful. It had a lot of responsibility. It put a lot of strain on me too.

The sense of accomplishment they gained from working was important to all women, regardless of class. This was consistent with a finding by Grace Baruch, Rosalind Barnett, and Caryl Rivers, that working women at midlife have a greater sense of "mastery" than homemakers.[20] Sometimes a feeling of achievement came from helping others, another important benefit of working. This was true for Laura, who talked about caring for a young woman with cancer:

> I went and took care of the girl. I took care of her for like a year. I did physical therapy with her. I did occupation therapy with her. Even though they had people coming out. I watched what they were doing and I did it. I got the girl to walk when she did not feel comfortable with the P.T. woman that come out. Because, I mean, they sent this woman out, she couldn't have weighed any more than 90 pounds, and Nancy was like 240 [pounds]. And this girl would put a belt around her waist and just hold the belt and expect her to walk. Well you don't feel confident enough or competent enough to do that. And I'd put my arms around her, and we'd walk step by step. I got her to walk to her mother for the first time in like about a year and a half. And common sense will tell you how to do it. And that tells me I'm in the wrong career right here because I love to work with people that are sick. I love to work with people that are sick.

Judy gained a sense of accomplishment from having mastered all the separate processes on the assembly line at her cosmetics factory job. Packing cosmetics is not easy; in summer, the metal buildings are hot and the machine that shrink-wraps the cosmetics uses intense heat. In winter, the buildings are cold, and stiff fingers refuse to move as they should. Until calluses toughen them up, women's hands are cut to pieces by the cardboard boxes they unfold by the hundreds. Judy was so highly skilled that she could take over any job if she was needed, and she could help other workers. She had every right to be proud.

Sherry described the sense of accomplishment she gained from her job as a clerk. "It's weird," she said, "I guess I feel good that I'm accomplished with the job, and I've done it well. . . . We've been growing since I got there, and I guess I feel kind of important because I've been there the longest out of everyone. And you know, different things that they need to know, I know. So it's kind of like a challenge, kind of thing. There's never a dull moment."

Buying a car, getting a driver's licence, meeting new people, many of these benefits of working shared a common thread; women were rewarded by functioning in the wider world outside the walls of their own home and the boundaries of their neighborhood. For Judy, work opened a window onto a hidden world, and she relished knowing how it worked:

> We do Cover Girl. We do Max Factor. We do a lot of their Perfect Point pencils, their Soft Radiant pencils. We do a lot of their liquid liners. And then we package it for them. . . . Now Proctor and Gamble is in with Noxell. So they, like, merged. So now we're getting a lot of Max Factor stuff, like their Splish Splash, their Skinny Minny pencils. Most of it is eyeliners. I'd say 90 percent of it is eyeliners. It's amazing. It's amazing how much you have to do a day to get out. It's so amazing.

Women felt enriched, strengthened, and empowered by this involvement in the world. Cora spoke for most other women when she said, "I realize now that there is more out there in the world besides just staying behind the door all the time."

Making a contribution to others was another benefit of working. Traditionally female occupations that involve caring for others remain popular; in part, this is because there are barriers to less traditional occupations, but it is also because many women find caring work enjoyable and meaningful. The teachers in the study, for example, felt hamstrung by the bureaucracy, but still found their work rewarding, because they felt they could make a difference in the lives of children. The work of caring for others was often what women said they would do if they didn't need money, and some women found this work so rewarding, especially when children were involved, that they were prepared to do it for minimal pay. Nina, who is described in the next section, was an example. Nina's family could have used a larger wage than the small and unreliable amount she brought home from her part-time job at the local school, but she knew that no other job would offer her the same satisfaction.

Works and Lives: Four Personal Stories of Meaningful Work

The survey questions could do only partial justice to the different meanings work held, because each woman's life was unique. The feeling of achievement Trudy gained from her job, for example, had a very special meaning for her because she suffered from serious depression; her job, she felt, quite literally kept her alive. "I think that quite a bit of my self-esteem is tied up in my job that I do," she said. "I just have no idea what kind of shape I would be in, because just having a job and having to get up and go to work in the morning is what keeps me going. If I didn't have to do that, or didn't have that—I don't know. It's reassurance that I'm an OK person." And the increased confidence brought by working had a special meaning for Gina, who had lived on the same street her entire life and had never worked. "I'm more comfortable to go out," she said. "I'm really not experienced much at all in the job world. I'm not shy to go out now. You always feel a little bit strange whenever you start a new job, especially if you don't have a friend or a family member who works there too and all. But it just does-n't bother me as much now. To start a new job that's all different." The four stories that follow are examples of the intensely personal and individual meanings women found in work, meanings we can only understand if we understand where work fits in the overall pattern of their particular lives.

Nina

Dressed in a faded corduroy jumper, her brown hair lightly streaked with gray, Nina opened the door of her wooden row house with a grimace. A heavy-metal thunderclap crashed and boomed above us, shaking the fragile little house to its foundations. There was nothing she could do about it, Nina explained apologetically; the family who lived upstairs refused to turn the music down, and she had given up asking. She invited me in, and we began the interview, but we soon decided we would need to reschedule. No sooner had we done this, however, when suddenly the music stopped, heavy boots thumped down the stairs, the front door slammed, and all was quiet. We both sighed with relief and decided to seize the chance and do the interview after all.

With her truck-driver husband, four of her six children, and a foster child, Nina rented the ground floor and basement of the house, which was in the middle of a row of identical houses, cottages really, built originally for dockworkers. The living room we were sitting in doubled as a bedroom for two of her children; Nina showed me how she created some makeshift privacy at night by pulling across curtains. They didn't have much, she said, but she was happy with what they had. After all, as the daughter of a carpenter and one of ten children, she was used to being poor. "I remember one time," she said, "we . . . had oatmeal a lot. It was still in the era of the coal and wood furnaces. And we didn't have any coal and we didn't have any money to buy any, so my dad chopped up the piano. This was when I was a child. That kind of thing, seeing your dad chop up the piano, kind of sticks in your mind."

Nina had a warm, loving relationship with her father, but with no one else in her family. Her mother was chronically depressed and was hospitalized after many suicide attempts; in one of these, Nina came home from school to find their house smelling of gas and her mother lying on the kitchen floor with her head in the oven. She always believed that her mother disliked her; an aunt had told her, when she was very young and about to cross a busy, dangerous road, "It doesn't matter if you get killed or not, because your mother doesn't want you," and her mother subjected her to constant verbal abuse. "She used to call us a whore a lot," she said, "and I didn't know what that meant, so I would get the dictionary. You know, it would be 'whore' and 'bitch' and things like that."

With no protection from her mother, and her father absent at work for long hours, she was defenseless against sexual predators in her family, and was sexually abused—by her uncle, her grandfather, and her brother:

> A lot of things happened when I was a child . . . you know, I told you I was molested by my [uncle] . . . he tried and tried . . . and my grandfather . . . and my grandfather tried to molest me, and I did tell my father. I did tell him then. And my brother also. Did. So it's not been a . . . that subject then . . . I, you know, that was the first, and I didn't realize that it wasn't something that people didn't do because, like I've said, that kind of thing was not ever really discussed back then. . . . I kinda blame my mom, but now, I mean, when I was younger I really blamed her.

Nina had been "the responsible one" in her family, and it was her job to care for her younger brothers and sisters. "I don't think I was ever a child," she said. "From the time I was five, I was doing for other people." Her sisters had left home as soon as they could, but Nina remained long enough to graduate from high school. She then worked as a clerk, a live-in nanny, a cook, a waitress, and a packer in a vegetable-packing plant before her marriage. After her marriage, her energies were absorbed by her rapidly growing family—six children in as many years—and although her husband's paycheck could barely feed and clothe her family, she was quite happy during those years. When her youngest child was in elementary school, however, she became concerned about his progress, and decided to volunteer at the school to make sure he was getting enough attention. From these almost accidental beginnings, she began her career as both a volunteer and employee of the school system. She started out as a classroom aide:

> I worked in the office as an office aide, and then the secretary left. She retired . . . and they didn't have a secretary to come in so I was the secretary of the school for all of that school year. The first year it was [volunteer]. [Then] the principal paid me. Because it is a city school, and this area is out of the way. . . . People don't want to come down here. And so he couldn't find anyone to come, so I got paid money, yeah.

So then, let me see, so then they got a secretary, and she came. . . . I was working in the office with her, showing her the ropes, because it was the first time she had ever been secretary of a school. But she had worked in the city system, and they had transferred her from one place to another. And she was there about six months and she was suspended. So I worked the rest of that school year and the whole summer, and the next year.

The school found a new secretary, and Nina became a volunteer again. For a while, she continued to volunteer, and was also paid to tutor children. Soon, however, the new secretary quit—"because nobody wants to stay there"—and she was asked to return to the office for the remainder of that school year. "Nobody wants to come to this area, because it is far out," she said, "but it is really considered as a safe area. People will say, 'Oh I don't want to go there, it's too dangerous, too dangerous,' but it's not really. It's just the idea that they have to go over the bridge. You know people [don't want to go] over the bridge."

So continued Nina's career; when there was money, she was an employee, when there was not, she was a volunteer. When I interviewed her, she had just heard that, once again, her days as a paid employee were numbered. On paper, she was employed as an attendance monitor, but she still worked as a volunteer, and supervised twenty-five other women:

Of course it started out as a little job, you know. Keep check, if a child misses a certain number of days, call home, see what's up. Then it got [more complicated]. There's all kind of paperwork. We keep a chart of every child in the school and when they're absent. The chart has the child's name and the pupil number and their address and their telephone number and all that stuff, and every day that they're absent, we mark that they are, and if they're late, we mark that, and when I make a phone call, I make a notation on the bottom of the paper there. When I send a letter out to them, I make a notation. Now, it's gotten so we make home visits. So it gets to be a full-time job. Then the city, they send letters and they'll say, "Give us the names of the children who've missed more than x amount of days and stuff like that." It's a full-time job. It really is. We have 500 children in the school.

Usually I'm there from eight-thirty until about three o'clock. Because after I'm finished the attendance books, teachers always have papers to run off, papers to be checked, things to be laminated. A lot, you know. Letters to be cut out. All kinds of stuff. We belong to the PTA and a couple of years ago, we bought a machine—we call it the letter cutter—and it has the letters, and you punch them, you push it through. It's really neat. It has uppercase and lowercase, and there's the symbols and things like that. And we bought a laminating machine, and of course the teachers like everything laminated.

We cover classes when the teachers have meetings. We work in the cafeteria. And we go outside with the kids sometimes. If it's cold, we stay inside with the kids in the auditorium, and they watch movies. People don't realize how many things there are in a school to do. You know, placate an angry parent. Sometimes the only time they ever come is when someone says something about their dear child, who is such a holy terror anyway. That's the only time they ever show up. They kind of look to me because I know a lot of the people in the community.

I'm involved in the school and the church and between that and the community association down the street, I know most of them. And the principal—she's new this year—she'll come and get me and say, "Mrs. Brown, come down here." Like yesterday. We had one of the parents standing in the middle of the hallway screaming at one of the teachers. She's not a nice teacher anyway, she really isn't. I said, "Pam," I said, "Whatever you're screaming [about], whatever you're yelling about," I said, "Just talk first. Calm down." So I got her calmed down, and the vice-principal came down and I said [to her], "This is Pam. Her little boy . . ." So then I said, "Talk to [the vice-principal], tell her what your problem is," I said. "It isn't going to do you or anybody [else] any good standing in the hallway and screaming."

I don't like the sad situations that I see the children are in. My husband, you know, he'll say, "What are you thinking about?" I'll say, "Well, I'm thinking about . . . " And I'll sit there and I'll tell him what happened at school today, what happened to this kid. And so he's kind of my sounding board. You know, I don't like knowing what these children go through. People don't realize how physically and mentally [abused they are]—and all the kinds of abuse that they get. Even children who aren't physically abused—and I yell at my kids. I won't say I don't, but children are abused, and they don't have to be touched to be abused. And they're abused by parents and teachers. You know. And I don't think it's really meant to be, but it happens though. And you know, and it's kinda, it's . . . in a way, it's better that, you know, that you live in a community, because you know what the kids are going through, but then it's even harder because you know that so-and-so's mother is a drug addict, and another [parent] is doing this, and [another one's doing that]. But then you can see their situation better.

People have no idea what children go through. None! I see it at school all the time. Children come to school and they've not been fed and, you know, lots of kids get up and they don't even see their parents or guardians or whoever's taking care of them. They get their self off to school and they go to school without breakfast. And they go to school dirty and [with the] same clothes on. I remember one time, a little boy, he came to school and he had . . . I don't know why I take notice. I guess I like kids. They make me upset sometimes, but I guess I really care what happens to them . . . and [this little boy] had the same shirt on, and the next day he turned it around and the next day he turned it inside out.

It's a trip. People want to know why they are so bad. I mean, there are some kids that are just like . . . the school's right there at the top of the hill . . . and seven o'clock in the morning . . . school doesn't start till eight-twenty-five . . . but seven o'clock in the morning there's children walking up the hill. And the reason why I think they do it is because there's people there that at least care what happens to them. You know, it's a job!

I like working with kids. And I like knowing that I did something to make their day better. . . . I try to always give them a good outlook, you know, instead of saying, "I'm going to tell your mother." Because there are people who do that. There are people who—for some weird reason or another they work with children, but that's all they ever do is—belittle kids and always tell them, "I'm going to tell your mom, I'm going to tell your dad. This is gonna happen to you. That's gonna happen to you."

As far as Nina was concerned, caring was not just a job, it was a moral imperative; she believed it was her calling to make a difference in the lives of the children no one else cared about. She was heavily involved in her church and community association and she had also informally adopted an emotionally disturbed child who had been abandoned by his mother. His mother had never asked for his return, Nina said, adding "I don't think she likes him":

She gave him away about—I hear—about five different times. She's called Social Services and told them to come and get him. [She] can't stand this child. But she wouldn't let the father have him. But she would let him come visit me. And so then we tried to get him from the Social Services. One day the man called. I remember it was a Friday afternoon and he said, "Do you still want this child?" I said, "Yeah." I said, "You can bring him here."

And the funny thing was, the man said, "I came up the street and went past your house and he started having a fit, saying, 'That's grandma's!'—because he calls me grandma—'You went by my grandmom's house.'" And so [the welfare worker] turned around and came in, and the first thing Paul said was, "I need to go to the bathroom." I said, "Paul, you know where the bathroom is?" And the man looked at me and said, "His mother said he'd never been in this house before." I said, "Well, you tell me how he knew where the bathroom is."

I just feel like he's a street person, that we've pulled him back. She never taught him, I mean honestly, never taught the child. I don't think she likes him because he looks so much like her husband. And apparently he had a hard time being born and I mean, she really didn't teach him anything. You know, most of the time when somebody says a word wrong, you at least think in your mind, "That's not the way you say that word." But she never taught him how to speak, she just let him do whatever he wanted. I mean, we still have trouble getting him to wipe himself because she never taught him.

I mean, we don't have a lot, we don't have a lot. But we have more than this child. Yeah. I mean, [my kids] at least know that their mother and father love them. And he knows that his mother doesn't.

Her foster child caused havoc in the house, but she would never send him away. "He needs to know," she said, "somebody at least cares enough for him, that they aren't going to put him out on the street every time he does something wrong."

Nina recognized no boundaries between work and home, or between work that was paid or unpaid. She had turned her own sad childhood history of poverty, abuse, and neglect into a priceless asset for her community, and in the process, she had found rewarding work that helped salve her own wounds and gave them some meaning. Who could better understand how it feels to be defenseless, rejected, and abused? Without work, she said, "there would be an empty place."

Anna

At 10 A.M. on a rainy Saturday morning, Anna was sitting at her dining-room table preparing party favors for her sixteen-year-old daughter's baby shower later that day. A small, unassuming woman with a sweet smile, she was surrounded by piles of candies, tiny umbrellas, pale pink plastic baby dolls, and other miniature toys waiting to be stuffed into small, colorful paper bags. She made up an assembly line of one, hard at work while her elderly mother-in-law dozed nearby in a rocker, and her husband watched television. I offered to come back another time, perhaps when she was alone and not so busy, but Anna said now would be fine, so we talked and I helped her stuff bags.

Perhaps prompted by our work, we began by talking about Anna's own childhood and early marriage; she had married at seventeen, was a mother at eighteen, and bore six children over the following fifteen years. Looking back, she said, it seemed she'd always taken care of children. It had begun when she was scarcely more than a child herself, one of thirteen children in a very poor family headed by her dump truck driver father, and her waitress mother. Anna was placed in foster homes for the first seven years of her life, and later, after she had returned home, she didn't get along with her mother and "never had much to do" with her.

When she was fourteen, in "special education eleventh grade, regular school ninth grade," Anna was again sent away by her parents, this time to West Virginia, to help care for her older brother's children. She remained in West Virginia for two-and-a-half years, attending school whenever she could. At sixteen, back from her brother's, she returned to her old school, but found it too hard to catch up, and failed. At this, her mother told her to leave school; since she didn't seem able to learn anything, there was no point in keeping her there—she might as well do something useful. "Something useful" turned out to be helping her sister, who had six children. "I babysat and helped the neighbors," she said. "I helped with fifteen nieces and nephews."

Anna had been sad to leave school. "I liked school," she said. "I still do. I liked all of it, I had trouble understanding some of the stuff, but I liked it. My grades were good in elementary school. My grades were better than my sister's but they passed her and kept me back. I lost interest in trying to learn. When I was down at my brother's, I started to get into it again. It was in sixth grade that they kept me back. It was heartbreaking. When I came back here I just couldn't get with it."

Upset at being forced to leave school, Anna had little choice but to live with her sister and help take care of her nephews and nieces. At the same time, she cleaned house for an elderly man who was a friend of her sister's husband. This arrangement lasted for several months, but for much of this time tension was simmering between Anna and her sister. Eventually, these tensions erupted in a violent disagreement, and Anna was forced to leave. She was reluctant to return to her parents' house, and had nowhere else to turn except to the elderly man, who agreed to let her stay with him. She did this for a year, then was married.

At eighteen, Anna was unprepared for motherhood. "At first when I first started having children," she said, "I had problems that I had to have some help with because some things didn't go right when I lived at home. So I had to have some counseling because I mistreated my children when they were small." For many years she felt trapped and isolated at home, cut off from the outside world. During these years she had done some babysitting and took in laundry and ironing:

> I've done babysitting in my home ever since I remember. I've always taken care of children. Even with my boys, I babysat and did laundry for people maybe three or four days a week, and in between that time I [looked after] children. The most I had—with my son I had three little children that came every day. Sometimes I had them a whole day, sometimes I only had them half a day, depends on what the parents would want, because they did volunteer work or other jobs. I did that with all of my children.

At one point, she followed up a television advertisement for training as a beautician, but was disheartened when they said she was "too old." She came to believe that domestic work was all she would ever do. Three years before our interview, however, she had learned of a part-time job in the cafeteria of her local elementary school. Encouraged by her daughter, she applied for the job and, much to her surprise, she was successful. Three years later, she still worked there, and loved it:

> They have me baking now. Monday I baked three cakes. They had a birthday. They're

starting a thing with the children's birthdays. From the first day of school starting in September, up until yesterday, they was taking all the children—two hundred and something of them—and they have them a little party. Cake and fruit juice. I fixed the cakes and iced them yesterday, and helped give them out to the children. That was before we all left, and before school let out.

The week before that I did apple cobblers. I made five of them. And my boss is bringing the children in to learn how to work with food and stuff. Because they like to know what goes on in the kitchen. So the kids have to put the ingredients in the apples to make the baked apples, which they have for lunch. We make baked apples, the children and I. And we made the apple cobblers. Let's see—and we made the cakes. I made the cakes myself the other day. I help set the steam table where I serve the food.

Anna's work had changed her life. "Before I started working," she said, "I was getting to the point where I was getting depressed and bored with myself. I'd do my housework, and I had nothing to do the rest of the day." Now, with her own car, and a job, she was growing more confident and learning new skills every day. To illustrate, she told me how she'd handled a recent incident at her school:

The other day the man that works in the cafeteria had these three young boys help out clean the cafeteria. The one boy took the broom handle off the broom. He was swinging it around like a baton. I know children do these things. I mean it's nice to show interest in doing things like that, but the thing of it was, the way he was swinging it, he just about hit me right between the eyes like this, and I ducked, because I felt something coming toward my face. And he almost hit two of the little black boys in the face. It was a white boy.

Anna took the stick away from the boy:

I says, "You hit me, and I'm going to hit you back." It's just a reaction I have. I don't think when I get hit. I have a reaction and it works pretty bad sometimes. When I was younger, I had a lot of kids used to pick on me all the time. And because of it I just learned to defend myself. There was these kids that used to walk by, they'd take a stick and punch at my shoulders and things. I'd say, "What's your problem?" They'd say, "We want to see how you react." I used to go home and tell my mom all the time. Then I had bigger brothers. But they said, "You have to learn to defend yourself. You can't depend on us being around all the time." Then it started. I was known as the bad kid of the neighborhood. But once they found out that I was fighting back, they left me alone.

But, every once in a while, like, the kid did that [swung the broom] Thursday. I almost hit the child. Which I didn't want to do. I had a mop in my hand. A wet mop!

Well, if I had have hit him, it would have just been the wet mop part, not the other part, the metal.

And I took the young man, Thomas, who works for us, I says, "Look," I says, "you're going to have to talk to that boy. I took this stick away from him." And he says, "Don't bother me now. I'm busy." This kind of upset me a little bit. And he says, "Leave him alone. Leave him alone."

I don't try to pick at children, but the thing of it is, when they almost hit you in the face, then it's time, you know you have to stand up and talk to them. And after [Thomas] finished what he was doing, I went back and I talked to him, because this is the way we do it. We talk about things that upset us. And I said, "This boy almost hit me between the eyes with that stick."

Anna said the school staff had been taught to talk about things that upset them, and she was proud to have put this learning into effect. Faced with the mop-wielding boy, she had mastered her first impulse, which was to hit him, and she had ignored her coworker's attempts to shrug her off. More confident than ever before in her life, she had asked one of the teachers to coach her for the GED, and she'd also been working eight hours a day, instead of the four hours for which she was paid, because she was determined to prove she could do the work. "At my age," she said, "they didn't want to hire me in the first place. Other people wouldn't like what I'm doing," she said, "but I do."

Carol

Carol and her husband, an electrician, lived in a spacious colonial-style house high on a hill surrounded by an acre of well-clipped lawn. She was an attractive woman—pretty, articulate, smart, and vivacious—who managed a recruiting office. She explained her job: "The firms will pay our service. In other words, if your job that I find for you starts at $15,000 a year, which is entry level, they'll pay 15 percent of fifteen thousand and with each thousand it goes up a percentage, so with $16,000, [it] would be 16 percent. Anything fifteen thousand and down is really very entry level." She explained that the average salary for jobs she staffed was between $19,000 and $30,000. "I get positions in for accounts payable and receivables, full charge bookkeepers, entry level clerical to executive level secretarial, medical, legal." She also "wrote advertising copy," and "was responsible for budgeting, supervising, and training new staff" and took over many of the functions of a human resources department, including advertising and screening. "They call in [and] they tell me exactly what it is they're looking for, what skills this person has to have. We test them." What happens if the person leaves? "They don't leave," she said. "I'm a good interviewer."

Carol specialized in office workers, but she was preparing to branch out:

This week [a client] needs a forklift mechanic; I've been interviewing for one and I said [to my husband], "Give me a real quick education on how to interview for a forklift mechanic." I don't want to sit there and feel stupid talking. So I've learned there's electric forklifts, there's gas, there's diesel. They should be certified. I said, "Give me a salary range for someone with, say, five years experience," because you don't want to refer someone whose looking for more money than what the job is really going to pay or what his skills warrant. Actually I was very proud of myself—I started interviewing Friday of last week and I think I have filled it today. I did not enjoy that. I was uncomfortable because I wasn't confident that I knew enough to interview and ask the right questions. You don't like to wing something because if a person comes back and . . . if they have a question for you and you don't have the answer to it, it makes you feel kind of stupid.

Carol was obviously a quick study. It came as a surprise, then, to learn that she had dropped out of high school in the tenth grade because she had a "hard time" in school. "I had a short attention span," she said. "I knew I wasn't stupid, just wasn't real bright." Not real bright? Here is her story:

One of three children in a warm, extended, Italian-American family that consisted of her father, a house painter, her mother, a secretary who worked for a bank, and her grandmother, a seamstress, Carol felt secure and nurtured at home. But not at school. As she described her school experiences, her voice shook with barely suppressed anger:

The Catholic elementary school was horrible. They were abusive nuns. They were awful. I can remember having flash cards shoved in my mouth, being thrown in the cloakroom. I had a horrible time with math, and she would have little flash cards, and I still, I couldn't do it. I'd get hit. You couldn't say one word.

The discipline was tough. If you were a child that was struggling, it was because you didn't study, so they would hit you. Hit you! That was the answer. [They'd say], "Go sit in the back of the classroom." "Why don't you know your facts?" "Why can't you do this?" "You can't do it because you didn't study." "You were not listening."

I was listening. I wasn't comprehending. Big difference. So it was a real struggle for me. . . . Then I went into the public school from the Catholic school. I spent the first six months or so, and they decided that I needed to repeat the grade. Now that I have kids, and I worked with kids, and with my own children [I know] I didn't need to repeat the grade. I needed a little help.

I wasn't a bad kid. I was a good girl. I did what I was told, and certainly didn't have behavior problems. I had a lot of friends. But it just didn't come as easily as it did to the next kid. I didn't understand.

Finally, in tenth grade, Carol quit school. "I couldn't wait," she said. She found a job as a receptionist, met and married her husband the following year, and gave birth to their first child, a daughter, a year later. She then stayed at home caring for her daughter and later a second child—another daughter—for a total of ten years. But when her second daughter turned six, she decided it was time to go to work, and with some trepidation, she took a part-time job:

The only reason I did it was because I had been home with my kids for so long and I was doing all kind of volunteer things in school and the kids were getting too big for Mom to be running to school; they didn't want me in a classroom and with field trips anymore, and I just felt like I needed a little bit more than constantly dealing with children. And I just wanted to see how I could do if I went to work.

I went to work for Sears. I sold furniture part-time, saw that I had a good knack for sales, and I stayed part-time for maybe the first year and a half. Then they wanted me to come on full-time. We had moved, and I didn't want to do retail anymore, thought I would try something else, so I did. I went to work for an employment agency, not knowing anything about employment agencies. I read an ad and it said, "Receptionist, Light Typing, Answering Phones, Fee Paid." I had no idea what that meant. So I went in, and I talked to the woman, and she said, "How would you like to work here?" I said, "As a receptionist?" It was a nice office in Owings Mills. She said, "No, I would like to train you to be a recruiter." I said, "Well, tell me [about that]." I had no idea what recruiting was. [She told me] filling positions, filling jobs within offices, placing secretaries from medical to legal. So I said, "Sure." I did it and I was very successful.

So I stayed there for, I guess, a year and a half, and got excellent training. They were very nice to me. They pay you a salary in employment agencies plus a commission. I was making a base salary and then they paid 10 percent of whatever monies you were able to get in at the end of the month. But you had to get $10,000 in collections from fees from these companies for your applicants that you place, in order to get 10 percent commission. The fees were based on salary, they're 1 percent per thousand of a person's starting salary, so if you came to me for a secretarial job and I had a law firm [as a client], and you had a legal background, I could send you there, and if they decided to hire you, if you were making twenty thousand a year, they would pay a $4,000 service fee for you to come in and work there.

So after I was there, I did very well. I brought a lot of money into the company and I went in and asked [the manager] for a base raise and he said, "Why, you're in the top 10 percent here every month. Why, you're doing wonderful." I understood that, and I liked the job, but I felt like the commissions and the money I was collecting were a result of my work and my efforts, and I just wanted to know that I was going to be compensated for being there and producing. I wanted a raise. And he said, "Well all right." He tried to pacify me, "Let me give you fifty cents an hour." I said I wasn't thinking about fifty cents an hour.

I had signed a no-compete contract, meaning when you leave an employment agency, you can't work in another agency for one year after you leave. So he said, "We like you here. You're not going to be able to work." I said, "I know that. I'm going to take a year and work, do something until my contract is up, and then I'm going to try another employment agency I like."

So I did. I went right across the street, found some doctors, and I just helped out [at] the front desk, scheduling patients. Actually they were teaching me how to take X rays. I wasn't certified but I did anything that I could do to help. When my contract was up in July, I knew what day it was because I had a job the following day. I went to another agency and I've been there since and I now manage it.

Determined her children should succeed in school, Carol kept her school dropout secret. "I'm always paranoid, [my daughters] will ask a question," she said. "My husband says, 'Why can't you tell those kids? Why do you have a problem with that?' It's because I'm setting an example here. I want them not to do what I did. I don't want to tell them, 'Well, your mother didn't [finish].' I just don't want to. In this house it's a must that you finish school."

Carol had come a long way, personally as well as professionally. She had proven she was not stupid; that, in fact, she was very smart. "I would be depressed," she said, "if I still felt the same about myself as I did in school. I would be very depressed. I can't imagine growing up and being an adult who thinks that she's stupid."

Colleen

Twenty-five years after she first planned it, Colleen was at last close to graduating from college, with a degree in industrial education. It had been a long, hard road. Her father, a carpenter, and her mother, a cake decorator, had split up when she was eight, and she had then lived with her mother, who suffered from an illness that Colleen didn't name. Her mother was "always the odd one in the family. She had a very winning personality, and she was beautiful. Yet on the other side, she had this dark side. . . . My mother was that type of person that—she would tell stories so often that they became truth. You know. But familywise, everybody loved her, although they knew that she was unusual."

Colleen's hopes for college were dashed in her junior year of high school when her mother's illness took a turn for the worse, and she was forced to move out on her own. "My mother, she wasn't very good with children, that type of thing. She liked to be on her own pretty much. The last year and a half in high school I was on my own. I was by myself, supporting my own self. Because of the situation with my mom, which is something else again, I was sending money to my mom. . . . There was times when I had very limited food, things like that, because I was paying for her."

Living on her own in Florida, Colleen not only finished high school but did well enough to win a college scholarship: "But I couldn't afford books and things like that . . . so I went to beautician school, and lived with my half brother. My mom was very ill." About a year after she graduated from high school, she was married; two years later, right after she and her husband had bought a beauty salon, she discovered she was pregnant. They went ahead with the salon anyway:

> It was fine, no problem. What happened was, I didn't have him until the end of that year, and we had pretty well done everything. We had painted the shop, and my half brother and my father-in-law helped paint the shop. It was one of those community, family things. And we had the shop for about fourteen years. Then we sold it.

During the fourteen years they owned the business, Colleen worked long hours in the shop and her husband worked in two—sometimes three—jobs. During those same years, she taught classes in cosmetology at a private hairdressing academy and enjoyed it so much she decided to teach in the public schools. She began substitute teaching on an occasional basis and when a full-time job came up in a distant county, she snapped it up, in spite of the commute. At the same time, she logged hundreds of miles driving to the state university several times a week to take courses: "I'm still doing that. I don't need to do it, but I would like to get my advanced credits in industrial education. You have to have a certain number of credits. I'm well advanced in that, but I do want to finish it up, just to get it done."

Colleen hadn't planned on becoming a cosmetologist; in high school she had wanted to become a dress designer. In the end, though, she felt she was doing "pretty much" what she wanted to do—"I always liked doing hair," she said. "You can veer off and still be happy." She was able to find in hairdressing the same quality that had appealed to her about dress designing, and it was what she most enjoyed about her job: "The creativity. And being able to influence a young person, molding them to do a job better." If she didn't work, Colleen said, she would feel "not as useful."

Work as a Second Chance

The experiences of Nina, Anna, Carol, and Colleen illustrate how difficult it is to capture with predetermined categories the meaning and experience of work for women. Each woman's work had a very personal meaning, whose particular quality could only be understood in the context of her individual life story. As a young girl, Colleen had loved to draw and dreamed of becoming a dress designer. With creative parents—one a carpenter who custom made beautiful furniture and one a cake decorator—she longed to do something creative. Bitterly disappointed when she was unable to go to college, she had changed direction and found other avenues for her creativity—first hairdressing, now teaching. During high school she had always assumed she would get a college degree, and at long last, she was about to graduate. Having endured endless humiliation in school, Carol could at last prove she was not stupid, and the feeling of mastery she gained from her job was like no one else's. After a lifetime of poverty and isolation from society's mainstream, Anna could finally work in the outside world and gain some respect and recognition in that world for the first time. And having been neglected as a child and abusive as a mother, working with children in a structured educational setting gave her an opportunity to become a different kind of person. Her self-esteem was growing day by day. Nina's work, too, had special meaning. As a child, she was always the responsible one in her family, the one assigned to take care of her siblings, even when her older sister still lived at home. Later, when she was taking care of her own six children, she often took care of nieces and nephews too. "We've always had a full house," she laughed. Now, she took care of the children no one else cared about. A very religious woman, Nina felt that caring was her calling.

By the time Nina, Anna, Carol, and Colleen left high school, they had faced formidable obstacles, and only two of the four women had entered adulthood with an educational credential of any kind. Nonetheless, by the time they were in their forties, they had all found meaningful work—and they had done it on their own. Nina turned volunteering in the local school into work. Anna was rebuffed when she made enquiries about cosmetology, but finally found her way to work. Carol, lacking in confidence after her disastrous experience in school, found the courage to apply for work she knew nothing about. And Colleen, forced to support herself through her senior year in high school and give up her college plans, had attended cosmetology school instead, but held onto her college dream; she had combined her training as a beautician with her desire for a degree and was now teaching her trade.

These women were creative, persisten, and plucky and they fashioned rewarding lives in spite of the limited choices imposed on them by their working-class backgrounds. Who knows what path Colleen would have followed had her mother not become mentally ill? Or Carol, had her teachers not forced her by their cruelty to leave school? Or Nina and Anna had their families not been poor and unable to provide them with a safe, secure childhood? All four women had carved out their own path to meaningful work, but the path had been long and difficult, and, for much of the way, they had followed it with no guidance.

Their beginnings in poor or working-class families (and in Carol's case, in a parochial school in a working-class area) had shaped the direction each woman was able to take. This was especially true for Nina and Anna: both women were from very poor families whose parents were unable to give them emotional or financial support, both left school with no clear plans about what they would do, and both had been abused and rejected. Like so many poor young women, they fell into marriage, rather than chose it. Later, when their children were older and more independent, and they began to seek out work opportunities, their choices, especially Anna's, were severely limited. In this, they typify what was a common pattern among women in the study, which I will elaborate on in the second part of the book. Many women, having spent their earlier married years focusing on children, were beginning to turn toward work as a source of meaning; as one said, "there was no point staying home when no one needed me." Turning toward work, however, they felt the full force of their lack of experience and lack of education. Moreover, psychologically painful childhoods were not scabs that healed once and for all; in the words of Eliot, "Time present and time past are both present in time future," and, as we will see in the second part of the book, many women carried the scars of childhood into their adult life.

The experiences of these four women tell us something about fluidity and change over the life course, but also about the nature of success. All four women had been successful in finding meaningful work, and they were all contributing to the well-being of their communities. None was alienated by her work, slaving in a job she hated, producing a product she cared nothing for, taking orders from a boss who cared nothing for her.

In this, they were all a success. But in terms of prevailing ideologies of success—getting ahead, moving up the ladder, getting rich—only Colleen and possibly Carol could be described as successful. Both women were living in a comfortably middle-class style, and both earned good incomes. Nina and Anna, on the other hand, were, if not poor, close to it. Nina's husband was a truck driver, but he was not always employed, and Anna's husband was retired; they lived on her mother-in-law's and husband's social security income and the few dollars she earned working part-time at the school. Both women worked in jobs that were low in status and low in pay—in fact, often they were not paid at all. In society's eyes, they are not worth much; they are worth enough to use as low-paid or unpaid labor, not enough to pay a decent wage. But in their own eyes, and mine, what they do is beyond price.

Work (f)or
F a m i l y

Mother had an MBA but didn't work after her children were born. I remember
her saying, "If I ever have to play another bridge game, I am going to scream."
To me, it was frustrating, because she was always a very smart lady. . . . I think
she was very ambivalent about [being a housewife] but . . . she felt that [it] was
the appropriate role.

—Eileen

[My mother] worked all of her life as a counter girl . . . counter girl, that was
basically about it. . . . She disliked her work very strongly, but she had to make
a living. That was all she knew. I hated her working. She wasn't there.

—Rhonda

As young girls, Eileen and Rhonda saw very different images of the work mothers do,
and they developed very different ideas about what they would do when their time
came around. Eileen had resolved to pursue a career; the last thing she wanted was the
life of a bored housewife, wasting her intellect on bridge games and coffee mornings.
Rhonda had resolved to be a homemaker; she didn't want the hard, thankless, daily
grind her mother faced every day. Yet, in spite of their different early examples and different early plans, both women ended up following identical work and family paths;
they were among the minority of women who worked continuously and full-time
over the course of their adult lives. But this similar work and family behavior, as you
might guess, had very different meanings for different women. Eileen, a middle-class
daughter who grew up and stayed in the middle class, was following a path she will-
ingly chose, and that she embraced with a passion. Rhonda, on the other hand, a
working-class daughter who grew up and stayed in the working class, was pursuing a
path she "chose" only by default. "I never had the choice not to work," she said.

In this and the following chapter, I turn to women's family experiences and examine how they interacted with their experiences at work. In this chapter, I will explore
how they made decisions about work and family over the years, and try to understand

what factors shaped their choices. Eileen, Rhonda, and the other women I interviewed had adopted four different work-family combinations: eleven women (nine working-class women, two middle-class) had worked continuously and full-time; more than half the women had worked off and on; one in three women had deferred work; and a handful of women had worked on a part-time basis for many years. As you will see, how the women managed what one psychologist has called the "dilemma" of women's two roles mirrored the way they experienced work; middle-class women's choices were dictated by preference, working-class women's by necessity.

Work Centrality, Role Conflict, and Other Middle-Class Myths

Psychologists and sociologists have extensively studied the centrality of work for women, usually defining centrality (or commitment) in terms of the importance of work for women's identity. Thus one psychologist defined it as "an attachment that is initiated and sustained by the extent to which an individual's identification with a role behavior, value or institution is considered to be central among alternatives as a source of identity." Another described it as "the relative distribution of interest, time, energy and emotional investment in work in relation to other life sectors and notably to family life."[1] By these definitions, women's investment in work is measured against their investment in family, and the relative importance of work or family as sources of identity are compared.

Responding to reported differences in the centrality of work between women and men, researchers have suggested that women may invest work with less importance because early gender socialization causes them to put family first, work second; if this were the case, women's orientations would be unconsciously learned in childhood, not consciously chosen in response to adult circumstances. An alternative view is that women's orientations are the result of rational choices they make as they assess the rewards available to them from work and family.[2]

In an interesting study of midlife women, Kathleen Gerson, a sociologist, explored how women's orientations to work and family develop. After interviewing women who were enrolled in a community college in a working-class area, she described a family or "domestic" orientation as one in which a woman "is or expects to be a homemaker or mother with loose, if any, ties to work," and a work orientation as one in which a woman is oriented "either toward full-time work or career with no plans for children or toward full-time work or career in combination with one or two children."[3] In her study, she asked whether women's orientations had been fixed since childhood or had changed in response to changing family and work circumstances.

Gerson found both to be true: some women's orientations remained the same but others changed in response to adult work and family experiences. Positive experiences at work—for example, being promoted—or negative experiences at home led some women to redirect themselves from a "domestic" to a work focus; this happened less often when women had positive family experiences and were in stable relationships with men who provided consistent economic support. Women who were disappointed in work sometimes made the opposite change in direction and became more oriented toward domesticity; among the women she interviewed, "blocked work opportunities" were a major reason women withdrew their investment in work. Gerson noted that "because there is usually a delicate balance between economic need and how much a woman is motivated to work, job commitment persisted only for those who found satisfying employment that fed their egos as well as their bank accounts."[4]

The life experiences of some of the women I spoke with were consistent with Gerson's account. Helen and Jill, for example, had followed two of the paths she described. As home became less rewarding and work became more rewarding, Helen invested more of her self into work. By contrast, Jill, had always had a "domestic" orientation, and continued to find her home life more rewarding than her work life.

Gerson's work shows us that women's orientations can change over the life-course in response to their changing life circumstances, and the title of her book, *Hard Choices,* reflects how difficult these choices are for many women. But the women she spoke with all had a high school diploma and were enrolled in a community college; were the same opportunities for change and choice available to a broader cross section of working-class women, particularly women who are poor and lack educational credentials?

As we saw earlier, the orientations of the women I interviewed were too complex to be described in terms of "domesticity" or "work," nor did it seem common for women to turn toward one when the other proved disappointing; on the contrary, women who were satisfied with their jobs were usually satisfied with their family lives, and many women preferred a balance between work and family, with neither making too many demands. To explore this question further, I had asked women to rate their family and work roles in terms of their importance and the satisfaction they gave; they rated both family and work roles as highly important, and higher ratings for one were not associated with lower ratings for the other.[5] Furthermore, when working-class women worked, it was work *for* family, not work *or* family. "My job hasn't interfered with my family life," Ann said, "because if I have to be elsewhere with them, I am." "A job is a job, that's all that is," she continued. "That's a job. I can get that other places. This family I will never get again."

It appears that for working-class women, work and family were not competing roles that vied with each other for women's attention and emotional investment, nor were they sources of the psychological role conflict that is a leitmotif of the work and family literature. At issue for working-class women was the physical impossibility of being in two places at one time. As Phyllis Moen has pointed out, "It may be that [role] conflict is more a problem for middle-class women, who have the financial means to provide for child care but who still worry about the effects of their employment on their children, while women in working-class jobs may suffer more from role overload, struggling to manage child care costs and time tables on a limited budget and with little flexibility in working hours."[6]

Without a doubt, the women I spoke with felt pulled in two directions. Most women and their husbands worked in jobs that offered little flexibility, so meeting family needs was more difficult for them than for middle-class women. One in four women, for example, said they had been unable to take time off work to see a school game or play, and the same proportion had sometimes needed to leave a sick child at home alone when they went to work. Four in every ten women had, at times, been unable to leave their job to pick up their child from school. To illustrate, Dorothy told me how she was refused permission to go to a school ceremony that celebrated her daughter's acceptance into the honors society: "I resented it, very highly resented it," she said. "She was the youngest ever, and I couldn't go. I was livid. I was livid. I offered to walk off. I just threatened. I said, 'I'm walking off this job right now.' And [my boss] said, 'You do, and don't come back. Because I'll fire you for insubordination.' And I didn't want to lose the job. But I cried through the rest of the afternoon because I was missing it."

Dorothy was sad and angry, but not conflicted or guilty; she had no choice. As we will see in the stories that follow, acting upon one's preferences or orientations is a luxury not usually available to working-class women; shifts in the balance of their families' economic, emotional, and physical needs, not in their orientations, determined whether and when they worked. This, as we shall see, was the main difference between middle- and working-class women: middle-class women could work or not, depending on their preference. Working-class women, especially poor working-class women, were often forced to work, motivated by need not preference.

Dorothy

Perhaps no one better illustrates the folly of thinking in terms of a work *or* family orientation than Dorothy. A tall, stately, and vigorous—or, as she put it, "hyper"—woman of fifty, who looked remarkably like Lucille Ball, Dorothy welcomed me into her cheerful dining-room on a cold, bleak January night. Her house was immaculate—she and her husband had just hammered the last nail on their most recent addition—and Holly, one of her daughters, had hurried home from school to cook dinner and straighten up afterward so the house would be tidy and her mother relaxed for our interview. This, Dorothy said with obvious pride, was not unusual. Holly was one of Dorothy's three children: two teenage girls from her current twenty-year marriage to Don, a mail carrier, and a son in his twenties from one of her two brief earlier marriages.

Dorothy had always sought advancement, and she had always found good jobs. Work was important to her, but so was her family. In fact, it is hard to imagine anyone to whom family could have more meaning; because her own was unhappy, making her children's family life loving and secure was one of Dorothy's main aims in life.

Dorothy's parents were divorced when she was six months old, and her father was awarded custody. Because he worked (as a carpenter), he was forced to place her in a foster home during the week, and bring her to stay with him on weekends. She stayed in a succession of these homes (called day-care homes) from infancy until she was seven years old. It was "very similar to what people do today," Dorothy said, "only their child is picked up every day. I wasn't picked up, I stayed there." Her eyes shining with unshed tears, she told me what she remembered of that time:

> I hated it! I hated it! I gained a great deal of insecurity from it. I had a phobia about loving. About caring. Because . . . I get upset just thinking about it, Jennifer. I just never felt . . . I always felt that anything that I would love would eventually be taken away from me. Because I learned to love these people at these different places. Not all of them, but some of them. And I began to have a closeness with them, because I so dearly wanted a mother. And I would have a relationship and then something would happen. It's incidental what it was. Either he didn't pay on time or they got tired of, you know, taking care of me. The reasons were varied. And I would go and be put into another one.

When she was seven, her father remarried, and Dorothy went to live with him, her sister, and a new stepmother and stepsister:

> And we were all put together as a family. My older sister was also put there. I had an older sister of three when my mother divorced my father. We were all in together, a stepmother, a father, and three girls. And it was his, hers, and ours. And then my brother was born, so we had children from three different marriages, all in the same house. So it was difficult. My stepmother was a good, good mother, as far as taking care of me, and providing for me and all of us, but she was a woman that didn't have—she didn't show compassion. She didn't show love.

Because of her early experiences, Dorothy vowed that her own children's experience would be "a complete reverse" and that they would never doubt their parents' love. "I did it intentionally," she said. "It didn't happen. I made it happen!"

> And my children know that they are loved. I mean Dana is going to be eighteen, Holly is fifteen, my son will be twenty-seven, and they never leave this house to go to the store unless they kiss us both goodbye. They go to bed at night and they kiss us both goodnight. We're their best friends. They come to us and they talk about anything. My children have never been in any serious trouble, never been involved in

dope, drinking, partying, bad friends. They've been kept in church, they've been told they have to go whether they like it or not. They go. And they respect the fact that that's the way it is. That's all stability. That all gives stability to your life, because I know what happened to me.

Dorothy put a lot of thought into parenting decisions; she said it was by "willpower, sheer willpower" that she had become an effective parent: "I just learned from experience. I knew what the experience was. I knew what it did to you as an adult. I knew that if I did not change it, they would make the bad decisions I had made, with two bad marriages. And I did not want them to do that. I did not want them to live those experiences. I didn't want them to have to learn that way. So I just made it a fact that it didn't happen. And it hasn't!"

For Dorothy, caring was meaningful work:

Holly kept me up till two o'clock in the morning the other day because she just had to tell me this long story about her friend at school and how terrible his family life is. She had to give me the whole entire story, and we were up till two o'clock in the morning. And I really was interested, but I was so tired. I'd had an extremely bad day that day. It was Friday, one of the busiest days of the week, and I was just so tired. I just wanted to close my eyes and go to sleep. And I said, "Holly"—about a halfway through, maybe an hour into it—I said, "Holly, do you think maybe we could finish this tomorrow?" [She said], "But Mommy I really need to talk to you now."

Dorothy stayed up, she joked, even if she needed toothpicks in her eyelids to keep her awake. Next day, at 8 A.M., after five hours sleep, she was at her desk, well-dressed, perfectly made-up, and ready to say, "May I help you?" to every one of the callers on the sixteen incoming lines of her switchboard. Dorothy described her job as "chaos," because as well as answering and directing all the calls that came into the office of the factory in which she worked, she transcribed dictation and did word processing. "It's mentally taxing," she said. "It's tiring. It's not hard, it's just tiring. It's a lot to get done all at one time, and I don't usually feel it until I'm home. And I've stopped. That's when I feel it."

Dorothy's family came first, and, in a number of ways, her work helped her family. She said—and her husband agreed—that she was mentally healthier when she worked. Her immaculate grooming—hair carefully styled and tinted, nails polished, makeup skillfully applied, pumps unscuffed, dress unwrinkled—as well as her attractively decorated, clutter-free house, its mahogany furniture polished and its wood floors gleaming, suggested a perfectionist who could not easily relax. What would she do if she didn't work? She laughed: "I mean, you can only clean so much! I'm not into soap operas or none of that. When I was home recuperating from back surgery, I mean, oh

God, I went crazy! After the first two weeks, and then you start to feel better, you know, and then I was allowed to get up and move around a little bit. Of course I was slow, but I could move around, but oh it was awful! I just hated it, I hated it! I don't like it. I'm an active sort of person. I'm hyper. I just can't be [doing nothing]. No."

Work kept her busy, but it had other benefits; she valued the opportunity it gave her to mull over problems at home. "Because," she said, "sometimes you don't see things clearly when you're close up. If you back up a little bit it looks a little bit, it has a different perspective. It takes a different shape. You know. It's sort of like being on the outside looking in. Yeah. Yeah. Sort of like that. In fact sometimes I work things out in my mind [at work] through the day. You know, a little bit at a time, and by the time I come home I sometimes have a solution." Laughing, she added, "It may not be one they want to hear!"

And working gave her money of her own, which helped her to live the way she wanted to live. "If I want to blow it," she said, "I can blow it." For all these reasons, she liked working, but for all these reasons, too, she had accepted a job that was a step down from her previous work as an executive secretary. This was an unusual move for Dorothy, because "advancement" had always been important to her. However, she had decided that the time had come to trade money and prestige for reduced stress; what mattered most was having a job that helped her and her family live healthy, happy lives, and that allowed her to come home from work physically tired, but not emotionally drained.

Dorothy had recognized that her energy was not limitless, and she was determined that she would always have plenty available for her children; even when she was at work, she wanted to be able to think about family issues during spare moments. "It's hard for me to separate," she said. "I don't separate. See, in my life, my family is my priority, and it doesn't ever take second place to anything. So, it's just hard for me not to worry. If I'm going to worry about my family, I'm going to worry about it all the time, you know." Work helped Dorothy take care of her family; she was able to earn the money she needed to secure a comfortable standard of living, and—this was equally important to her—work also helped her be a more stable, healthy woman, and a better parent. Work was not at the expense of family; quite the contrary, it was better in every way for her family that she worked.

Working Off and On

Working off and on was the most common pattern followed by both middle- and working-class women. Although women in both classes worked off and on, however, the similarity is only superficial; middle-class women had fewer—and more predictable—periods of work, and when they worked, it was by choice. Working-class women, on the other hand, were more often pushed into work by economic necessity. To illustrate the different meanings of working off and on, I have included in the following pages brief—and in one or two cases, lengthier—excerpts from middle-class women's stories and have identified them as such, when necessary.

Kate

Kate had worked off and on but she had only two "on" periods before returning to work permanently. After graduating from Mt. Holyoke with a major in French, she had taken a master's degree in teaching and taught for two years. She soon discovered, however, that teaching was not for her—"she didn't like doing the song and dance"— so she moved into publishing, which she "had always had in the back of her mind that she would like to do." She went to work for a local press as an editor and worked there for six years until shortly before the birth of her first daughter. Twelve years later, she returned to her old job, and had been back a little over five years when we talked. In between she hadn't held a job until she was pregnant with her second child, then she babysat two other children for a year. When her son was three, she started working in his nursery school as a substitute, and when he moved on to elementary school, she went too, as an assistant.

Kate took the babysitting and school jobs because she and her husband needed the money, and they allowed her to be with her children. But she always thought of herself only as an editor; the other jobs never became part of her identity. "Now I think of it as 'I am an editor,'" she said. "When I was home with my children, taking care of other children, [it wasn't] 'I am a day-care worker.' Even a nursery school teacher—I really wasn't. [It was], 'I am a mother.' Mother was my occupation I put on my tax return. And I was happy with that, but I don't think that was the way I define myself. At the same time I thought it was very important for me not to be working at a paid job while I was raising my children. I guess I'm old-fashioned that way but I just felt like if we could—and we really did have our living standards decline—but as long as we could manage it, I wanted to spend that time with my children."

Harriet

The working-class women who had worked off and on zigzagged back and forth between work and home, sometimes so often they could only guess how many jobs they had worked in. Harriet was an example; she had quit school in the middle of ninth grade to take a job as a waitress. A few months later, when she found she was pregnant, she left her job and got married. Soon after, her son was born, but he was premature, and she was told he would be developmentally disabled. Wanting desperately to stay home and take care of him, she got her husband to agree.

Turning a blind eye to the growing pile of medical bills, she and her husband managed to get by on one income until he was laid off from his factory job—one of a long string of layoffs that would follow over the years. At this point in her life, Harriet climbed on the seesaw of work and family she was still riding. It went like this: Need money. Find job. Work until family crisis. Quit. Need money. Take job. Work until laid off. And so on.

When Bill, her husband, was laid off that first time, Harriet went to work in a local department store in what seemed to be a great job—clean, not too demanding, and in pleasant surroundings. But her baby needed physical therapy daily and often had to be rushed to the emergency room, so before too many months had passed, she was fired for taking time off. Luckily, the financial pressures eased when Bill found what seemed to be a steady job, so she decided to stay home and take care of her child full-time.

A year or so later, she and Bill had a child of their own, but soon after this baby's birth, Bill was laid off yet again and Harriet went back to work, this time at McDonald's. Her son was "just an infant," she said, but "I didn't have much choice." Harriet worked at McDonald's until she found a better-paying job, working on the assembly line at a plastics factory. This job worked out fine for a while, until she was told she would have to work the midnight to 8 A.M. shift. This was impossible, so she quit.

Harriet's first son died when he was six in a house fire. Grieving, she stayed home for a year or so until the bills started to pile up again. She then took a job assembling electronics, and stayed there for five years—five years that were remarkable because neither she nor Bill were laid off. But she wanted to spend more time with her second son—and she'd never really liked factory work anyway—so she decided to quit her job and try babysitting in her house. She did this for about a year and enjoyed it, but it didn't pay enough, so she took a second job, working evenings at Walmart. She was still at Walmart, but she had given up babysitting and was working in a factory during the day.

In her early married years, with a severely handicapped child, Harriet's family load was heavier than most women's but otherwise her situation was common. Over the years, she had faced a no-win situation, forced to choose between her job and her family. Recently, for example, she had wanted to take time off to drive her husband to a doctor's appointment, and to visit her son's school to discuss his poor grades, but the need for time off had already cost her more than one job and she couldn't afford to lose another. "They're not too crazy about you taking [it]," she said. Since neither she nor her husband had much formal schooling or job training, they were forced to take unskilled manual laboring jobs with high injury rates, and no cushion of benefits to help with the children's illnesses, school appointments, and all the other business of parenthood. Bill was home watching television while we talked, his foot propped up in front of him; he had broken a toe in an accident at work, Harriet said, explaining that she was now the sole breadwinner. Because of Bill's accident, she had been forced to take a full-time factory job during the day, as well as working evenings at Walmart. And if Bill wasn't back on the job soon, she'd have to take a third job to make ends meet.

Connie

Connie, one of six working-class daughters who had completed a college degree, had also adopted the off-and-on solution to combining work and family. Hers is an instructive story, because she had more of the guilt and role conflict that are so often described in middle-class women.

Connie appeared at the door of her comfortable old clapboard house looking flushed and somewhat harried. It was five o'clock on a school night right before Christmas—not a good time for a teacher who was also a mother—and she was about to leave to take her daughter caroling. She explained that the boxes piled up on the dining-room floor were all school supplies, waiting to be sorted for her class's Christmas party the next day.

In high school, Connie said, she was an A student, which had made her a nerd in her working-class neighborhood. She was desperately unhappy as a teenager, socially isolated, and rebellious, so when her parents wanted her to go to college, she refused and enrolled in a "baby nursing school" instead. She soon grew bored with this nursing school and spent two or three years trying one job after another—"too many to recount"—until she became pregnant with her first child, a daughter. As a single working mom, she settled down to support her daughter, but after a few months, she met and married Peter. After they were married, she taught in an early childhood center for two years, switching to part-time when they had a child. Four years later, when her third child was born, she left teaching and did part time telemarketing on and off for three or four years. Since then, she had mostly taught—sometimes full-time, sometimes part-time—and for the last three years she'd been on the full-time staff at a city public elementary school. For most of this time, she had also studied part-time toward an early childhood degree and, finally, sixteen years after first enrolling in college, she had graduated.

Connie wanted to be a "more nurturing mother" than her own mother; as a child, she had resented her mother for working when, as she saw it, they had no real need of the money. Connie said her mother had always enjoyed working, and she went to school for a GED—even though she had a "perfectly good job without it."

Connie so disliked her mother's working that she resolved not to work when she became a mother. "That was a real strong part of my life," she said, "making a commitment that if I ever had children I would be there when they came home in the afternoons. She was not there. . . . I remember wanting to have one of the mothers that baked cookies and that sort of thing. . . . I've tried very hard to be that kind of a mother," she said, "because that was what I wanted. But now it's out of sync with the times. But that was a real strong part of growing up."

Connie stayed home with her children, trying to be the kind of mother she felt she had lacked, but ultimately—and ironically—she returned to work earlier than planned, and her daughter was the reason:

> [Kelly] was an extremely rebellious teenager. . . . It took me a long time to understand that they were classifying her as depressed, and we were dealing with yelling and screaming and running away and all this other behavior. . . . [She] was hospitalized in [Pleasant View Psychiatric Hospital] for fifteen months when she was age fifteen. Which of course has had an impact on our family in various ways. At the time that she was hospitalized, that was the point at which I went back to full-time work because I was feeling very badly about myself as a mother, and a friend offered me a job in a day-care center, and I took it even though I might have waited a while had I not had that happen. I needed to feel that I was competent. And so I went back to work. . . .

Connie still wrestled with ambivalence:

> In fact I have to make a decision soon, because if I'm going to stay in a public school system, I must get my master's within five years. So I have not yet started. I've put that off, and so I have to decide what I'm going to do about that. So that's a very current question. I have one course to take before July. See there's two places at which you must renew your certification, so I will renew it in July and I'll be OK, but then in five more years, if I don't have my master's, they won't renew it.
>
> Normal people would have started long ago, but I waited! In recent years I haven't wanted to. . . . When I went to school at night when the children were young, I wasn't taking that much time away from them because I would do studying during nap time, and they'd go to bed early, but now that they're older, there's almost more time that I need to give to them, and I can't and don't want to take it away for me at this point. I'm not sure. I may drop back and do something—teach, but not necessarily in public school, I might go to Head Start, which I like anyway.

These four different women, like many other women who worked off and on, believed that young children would suffer if their mothers worked; thus their ideal when they had young children was to work full-time in the family. But the extent to which they had been able to do this depended, in part, on their family's financial needs. Muriel, the most upper middle class among the women who worked off and on, and whose husband worked in a very highly paid profession, had only one "on" period before she ultimately returned to work, and then it was only because a friend offered her a rewarding chance to help out in her business. When she finally returned to work it was for psychological not financial reasons.

Connie and Kate (a middle-class daughter) were less financially secure than

Muriel. They were from less high-status families—Connie's father was a foreman, Kate's was a white-collar sales representative—and their husbands were in less high-status jobs than Muriel's—Kate's was an accountant, and Connie's was a computer programmer. Although Connie's return to work was in part motivated by her daughter's adolescent crisis, she had also, over the years, worked in response to financial need. Harriet had never had much choice; even when she had a disabled child and wanted to stay at home, she was forced to work.

When middle-class women returned to work, it was usually because they felt they and their children were ready and they looked forward to the stimulation of a job. When working-class women returned to work, there was often little choice involved. Their moves in and out of work were more frequent and crisis-driven; they went to work when their family's most urgent need was for hard cash, and stayed home when it was for hands-on care.

Both Harriet and Connie worked when their children were young, and both still worried about their children; however, they experienced this worry differently. Because she had exercised some choice and because she was more attracted to work, Connie's worry was tinged with guilt; she constantly questioned whether she was doing the right thing. But because she had no choice, and did not really enjoy her job, Harriet's worry was free of guilt. Guilt was not an issue for Kate either, because she had stayed at home while her children were young.

Putting It Off

Middle- and working-class women who put off going to work, like women who worked off and on, had adopted a similar combination of work and family. The women themselves, however, were very different. Among the working-class women who adopted this solution were some of the poorest women in the study—and among the middle-class women were some of the richest.

Many of the working-class women had dropped out of school because they were pregnant and others had married very soon after high school graduation. Several were in their first job ever, most had very few skills, and many were poor as children as well as adults. By contrast, middle-class women who put off working were usually married to highly paid professionals and lived an upper-middle-class life. They gave up their jobs when they had children, with little real financial sacrifice, because their husbands' earnings were much higher than their own. Usually, they had completed a college degree and worked for a year or two before giving birth to their first child, then returned to work only when their children were old enough to be fairly independent. Denise, for example, was married while she was still a graduate student at Vassar, and she and her husband had decided to start a family right away. She became very involved in volunteer activities for a number of years, but when her son was preparing to leave for college, she decided she'd had "all of the growth" she needed from "the volunteer sector" and wanted to go to work. She described herself as very bonded to her son and she "wanted to be prepared for a whole new stage of life before it hit me over the head." She went to a career counseling service where they helped her develop a résumé, then she spent the spring and the summer of her son's graduation year job hunting. She was offered a job after her first interview, but turned it down because she had not yet decided whether to work full- or part-time. Several months later the executive director of the organization she now worked for as a volunteer coordinator called her, and she had worked there ever since.

Judy

Still in her first job, Judy was one of the working-class women who put off working. Poor as a child, and with an alcoholic, abusive father, she had quit high school when she was sixteen and in tenth grade. She was married within the year, and for the next sixteen years remained a stay-at-home mother. It hadn't been easy, but she and her husband had managed to live on his wage as a concrete laborer. When the second of her two sons turned thirteen, though, and "didn't need [her] any more," Judy thought, "Girl, go out and do something for yourself." She immediately took a job with a temp agency and was assigned to a cosmetics packaging plant, where she still worked.

Judy had no regrets about her choices. "You see, with me, my family has always come first," she said. "My family has come before my job or anything. OK? And what I mean by my family is my husband and my two children. OK. So if it meant—say if one of my children became very ill and it meant for me to quit my job, I would quit my job. My bosses know this. I tell them, 'Hey, I would leave this job tomorrow if I needed to for my children.'" Nor did Judy regret having started her family at seventeen. "I had both my children when I was young," she said, "but by the time I'm in my forties, they're gonna be grown. And I still can live my life. That's one of the benefits. I don't regret it. Because now I'm thirty-five years old, got one who's eighteen and one sixteen. So I'll be done in another two years at the most. And then I can do what I want. So I'm lucky on that. I see other people wait until they're twenty-five and twenty-six years old."

Phyllis

Phyllis had also postponed going to work until her children were old enough for school. The daughter of a policeman and a bookbinder, Phyllis still lived in the old working-class neighborhood she grew up in, an enclave of tiny houses that clung to one another in a maze of small winding alleys, called "ways," too narrow for cars, but tucked away under a freeway. Postage-stamp backyards open off the ways, some boasting a rose bush or two but most strewn with old bicycles and the other odds and ends that spill out of houses that are too cramped to contain the accumulated detritus of family life.

At thirty-five, Phyllis was the mother of four children, the first of whom was born soon after she quit school in eleventh grade. She had put off taking her first job—as a machine operator in a box factory—until her eldest daughter was old enough to babysit the younger children. After she passed the GED, she had moved on from the box factory to her present job at Southern Foods, the supermarket where she worked as a cashier. Her daughter still babysat. "I'll fix dinner," she said, "and then she'll cook it and then she feeds them and makes sure they get their homework done. Because her father works night shift too. He leaves at three. And he doesn't get home until two o'clock in the morning." Phyllis said there would be no point working if she had to pay a babysitter.

Phyllis said she worked entirely for financial reasons; first to help buy a new car. "We decided to get a new car," she said, "and they were going to be taking $150 a week out of his check so I had to get a job to make up the difference. So that's basically how I started working. Because otherwise I probably still wouldn't be working. You know what I mean?" Now she worked to pay private school tuition for one of her children, who has learning disabilities: "Stacey was in the gifted and talented program, OK, so I didn't have to send her [to parochial school]. I had other options. [But] Jack, that's my oldest boy . . . my [only] option was to put him in a private school, so that's what I did." If she won the lottery, Phyllis wouldn't work, she said; she would volunteer at her children's school.

Social class aside, Denise was not so different from Judy; both women chose to stay at home when their children were young and both went to work for the first time when their children were older. (Phyllis, on the other hand, was driven into the workforce earlier than she would have liked, because her family needed the money.) What was different, however, was their freedom to choose. A number of the women who put off work had very few options to choose from because they had very little formal education; twelve of the twenty-one women who chose this alternative had dropped out of school, several when they were very young—Liz, for example, at fourteen—and often because they were pregnant. Five of these women were the victims of childhood abuse or neglect, and motherhood and marriage had represented escape. A number of the women who put off work had been very poor during much of their adult lives, but because they had started childbearing very early and because they had little to offer on the job market, they had little to gain by working.[7]

Working "Like a Man"

Working "like a man"—continuously and full-time since leaving school—was uncommon among middle- as well as working-class women, and in some ways, regardless of class, the women who followed this path were similar. They had all limited the size of their families to one or two children,[8] which, for working-class women, meant they could depend on family members for childcare. The two middle-class women who worked throughout their adult lives were the most highly qualified women in the study. Eileen, whose story appears in this section, was an attorney with an MBA, and Alice was a professor. The nine working-class women who worked continuously throughout their married lives all had high school diplomas, and good jobs with benefits. Among working-class women, therefore, they too were well-qualified. Eileen and Alice had exceptionally fulfilling work for which they had spent long years training. Similarly, all the working-class women who worked continuously had interesting jobs they enjoyed. Regardless of class, then, these women had much to lose by giving up paid work. [9]

Middle- and working-class women who worked continuously and full-time had one more thing in common. With one exception, they all agreed that working *improved* their relationships with their husbands, and they all had supportive husbands who encouraged them and enjoyed talking with them about their jobs. So if these women were more committed to work, it was surely not because they were less committed to their families or less gratified by family life. Indeed, the commitment of their families helped them work.

Karen

Karen was one of the few women who "did it all." She had worked at Sears ever since her marriage twenty years earlier, with one brief period off work after the birth of her son. Before our interview, Bob, Karen's husband, took me on a tour of their brick cottage, which was filled with the comforting fragrance of the cinnamon potpourri he had set to simmer on the wood stove. When Karen was ready, he made us a cup of tea and left us. Karen clearly thought her work history was no big deal. "Once I got out of school," she said, "and I got a job, and I liked working there, and I liked the people, I just kind of figured maybe I should just stay here." She had always expected to work, enjoyed the people she worked with, and liked having the freedom to work at her own pace.

Bob was one of the reasons she could cope with working full-time. She said they were very close and worked as a team:

> Well, he'll cook and you know he'll take turns going to the grocery store, or we'll take turns washing clothes. He will go and find a little chore list that I leave. We kind of think, like, the same. You know, if we come in the house and I say, "You know what, I'd really like to do something with that wall," and he'll say, "Saturday, why don't we go out and we'll look for like a painting or something and then we'll hang it up." It's like we're always thinking together. And we do, we split just about everything. If he cooks, I'll do the dishes. If I cook, he'll do the dishes. If I wash the clothes, he'll take Robert Jr. to work. He loves to grocery shop and he loves to cook. He cooks everything. Do you know what he gets for Christmas and birthdays? He gets cookware and bakeware and bowls and dishes. He loves it. I mean, Saturday and Sunday, he'll

cook. He made a big pot of chicken noodle soup, he made a big pot of beef barbecue and spaghetti meatballs. And after they all cool down, he'll section them all up and put them in his little freezer bowls and mark them and stick them in the freezer. So that during the week if I have to bowl, or like he has to—like tomorrow night—he's got that spaghetti dinner, so Robert Jr. can just come home and he can just plop it right out of the freezer and put it in the microwave. And then nights when Robert Jr. works—he's gotta be there at five, and I don't get home till almost five, just in time to pick him up—he's always got a hot meal that he can go in there and eat before he goes in to work. He loves it, his dad's a cook. He loves it! I mean, he makes a heck of a mess, but I've even got him cleaned up on that. I'll say, "Look we have so much mess here." So he'll clean up the kitchen. Sometimes I'll come home and sit on the sofa and smoke a cigarette or something and he'll just stand over there and cook for me.

Karen's job paid well and offered good benefits. It was near her home, and because she had always enjoyed plenty of backup from her extended family, childcare had never been a major problem. When Robert Jr., her only child, was born, she had taken six weeks off work, then left him in the care of her sister-in-law. Even now, if she and her husband had to go out of town, family members would come and stay with their son, or he would go and stay with them. "Because Rob is really a good kid," she said, "but I think if you leave too many kids in the house, there could be trouble. Especially when they're sixteen or seventeen."

Karen was one in a family of six children that was always short of money; her father, a truck driver, had to work long hours to support his family. "I guess when he got that job," Karen said, "he put his whole heart into it, and made it, because he knew with all the kids coming, that he had to find something that he liked and wanted to do every day. And he did." Her father was not around much, but Karen always felt cared for and knew she was loved; she realized he was working for his family, and she was especially impressed that he had sacrificed and saved to send as many of his children as he could to parochial school—even though he wasn't a Catholic:

My dad, I guess, he had so many kids, he always had to be working it seemed like. . . . [They] put the ones they could through Catholic school. And I guess they really gave up a lot of their spending money so that we could have a good education. Like, my dad was never Catholic and we're Catholic, [but] he'd always get up on Sunday morning and make sure that we went to church. He always took us to church—communion—always made sure that we did everything we were supposed to do. And he wasn't even Catholic!

Karen and Bob had an egalitarian relationship that was also warm, loving, and good-humored—they enjoyed each other, their son, and their life. Bob did the cooking, she controlled the money, and they both shared childcare duties such as driving their son to his job. In addition, his parents were helpful, always ready to pitch in whenever they were needed. Over the years, there had been times when work and family clashed—school meetings that fell during working hours, for example—but one of them was always there. As a construction equipment salesman, Bob had more leeway than some other husbands, and, as a trusted, long-term worker, Karen could usually arrange some time off.

Was Karen "work oriented?" If so, she was also "home oriented." She enjoyed her job, and working allowed her to maintain a standard of living for her family that would otherwise be out of reach. Because she had always worked, she found it hard to imagine not working, "I've done it so long that it's just so much a part of me," she said. "I can't imagine myself not working." Karen's no-fuss attitude is probably not very different from the attitudes of many men; they work, not because they are work oriented, but because they want to support their families.

Eileen

For Eileen, on the other hand, work was a "central life interest." I interviewed Eileen in her office in suburban Bethesda, where she was the employer of thirty men and women. She was a stockbroker in a highly specialized field, with a law degree and an MBA from Harvard Business School. She looked in charge; her thick, dark hair was cut short in a no-nonsense, low-upkeep style and she wore square, tortoiseshell glasses that made no concessions to fashion. She entered the room at precisely 9 A.M., checking her watch to confirm it, and told me exactly how much time she could spare (though, as it happened, we went well into overtime—obviously, her warning was just in case). She told me about her work:

> Usually I'm out trying to sell to clients. I might make a call on two or three different businesses. I'll either be selling or presenting the findings. [I tell them] how to solve their investment problems. We try to teach them a different mind set. . . . It is the culmination of all the jobs I've had. It pulls [them] together . . .

What she liked most about her work was:

> Creating a new industry. Influencing people on a national and regional level. I like building a team, the way that I would like it to be done. I think the old way of doing business is dead, but they haven't recognized that. It does not take into account the needs of people in the nineties and especially women and minorities. And so basically I have the opportunity to do it my way . . . which is clearly a different way than most of the structures in which I have participated previously. In most of my previous positions I was never allowed to utilize all my talents. When I started, what I was

thought to be capable of was substantially less than what I really was capable of. And sometimes I was fortunate enough to be in an environment that allowed me to do it regardless, and sometimes I wasn't.

Eileen had long invested heavily in her work; she spent at least fifty-five hours a week in the office, but also read a lot at home, keeping up with the literature—"industry-specific journals . . . the business news, the [Baltimore] *Sun*, the *New York Times*, the *Wall Street Journal*." She dreamed about her work every night, and said she would have devoted even more time to it except that her husband objected. In fact, she had chosen her second husband, in part, because she could see he would be a helpful partner:

> When we got together, he had a much more flexible schedule than I did. And actually, one of the reasons we got together . . . was because I was an executive vice president, and he could come and take care of my children. He could meet them and make them cakes and so forth, and I decided that this was—we weren't married yet—this was someone that I would be very interested in having a relationship with, because he was very supportive and willing to do that. There are not many men, I don't think, who would be willing to do that. The car pool mothers were always amazed. So he was always pretty flexible.

Eileen's childhood was solidly upper middle class; her father was an aeronautical engineer who ran his own business, her mother an MBA. She attended a private Catholic girl's school where, she said, the teachers fostered the notion that girls could be whatever they wanted. Her parents encouraged her to be independent, competitive, and assertive. "I have always liked being in charge," she said.

> That's a personality characteristic. I remember as a little child going to my father's business, and I loved sitting at the desk. Playing office was important to me. I don't know why it appealed to me, but I remember sitting at the desk with all the pencils and papers . . . was definitely a role that I could relate to and liked. I thought that business was glamorous, because you got to travel and do a lot of interesting things.
> My family always emphasized hard work. Everybody always worked hard, so that was something that was valued. And I really like to do that. I do like—I mean to me, that gives me a lot of pleasure. And I was also a competitive swimmer, and I liked competition. I liked to win. Being encouraged to win and to be a competitor was not something that was a typical experience for a forty-year-old woman to have, but I have done that, and done that very successfully, and I like that, so I really do like to compete. My parents encouraged that a great deal. In fact, these would almost be my mother's key words: "Whatever you're going to do, do it well, and be the best."

When Eileen entered her father's work world, she liked what she saw—"glamour," "travel," "being in charge," and other "interesting things"—and she felt she was more like her father than her mother. Only later, when she herself became a mother, she said, was she able to fully appreciate her own mother; when she was younger, "it was frustrating" to her that her mother had given up her career when she had children. "I also knew that [she] was not satisfied with her life," she said. "I don't think that was a conscious thought until later on. She felt that was the appropriate role." I asked Eileen if she was guessing that her mother was dissatisfied, or if she knew for sure: "If you asked her if she disliked it, I'm not sure that she would ever say that, but my feeling, interpreting her behavior—yes, she really did dislike it."

Her mother had encouraged Eileen's academic goals and, unlike some of her friends' mothers, hers had not pressured her to marry at a young age. Instead, she encouraged her to get a teaching certification because "you never know when you're going to have to support yourself." This was common among middle-class women; their parents encouraged them to go to college and get an education but rarely talked in terms of specific careers. If they did, in most cases, it was teaching—so their daughters would have something "to fall back on" should the need arise.

Eileen's parents were rich in both economic and symbolic capital; their economic capital meant they could give their daughter every educational opportunity, and their symbolic capital meant they had the *savoir faire* to help her find the right career. First, her father's, then her mother's good advice had helped; when she decided she had no desire to be a teacher and would go to law school, her mother was dubious, but her father was delighted and encouraged her. "Go for it, you'll be terrific" was his response. A year later, it was her mother's turn to show the way:

> At the end of the first year of law school, I was seriously thinking of dropping out. It was very hard. It was very hostile. Very unpleasant. Then my mother said, "Go to Paris." (To do a second year abroad program.) Which is what I did. She said, "At the end of that time, in the worst case, you'll have a wonderful year in Paris, and you'll be two years, two-thirds of the way through, and it will probably be easier to finish."

It was easier; she finished and went on to do a business degree as well.

Eileen was assertive and smart, and, because she was one of the few experts in the country in her field, she was in demand. But working all along had been a struggle, even for her, especially when her children were young:

> What I worked out with all my clients was that when I took the cases, part of the fee arrangement was that I would bring my children along, and they would have to provide babysitting services. In retrospect, I can't believe I did it! . . . At one point I had a list of twenty-five backup babysitters. If the regular person didn't come in the morning, I would just keep calling until I found someone who could come.

No other woman in the study could call the shots the way Eileen could, and only one or two other women came from such a resource-rich background. She was exceptionally accomplished, and exceptionally intense about her work—more so than any other woman, middle- or working-class, and I suspect more so than most men. This, in itself, is telling; among middle-class women who could afford *not* to work, only she and Alice worked continuously, and both women were high achievers who were intensely committed to their particular field. Working-class women who worked continuously had good jobs—with benefits that facilitated staying in work—and they enjoyed working, but they did not share this identification with a particular occupation. They had good jobs, but not highly rewarding careers. Like Trudy, they had made a rational decision to work for the good of their families. "One thing that I at a very young age decided for myself," Trudy said. "This was like when I was like nine or ten years old, I decided that when I grew up, if I got married, I was not having any more children than I absolutely knew I could provide for. And that was monetarily and also emotionally and physically. Because I could see what a hard time my mother had. She had five children all by herself. And I just knew that I was not going to do that and I have one child."

Working Part-time

Only a handful of working-class women and two middle-class women had worked part-time over a long period. Polly was typical of these working-class permanent part-timers; she had started as a volunteer at her children's nursery school, began to be paid, then stayed on as a part-time worker because she enjoyed the work. In fact, however, she worked close to full-time hours, as did several other women who worked in schools. They chose to put in these hours and continued to work part-time because the work was extremely rewarding. The same was true of Margaret, one of the two middle-class women who worked part-time; she had built up her workload over the years, and, some of the time, worked full-time.[10] What women who worked part-time had in common was that in the beginning they had chosen to work part-time because of their children, but now that their children were older they continued to do it because they found the work enjoyable.

Margaret

A reserved, elegant woman wearing a slender silver bracelet and silver-and-lapis earrings, and dressed in black wool slacks and a royal blue silk shirt, Margaret lived in a neighborhood of Victorian houses perched on wooded hills. Hers had been gutted and now boasted skylights and soaring spaces. We sat and talked with the sun streaming down warming our faces through the glass. Margaret, a photographer, had worked at home for many years.

Margaret grew up in the Washington suburbs, the daughter of affluent parents—

her father was a lawyer, her mother an artist. She, too, was encouraged by her parents to teach:

> I didn't really find my career in photography until later. I never took any photography classes in college. I took a basic curriculum for two years and then you specialize. . . . So I never really majored in that. I learned it all myself. But I didn't really know what I wanted to do and my father was pushing me to teach. I applied to graduate school in teaching, didn't get in. I applied for one teaching job and didn't get it. I am not a teacher. I taught some classes at the Jewish Community Center. I don't enjoy it. I taught in the elementary school, volunteer work. It's not for me. I wish I'd had more counseling. Even in college there was no counseling.

After graduating from college, she worked for a year at the National Portrait Gallery as a clerk-typist, but quit when they refused to give her time off for her honeymoon. After her marriage she worked as a demonstrator of ceramics, and then for a computer company, designing visual displays of their information. After working for a "year or two" for this company, she and her businessman husband moved to Europe, where they lived for several years, and she gave birth to two children, a son and a daughter.

When they returned from Europe, Margaret began picking up a bit of work here and there, mostly working at night when the children were small, and as her reputation grew, so did her business:

> Gradually I started doing more photography and some graphic artwork. So as I had more time, I filled it up with working whenever I could. I do brochures, advertising. I've done that since. I work with a computer now. It's very professional. I have a scanner, a laser printer, a Macintosh computer with lots of memory and typefaces.

As well as her freelance photography, she produced a magazine that came out quarterly; she did all the design work, typesetting, and editing, and arranged to have it printed, mailed, and delivered. As the deadline approached each quarter, she often worked into the night, but, she said, she always tried to choose work that would allow her to put her family first. "Now that they're older," she said, "I try to make work more of a priority but I'm always open for them. Usually when the kids were younger, I wouldn't take a job that had a tight turnaround. I did a calendar twice [but] I'd have to stay up at night to do it in twenty-four hours so I decided not to do that kind of work." Her day was completely under her control. "I get up pretty early," she said, "and have breakfast and get everybody's lunch made and send them off to work. And then I don't do the dishes or anything. I take my shower and start my work. I start work at eight. I have a little lunch and then I work again. Now I've been waiting for people to come home before I make the dinner. Then clean up the dinner and then I might go back to work. Frequently. And sometimes my husband helps me at night on the computer. If I have a problem."

Margaret had faced some resistance from clients because she was a woman—and, she thought, because she worked at home it was harder to be taken seriously. "I'm extremely professional about this," she said, describing a recent conflict she's had with a difficult client. "I know, working at home, I want to be as professional as possible. So I've done everything correctly." Margaret really liked what she was doing. "It's a great job," she said.

Polly

Polly would love to work full-time, and, like Margaret, when times were busy, she put in full-time hours. But her employer, a local church-run nursery school, could not afford a full-time salary, so she stayed on, doing a job she enjoyed.

A high school graduate, Polly complained that her parents—her father, a skilled machinist at Bethlehem Steel and her mother, a former secretary who later worked part-time in her school cafeteria—"didn't really care what I wanted to be" and would not send her to college. So, hoping to save money to pay her own way, she went to work in a bathroom showroom, "doing a little bit of everything." Before a year was out, however, she was pregnant, soon to be married.

After her first child was born, Polly went back to work but it "didn't work out." She had good childcare arrangements but when her son started calling the babysitter "Mom," she decided to quit her job. She stayed home, first with her son, then with her second child, a daughter. When her daughter was old enough to join her brother in preschool, Polly started volunteering at the school two hours a day. Eventually, in her third year as a volunteer, she began to be paid—at first for only twelve hours a week during the school year, then gradually for more and more hours. Finally, she was being paid for twenty hours a week year round and was the director of the program. In reality, however, she put in numerous hours of extra unpaid time "throughout the week and at the weekend."

Polly liked her job. She directed a staff of twenty-five and was responsible for 140 children between three and four years of age. Among her other administrative tasks, she took care of the payroll and the parents' fees, produced a news bulletin for parents, and supervised staff. If she didn't work, she said, her self-esteem would be lower. "I always did enjoy working," she said. "I like being out with people. I'm not one to sit idle."

Polly was a quiet, unassuming woman whose calm expression and even, unemotional voice didn't change, even when she told me that her family was not the least bit supportive. Her husband was ambivalent about her working and was "grouchy and irritable and short-tempered." He disliked his job and seemed to resent that she enjoyed hers; he complained, for example, when she ran work-related errands on her time off and he told her that her work wasn't real work. "He thinks that I have a fun job," she said, "that it's not a hard job. He often says, 'I wish we could change places for a day. I'd do your job any day.'" (Her daughter, an angry teenager, also claimed that Polly's job was "not a real job.") On the other hand, her husband seemed impressed that she could handle it. "Maybe secretly," she said tentatively, "he's kind of proud of the fact that I'm in charge of everybody. He often says he knows no one else could do my job. I guess that inwardly he would say that I'm the best qualified."

But even if "secretly" he was "kind of proud," her husband made it hard for Polly to do her job as she would like and feel good about it. "My husband always feels I should be home when he is," she said. "If I have something else to do and it doesn't fit in with his home hours, it disturbs him a little bit."

Like so many other women, Polly had made a trade-off. On the credit side of her work-family ledger, she had achieved her dream of becoming a teacher, and she enjoyed her work. On the debit side, she was not able to earn a full-time wage or the respect and consideration of her family. Polly and Margaret were quite similar in their work orientation, but Margaret's career enabled her to be flexible, her economic resources enabled her to choose how intensely she worked, and her husband was supportive. Polly, with only a high school education, fewer economic resources, and an unsupportive husband, had to choose between rewarding work she enjoyed and a fatter paycheck. She chose rewarding work, and was forced to supplement her income by working two evenings a week at the church hall collecting fees for an aerobics class. It was a choice Margaret was not forced to make.

Working-class women were not alone in their belief that young children may suffer when their mothers work; Margaret, in fact, echoed the words of several of these women: "I don't have an out-of-the-house job," she said, "because my family comes first." Muriel and Kate, two of the middle-class women who worked off and on, shared this belief. In terms of beliefs, then, if not class, they were similar to Polly. Eileen, by contrast, felt this way not at all. Her beliefs were quite different from those of the other three middle-class women. But what the four middle-class women had in common was that they had been able to choose a work and family solution that conformed to their beliefs. This was the main difference between working- and middle-class women—not their orientations, but their ability to match their actions to their ideals. Middle-class women had choice, working-class women did not.

The Work of
C a r i n g

There's drugs. You know, there's drugs everywhere. . . . We have a drug dealer up the street. We had one last year across the street. One moved in across the street from us.

—Jill

I work days, evenings, and nights. I have been scheduled for some nights, which is fine. I'll just come home, get the kids up and get them dressed, and feed them and take them to the sitter's for a couple of hours while I get some sleep. Right now I'm working twelve-hour shifts and that's a killer.

—Wanda

I see my mother two or three nights a week. Some nights I really don't feel like it, but I do it anyway, because you don't know how often you're going to have them here, how long they'll be here. So I want to see her, but on the other hand I might be tired of different problems that she has, she'll complain to me about them, sometimes it's like you have enough of your own and you don't want to hear it.

—Patty

Jill is a mother who worries about whether her son and daughter will survive the dangers on her street. Wanda is a grandmother who finds herself, in her forties, with two young grandchildren in her full-time care. And Patty is a daughter whose mother is not yet elderly or incapacitated, but needs her daughter's presence. Jill, Wanda, and Patty are three women doing what women have always done: as mothers, daughters, grandmothers, wives, friends, and family members, they think about, worry over, plan for, and tend to the physical and emotional needs and well-being of those they love—or feel responsible for. Because its currency is love, not money, and because the bonds of love and duty are hard to disentangle, sociologists are only now beginning to call this unpaid caring that women do "work." Paid or unpaid, caring *is* work.

In the pages that follow, I discuss the women's caring work, focusing on their unpaid caring as daughters and grandmothers, as well as mothers; I will make the argument that while caring work is gendered, it is also classed; in both their paid and unpaid caring, working-class women do the most strenuous, dirty, and demanding manual work, and do it in a social and economic context that offers little support and few rewards.

Working-class women and their families often live in very stressful conditions. As mothers, working-class women must shepherd their children through the dangerous passages of childhood and adolescence; as grandmothers, they must find the economic and emotional resources to care for grandchildren as well as children; and as daughters, they must shoulder alone the burdens of elder care. Because of their stressful life conditions they may be faced with demands across multiple generations—caring for parents, troubled teens, and grandchildren too. Yet they must do this without the economic resources available to middle-class women, and without the ability to delegate the more onerous, less enjoyable aspects of their caring roles to others. It comes as no surprise, then, to learn that one study found that among mothers raising young children on low incomes, women who were more involved with relatives and friends experienced more stress.[1] Or to read, in another, that "women who have greater parental concerns and lower per capita incomes are more likely to report that they have a whole day's work at home on top of their jobs."[2] (In this study, too, compared to middle-class women, working-class women—especially women in unskilled gray-collar jobs—reported more fatigue and role overload.)

Mothers Care

As mothers, the working-class women I spoke with had to raise children in neighborhoods that were violent and drug-ridden, educate them in schools that were overcrowded and underfunded, and feed, clothe, and protect them in families that were short of money. In Baltimore, where most of the women live, the poverty rate for children, at 33 percent, is one of the highest in the nation, the percentage of high school dropouts and teen mothers is the second highest, and the juvenile arrest rate is the highest.[3] It is not surprising then, that, compared with middle-class mothers, more working-class mothers had serious concerns about their children's school progress, and about drugs and other urban dangers. A number of women, including Judy and Liz, were coping with one of the fallouts of these conditions: seriously troubled teenagers whose problems included depression and addiction.

Judy

A tiny woman with a prematurely lined face, Judy spoke softly, her eyes darting to where her son sat in the next room, watching the Saturday morning cartoons in the dark. Still shocked, she told me how she had first learned several months earlier that he was severely depressed.

One day, she told me, her factory foreman called her to the phone to take an urgent call from her son. He was afraid, he said; before school that morning, his older brother had threatened to hang himself, but thinking it was a joke, he had scoffed, "Yeah, right," then laughed and left for school. Now, though, at the end of the school day, he was home, the house was dark and still, and his brother was nowhere to be found. "You could hear in his voice that he was worried," Judy said, "because the poor child went to school that day with no socks on and didn't realize it until he came home from school."

"I got to go find [my son]," she thought, as she put down the factory phone and rushed to find her boss. When she told him what was going on, he was reassuring: "Take as long as you need." Sick at heart, she first tried to call the local emergency room, but when no words would come, she dropped the phone and ran to her car. The drive home seemed neverending, every light red, every driver a fool, but when she finally pulled up in front of her house, she sat in her car, afraid of what she would find inside. Finally, her legs like rubber, her heart thumping, she walked in the front door and headed toward the basement stairs:

> When I went down to the basement there was a chair there and the first impression I got was that he had hung himself. And I just could not go down into that basement. So I called my husband and I said, "You'd better come home NOW!" and I sent him down. I—could—not—go. That was a nightmare.
>
> Right. So, this happened on Thursday, and we put him in hospital that Thursday. This just happened in September. That's when they discovered that it was major depression. Because everything that he wanted to do in life was now being rejected. Him and his girlfriend had broke up, but they had told me that the fuse was burning for a long while, and it was just a matter of time. So, he was in there for like seventeen days.

Her voice little more than a whisper, Judy spoke slowly, with long pauses between her sentences, as if to show how she had gotten by, going through the motions of ordinary life, one foot forward, then the other. "And it was like—every night—I'd get off work—I'd come home—I'd drink a cup of coffee and run to the hospital." As long as she stayed busy, she could cope:

> See, with me, it's always been that when something happens, I get upset about it and it's like I'm running around and I can't fit this all into perspective. But then when it's like everything's calmed down, like seventeen days later when they let him come home from the hospital, that's when I broke down! So, I mean, when he came out and they told me that he was in a major depression, I didn't cry. But it was after it was all over with—because I guess it was like—you have to go to work. You have to go to the hospital. And I kept going and going and going. And then after it was all over with, I was doing something, I was up in the bedroom, and I just stood there and started crying.

The crisis was over, now, but Judy was still shaken, trying to understand what went wrong, and afraid the nightmare would return. It was all the more disturbing because it was so unexpected. "See it was hard for us, because they say when someone is going to take their life, they leave notes, and they start giving their worldly possessions. It's not true. As far as I'm concerned it's not true. Because he did this on a Thursday, and Wednesday he was sitting there in that room just fine and dandy. I mean there was no argument, you know? He didn't give any possessions away that I know of. I didn't find a note."

Judy knew full well her job was second-rate; there were no health benefits, the pay was lousy, and many of her coworkers were annoying. But she also knew her boss would understand if ever she had to leave in a hurry, and this was what mattered most:

> You know, people say to me, "You drive, you're crazy, why are you staying here?" But, you know, you have your good faults with it, you have your bad faults with it. Like if one of my children gets sick, OK, I mean they know about my oldest son, so if he calls me up and tells me he's sick, I go, "I have to go, my son is sick." [They say], "Fine." You know, and nothing is said. There's been times when he's been in hospital for weeks and weeks and weeks. And I've taken time and nothing is said. See what I'm saying? There's good drawbacks on it and there's bad drawbacks on it. Money wise, insurance wise, they're not giving it to you and you're not going to get it. But when it's a family crisis, they understand it.

Compared with her concern for her son, Judy's other family concerns seemed minor, but they added to her emotional load. She was responsible for her mother's well-being, and also her father-in-law's: "You know sometimes we don't have time to go there, so every night at seven, he has to call. Because he is up in age and he lives in a house by himself. . . . Sometimes it's like, 'Oh God, I wish they would all go away and leave me alone.' Sometimes I go upstairs and I just fill up the bathtub with hot water and just sit in it. Sometimes I tell my husband, 'If anyone calls, I'm not here.'"

Judy stayed in her job in part because it was flexible, and her boss was sympathetic; she knew this was unusual for a minimum-wage job. Sympathetic bosses were to be valued because with no job protections, mothers faced with family crises could soon find themselves out of work. This is exactly what Liz, whose story follows, had discovered.

Liz

Liz wept openly and often as she talked about the many tragedies in her life, and when she lit up one of the menthol cigarettes she chain-smoked, her hands shook. Soon, I understood why she was so distressed.

Liz began our interview by apologizing for her Christmas tree, which was still lit and standing in the front window in February. "We're keeping it up until Wayne comes home from the hospital," she explained, and went on to tell me how her son Wayne's crack cocaine addiction had forced her to give up her job at Barry's Video:

I sort of had a breakdown. . . . That was when we had Wayne put in [Baltimore Psychiatric Hospital], and he would call me from [the hospital] at the video store and cry and carry on on the phone, "Please Mom, please let me out. Please Mom, take me home. Please don't leave me here, Mom." And I got to the point where I was crying in the customers' faces and I couldn't count the money at nighttime, so I took a week off, and I was supposed to go back the next Monday and my husband came home and he said, "What's the best thing that could ever happen to you?" I said, "That I didn't have to go back to work." He said, "Good, you've been laid off."

Now, with her son still hospitalized but no longer in crisis, Liz felt able to cope with a job again, but not with stress. Her present job, as a doorperson in an office building downtown, exactly suited her needs. I asked her what she did each day:

I say "Good morning," read a book. The money is terrible, but that's what I need right now. And there's no stress to it. I like the part with no stress. Maybe after Wayne turns eighteen, I'll go find something stressful and challenging. Because it does get very boring.

At least for now, boredom was better than stress.

Judy and Liz had to cope with children whose problems were serious, but even the everyday business of caring for adolescents was often stressful. Judy's boss was sympathetic in an emergency, but he was annoyed if she took time off for more minor mishaps or appointments. She gave me an example: "Like, say, if William or Thomas gets in trouble at school, and they bring me this letter home [saying] 'You've got to be in school the next day.' You know, these people have got to be a joke. They work nine to five. They can leave and come as they want. You know, it's basically that." When her younger son's behavior recently prompted a letter from school demanding that a parent attend for a conference, Judy said she waved the letter in [her son's] face. "God," she said, "I hope you don't [misbehave] again." Judy's appointment, of course, was during work hours, and if her son was suspended, he would not be readmitted until she took him in to school—again during work hours.

Teachers and other professionals—physicians, therapists, and dentists, for example—are usually not prepared to give up their own evenings or weekends to meet the needs of other parents who work. Like Judy, therefore, women whose bosses would give them even unpaid time off knew they were well-off—relatively speaking. But because her job was "temporary," Judy's time off was unpaid, so every hour spent at her children's school or at doctors' appointments took a piece out of her paycheck. For this reason, she was sometimes forced to miss events she would like to attend.

Judy and Liz were at the younger end of the age range of the women in the study, and because they were not yet grandparents, most of their caring work concerned their children. But a number of women, including Maureen, whose story I tell now, had concerns as grandparents as well as parents, foreshadowing what many other women could expect in the future.

Grandparents Care

According to the 1997 Current Population Survey, more than five percent of all American children live with a grandparent or other relative, and two-thirds of these children also have a parent present.[4] As one study noted, because these grandparents must fulfill parenting and grandparenting roles that overlap and are not well defined, tensions over authority and responsibility are common, especially when they are associated with legal disputes over custody. As the author stated, "grandmothers deal with complex family situations about which they often have ambivalent feelings, especially toward their own children."[5] This was certainly true for Maureen.

Maureen

Maureen was in her early fifties, a fit, healthy, and vigorous woman, with the lithe body of someone who likes to swim. One of the nine women I spoke with who had live-in grandchildren, she had only recently become a grandparent when her sixteen-year-old daughter Roxanne, gave birth to a daughter. Maureen and her husband planned on caring for the baby while Roxanne finished high school.

When I arrived at their small, neatly furnished suburban house, Maureen's husband was the only adult at home; still in his underwear, he met me at the door, nervously jostling a cranky baby, and told me that Maureen was out on an emergency run for infant Benadryl.

Later, back home, with the baby now asleep, she told me how unprepared she was to become a grandmother—at least a grandmother who was responsible for the care of an infant. With her husband now retired and her daughters soon to leave high school, she had been looking forward to picking up the threads of a carefree life—bridge, dancing, weekends away. Now these were all impossible. "Sometimes I feel like I want to cry," she said, "because I feel tied down. . . . [One night], to be perfectly honest with you, I totally lost it. I walked away from [the colicky baby] and I just sat on the bed. And I was rocking her, and I was walking her, and then I just walked away. And [my daughter] said, 'Is she getting to you, Mom?' I said, 'I'm just tired.' I'd had no sleep. . . . I was just losing control and I thought I'd better just walk away."

Maureen and her husband had been locking horns with Roxanne since before her pregnancy. She had defied them by dating the young man who was now her child's father, and had not been deterred even by a court order. Her boyfriend was now in prison, and Roxanne had reluctantly promised not to visit him, but her parents still worried that she would start seeing him again as soon as he was released. They had disputes about this, and also about childcare responsibilities; at sixteen, naturally enough, Roxanne wanted to go out on dates, but Maureen and her husband—also naturally enough—saw no reason why they should babysit while she had fun. Maureen described one of their many conflicts. "I jumped on her last week," she said. "She was standing out in the kitchen. Now I'm taking care of the baby. Her responsibility is to make sure that he's got formula before she goes out the door. It wasn't being done, so I jumped on her. She was out there crying." Maureen, too, was often in tears; she was tired, frustrated—and angry.

Feelings of exhaustion and resentment such as Maureen's have been reported by other studies, and a grandparent in one of these studies echoes Maureen's words almost exactly. "There are parts of my old life that I miss," she said, "and there are times that both my husband and I are so tired we don't think we'll make it through the day."[6]

Wanda

Wanda was another hands-on grandmother. We talked in the living room of her inner-city row house, a narrow red brick dwelling in a seedy trash-strewn neighborhood. Her house was distinguished from its neighbors by its unbroken windows, neat shrubs, and lack of peeling paint. According to Wanda, the surrounding streets hosted a number of drug markets, and the sound of gunfire was an event that no longer raised eyebrows.

Wanda's eyes were shadowed with fatigue, and she smoked nonstop during our interview. She remained unflappable, however, calmly and unapologetically swatting an occasional roach with her sandal while we talked, and reprimanding her grandchildren's loud and boisterous play only when they threatened to hurt themselves. Her furniture was already shabby from the previous generation's wear and tear, so she let the two small children play on it with abandon.

The two children, she told me, belonged to her son and his wife, a heroin addict. Bobbie, the four-year-old, had been with her for several months, but she had just "snatched" the little girl two weeks earlier when she found her on the street. On the day of our interview, Molly, Wanda's sixteen-year-old, had stayed home from school to amuse the two young ones, but her babysitting skills were not equal to the task. As we talked, Bobbie, who was hyperactive, lunged repeatedly at the TV to try and start up Nintendo, only to be yanked back halfheartedly by Molly, who also kept interrupting us. Wanda's occasional attempts to gain control of the situation—"Shut up, Molly!" "Stop interrupting, Molly!" "Watch him, Molly!" and "Can't you get them out of here?"—were in vain, but she managed to maintain her good humor in spite of it. She described how she cared for the babies while also doing shift work as a nursing assistant:

Usually I don't mind [working long hours] because I really appreciate the vacation time, but now, with the two little ones, I'd prefer to be able to stay home. Because it's hard working a job and then coming home and having to take care of the kids. And [the house] is not child-safe now.

Wanda believed she was being treated unfairly on her job; she had applied to work full-time, but her employer had turned her down, then hired three men full-time. She was convinced her supervisor disliked her: "We don't get along," Wanda said, "because I don't take any guff off of her. Everybody else kisses butt, and I won't do that . . . I just tolerate a lot of bull to keep my job, because I need my job." In addition, she had been told she had to work sixteen hours every weekend or lose her job, but when she checked out the legality of this threat, she discovered they had no right to demand weekend work. "If I'd fight it, I'd probably win," she said, "but then they'd make your life so miserable and they'd find everything in the world wrong. They're like that."

I asked Wanda if she was able to take personal leave for family emergencies. "No," she replied, "I would get written up. I mean they're really bitchy. One day I turned around and said, 'Look, my family comes before this job.' Which it does, right? And I got pulled into my supervisor's office [about it]. And I said, 'I most certainly did [say that].' And she said, 'Well you'd better stop and think again,' she said, 'because you'd better make your job more important than your family.' Well, now she has a small child about eight months old, so that's OK. She'll learn won't she? And of course when this child has to go to the doctor, she takes off. If this child's sick, she takes off. I'm just waiting for an opportune time when something happens and I need to do that. I will go off and say, 'Well, it's fine if you take off.'" Wanda chuckled. "See," she said, "that's why she don't like me."

In a study of class and race differences in women's work and family experiences, in which they compared the experiences of LPNs and social workers, the psychologists, Nancy Marshall and Rosalind Barnett, noted that LPNs had greater concerns overall about their children's health and safety because, as working-class women, they had less access to health care and lived in unsafe neighborhoods.[7] This would not surprise Wanda, who might have added that working-class women have fewer job rights when it comes to taking time off to deal with family problems. She described another recent incident:

We had an episode last year where my youngest daughter was sexually assaulted. It was minor, so it wasn't as bad as we thought when I had her examined. I went into work and talked to the nursing supervisor that was on. I was due in [at] work the next day; well I had to take my daughter to get her checked, and a bunch of things. The nursing supervisor was fine. I only missed the one day. The one day I missed, that was the only day I missed. [But] I got pulled into my nursing supervisor's office, the nursing supervisor for the ER, and [she] warned me about missing time. That was a day where I just wanted to take my fist and pop her right in the face. It's a losing battle.

Wanda's husband was an added responsibility; he suffered from seizures as the result of an accident on his firefighter's job, so she had gained power of attorney to fight on his behalf for a full pension. A year or so earlier the city had sent them a bill for an alleged pension overpayment of $9,000, because her husband had worked part-time while also getting a pension. Furious, Wanda complained to the firefighter's union and her local councilman, and testified before the city council, persuading them to change an ordinance so pensioners could earn the difference between their previous earnings and their pension payment. "Paul is not a fighter," she said.

With two extra mouths to feed, Wanda needed to work as many hours as she could; on the other hand, she needed to be home to care for the children. And as an aide, not a nurse, Wanda lacked the bargaining power to negotiate conditions that would give her more flexibility and pay. A 1994 study by the American Association of Retired Persons shows that Wanda's predicament was fairly typical; the study found that 39 percent of grandparent caregivers had family incomes of $20,000 or less;[8] another study reported that many grandmothers must give up their jobs or reduce their hours because of their family responsibilities.[9] In fact, soon after we talked, Maureen left her job.

Martha's solution to the demands of multi-generational caring was to run a day-care center in her home; this enabled her to earn some money while she cared for her grandchildren and home-schooled her two learning-disabled daughters. Martha seemed not to share Maureen's resentment toward her grandchildren's parents, probably because they were older, married, and not living with her, but she resented her other grown children for making unreasonable demands on her time. "If it wasn't for my adult kids running in and out," she said, "it wouldn't be so bad."

Martha

Martha lived in a respectable, lower-middle-class neighborhood, one of the many that mushroomed after the war, built to house returning soldiers and their young families. The streets, lined with small, neat brick houses, crisscrossed what was once the major highway between Baltimore and York, Pennsylvania, but was now a long, traffic-clogged suburban artery lined with car yards, fast food outlets, and strip malls. A small, bustling woman, Martha welcomed me into her house and led me through the dining room, past several cots, changing tables, baskets of toys, and a couch on which a small child lay sleeping. Although most of her day-care charges had long since left, Martha was still babysitting her grandchildren when our interview began, at around 7:30 P.M., and two of the three toddlers were still at her house when we were winding down, at around ten o'clock.

"This is what my day is like," she said. "I have my day-care kids, but my big kids keep popping in. See [my grown son] is not working, so he's in and out [saying], 'Mom, can you watch the kids for a little while, I've gotta go do this. . . .' [I say], 'OK babe, bring them up.' And then he'll come and pick them up. And then his daughter will come up because she likes to play with my other grandchildren. . . . I've had those two grandchildren the whole time. In between [I'm] trying to home-school my own two and trying to help [one of Martha's older daughters] with her kids, and . . . then do day care on top of that." She went on to tell me about her two daughters' learning disabilities, her motivation for home-schooling:

> Julia is much more so than Joy. Julia has no memory. She has to relearn her math facts every morning. She doesn't have any math facts. It took me two years to catch them up when they left school. They have no long-term memory and very little short-term memory. . . . When we first started, I bought every home-schooling book I could find. I was hoping they were not learning-disabled, which it turns out a lot of kids are not; they're just stressed at school. But [my kids] are learning-disabled. . . . No one else in the family understands that I need to give [them] extra help. . . .

Martha had chosen to educate her daughters at home in part so she could prepare them for a job by teaching them how to care for children, but this added to her already stressful burden of care, and, because she was so stressed, she was annoyed when her healthy, grown children called to talk:

> And I have got [another] son who has his own business. He's not married. He doesn't have a girlfriend. So he's got no one to tell when he gets a great new deal or something. Now, he calls me about five times a day. I've got a daughter who's single, so she calls me a couple of times a day. And then [my other married daughter] calls, and she says, "Mom, how do you make this? Where do you get this?" I'm an expert at everything! And I can't, I don't want to say, "You can't call," but I've got other responsibilities. So it's really hard. I also owe the two at home. And I feel like [saying], "I've put my time into you guys. Let me have some time with these two. They really need me."

Notice how Martha unconsciously confirms what we all know about caring roles; now that her son does not have a girlfriend, he has no one to tell when he has exciting news, so he calls his mom. But his mom was about as busy as she could be and resented the phone calls; on the other hand, she believed she owed her adult children time and attention because she had shortchanged them by working full-time after her first marriage broke up. "It really affected my relationship with my children," she said, "and my ability to help with their problems." She now believed that working had prevented her from supervising them properly—she even blamed herself for her eldest son's depression. "I wasn't at home when they needed me," she said. "I mean, I would get home and find my living room full of teenagers. And I found out later that I needed to be home supervising and I wasn't."

Martha was stressed, too, because—paid or unpaid—she had no break from the demands of caring for children. And although she said she found it rewarding, I sensed she was making a virtue of necessity; she made a sharp distinction, for example, between caring for pay and caring for love. "Because you can do things for your own kids that you don't mind a bit, but for other kids grind you, get on your nerves. Your own kids can do things, that in anyone else's kids just send you right up the wall. . . . Your own kids are totally different. It's a totally different feeling."

Daughters Care

Working-class women can't afford help with their own unpaid caring work, so it is they, not paid workers, who do the work of driving, dressing, bathing, cleaning, and providing other physical and emotional care for their parents. Cindy, for example, took her mother shopping nearly every day and drove her to her doctors' appointments; Sheila visited her mother a couple of times a week in her nursing home; and other women dropped in to see their parents on the way home from work. Maureen's mother was in a hospital on the other side of town, which meant time-consuming hospital visits, and she also had to attend to the needs of her stepfather, an Alzheimer's sufferer. "My husband and I, we go once a week," she said, "and we shave him and give him a bath and take care of him and love him. He messes himself all the time. . . . He won't go to the bathroom, he won't go to the barbershop. And I go down there and I give him a bath and I shave him. We can't afford to put him away [in a nursing home]." This hands-on care was a significant burden, especially for women whose paid work was physically demanding and inflexible.

Maureen's comment points to one of the key differences between working- and middle-class women's caring work for aging parents; because neither they nor their parents had the economic resources to pay for physical care, working-class women's work was hands-on. Compare Maureen's elder care, for example, with Denise's. Denise, a social worker, had recently faced a family crisis; she had needed to fly to Florida to stay with her mother for a week when her father was unexpectedly admitted to the hospital. To prevent the same thing happening again, she was about to interview some geriatric case managers, who would be able to step in the next time there was an emergency. Thus, as a working-class woman, Maureen's caring work was manual; as a middle-class woman, Denise's was managerial.

Class and Gender in Paid and Unpaid Caring

Before the sixties and seventies, women's unpaid household work was considered to be irrelevant to their paid work. However, as more women moved into the (paid) work-force, there was a growing realization that paid and unpaid work is intimately linked—that women's ability to participate in paid work is limited by their unpaid work at home. The gender division of labor in the household was described in pathbreaking books such as Arlie Hochschild's *The Second Shift*,[10] and was cataloged in detail by time-use studies in which research participants meticulously record hour by hour their household activities. Initially, studies focused on housework and childcare, but more recently, caring—conceived more broadly—has also been recognized as work.

What is unpaid caring work? In her persuasively argued book on caring and justice, the philosopher Diemut Bubeck gives the following definition:

> Caring work involves looking after members of the household or the (extended) family if required by sickness, physical, or mental disability, or frailty. It is often restricted to limited periods of time but can be time-consuming and require constant availability. It also involves looking after elderly relatives, which can be a twenty-four hour job depending on their needs and their infirmity, and the meeting of emotional needs of all members of the family.[11]

As this definition states, women care for and care about family members. One classic depiction of this is Elizabeth Bott's description of London working-class life in the 1950s; here Bott describes how Mrs. Newbolt, one of the women she came to know, created and managed the social life and mutual support of an extended family:

> Mrs. Newbolt was the eldest of the third generation, but her cousins were growing up and marrying, and it seemed likely that they would soon begin to join in the activities of their mothers and aunts. Each of these women brought her children and to some extent her husband into relationship with the other members of the nucleus. It was these women who organized the large gatherings of kin at weddings, funerals, christenings and so on, it was usually these women who persuaded male relatives to help one another get jobs, and it was the women who did most of the visiting and small acts of mutual aid.[12]

For most women, caring extends beyond family to a broader network that includes friends and coworkers; but developing and maintaining social networks among family and friends is just one aspect of caring. Caring is also empathizing—for example, feeling for a friend whose husband just walked out, for a husband who was passed over for a promotion, or for a teenager whose acne makes her feel ugly. It is thinking about others, feeling concerned for their welfare, and giving serious thought and attention to questions such as the following: Is a child being bullied at school, and if so, what can be done about it? Will a friend's mother need to be hospitalized, and how will she pay for it? Will a coworker who lost her job soon find another one? Addressing questions such as these is part of women's everyday, scarcely noticed, unpaid caring work.

As well as all this unpaid caring work, many women do caring work for pay; in fact, with an aging baby boom generation and widespread workforce participation by women, caring occupations are rapidly expanding, offering new work opportunities for thousands of women. Over three million women work as nurses, for example, almost three million as aides, orderlies or attendants, almost three million as elementary school teachers, a million as teacher aides, and three-quarters of a million as home health aides. Interpreted broadly, then, to include elementary teachers, the essential work of caregiving is already performed by ten million women, one in every six women who work. A number of the women I interviewed worked as childcare workers, nursing aides, and teaching aides, three of the most rapidly growing occupations. By 2008, it is estimated that demand will grow by 24 percent for childcare workers, 24 percent for nurse assistants, and 58 percent for teaching assistants. For home health aides, the demand will grow even more; there were around 750 thousand home health aides in 1998, but this number is expected to grow by 58 percent by 2008.[13]

We need it, but do we value caring work? The answer is no;[14] nursing assistants, teacher's aides, childcare workers, and home health aides—the caring occupations that are available to women without a degree—are all among the lowest-paid jobs, in the bottom fourth of the income distribution. In fact, nursing, which requires at least an associate's degree, is the only well-paid "female" caring occupation.[15] Because of these dismal wages, turnover in caring jobs is high, and this affects the quality of care. In relation to childcare workers, for example, the Center for the Child Care Workforce recently noted that "with annual job turnover rates hovering between thirty and forty percent throughout the country, current market wages in the child care field have clearly been insufficient to secure a skilled and stable workforce or to guarantee high-quality services for children and families."[16] We should be concerned, then, on two fronts: for the welfare of the women who do caring work and that of those they care for.

Caring work as a whole is devalued, but working-class women's caring work is devalued most of all. Increasingly the caring jobs that are available to working-class women, especially women without a high school diploma, are "bad" jobs, not "good" jobs—jobs that are low in status, low in pay, and lacking in power. In health services, for example, doctors (whatever their gender) have higher status and pay than nurses, but nurses have much higher status and pay than aides. The paid caring work performed by working-class women, therefore, is doubly devalued; they not only perform the gendered work of caring, but the caring work they do is the lowest-paid, least attractive manual labor that has been rejected by others of their gender—but of a different class.

Public policy and union activism must spearhead social change so that paid caregivers can earn fair wages, and unpaid caregivers can afford help. But as users of caregiving services, middle-class Americans benefit from the "unskilled" labor of poor and working-class women in hundreds of unacknowledged ways. They take advantage of working-class caregivers by making unreasonable demands and paying poverty-level wages. Every six months or so, *The New York Times* publishes horror stories told by nannies who are paid low wages, expected to work around the clock, clean and run errands as well as care for children, or by maids who work under slave-labor conditions. Most middle-class readers will know of cases like this and others, where women with the least education, material resources, and skills care for the children and do much of the dirty work for women with the most; they clean their houses, shampoo their hair, bag their groceries, serve their food, scour their toilets, and wipe their spills from convenience store counters. Pay inequality persists because it is convenient for those with power—middle-class women as well as middle-class men.

Growing Up Poor
in Postwar
America

You have a lot of people out there that didn't struggle when they were growing up. They have a very big head about it, and I can feel sorry for them to some extent. Because they don't know what it's like to go to bed at night and want something, or need something that you know your mom can't provide. Those kids could get it.

—Laura

We had oatmeal a lot. . . . It was still in the area of the coal and the wood stoves—not stoves but furnaces—and we didn't have any coal, and we didn't have any money to buy any, so my dad chopped up the piano. . . . This was when I was a child, so that kind of thing, seeing your dad chop up the piano, kind of sticks in your mind.

—Nina

With my income being the only income right now, I had to take this job, even though I'm not satisfied with it.

—Ruth

The Different Worlds of Postwar America

In the postwar decades, America was an adolescent country enjoying a growth spurt. Cars, trucks, and appliances rolled off assembly lines and into showrooms; soil was broken for countless new houses, shopping centers, and schools; and interstate highways snaked across the land. Manufacturing wages soared, and for many working-class families, these were the best of times. Thousands of young couples flocked to buy new ranch houses, whose gleaming kitchen cabinets, split-level design, and pine-paneled rec rooms represented ideal family life—wholesome, efficient, prosperous, and modern. The manufacture of goods and the building of infrastructure produced an ample supply of jobs, and almost one in every three of these jobs were union pro-tected; secure and well paid, they supported families, and made workers proud.[1]

A mood of postwar optimism extended to ideals of marriage, childrearing, and family life. The stern behaviorism of Dr. Watson gave way to the benevolence of Dr. Spock, and television families showed us an appealing version of how life could be, with parents like stern but wise and kindly Ward Cleaver and June, ever smiling, neat, and prim in a sweater-set and pearls. How many of us envied these television fami-lies—families where father was good, kind, and "knew best," and mother was loving, warm, and always supportive?

But every coin has two sides; the prosperity, though real, was not universal. In the middle of the fifties, one-quarter of the U.S. population was poor and at the end of that decade, a third of American children remained in poverty. Whites were better off than blacks, families with two parents better off than those with one, but even among white, predominantly two-parent families, one-third were unable to manage on a single income.[2] As might be expected, the families of the working-class women in this study were not among the prosperous; most were just getting by, the better off among them able to comfortably afford a decent life, the worst off severely and persistently poor.

We know the "good" version of postwar family life; it was the one we saw on tele-vision and, as Stephanie Coontz notes in her history of the period, *The Way We Never Were*,[3] it is the one we like to look back on with rose-colored glasses. In this chapter, therefore, I only briefly sketch profiles from the shiny side of the postwar coin, before turning it over to examine its lesser-known underside. I do this because we cannot begin to understand the diversity among the women I interviewed without appreciat-ing the hardships some women suffered as children and young adults.

First, however, I begin with some of the many families that really do remind us of the Cleavers. Greta grew up in one such family. Her father was originally a cop who walked a city beat, but he was promoted several times over the years until, at the pin-nacle of his career, he became superintendent of the county jail. Sometimes he took his daughter to work, and Greta remembered those times well; she told me about one of her more exciting visits. "I remember going down to see him," she said, showing me a picture of her father in his uniform. "At the prison I went to get a candy bar and my father said, 'Don't go too close to those bars.' And I wasn't thinking and I reached in to get a candy bar, and this hand came out and went across my neck and pulled me against the bars! And I was turning blue, my father said, and he took his nightstick and he raised his nightstick and hit the guy. I seen this nightstick coming toward me and I closed my eyes, and my father hit him right there, and it broke his arm. I was eight-years-old. That was a wild experience, going down to see my daddy at work."

Greta and her father enjoyed many good times together on weekends too. "I used to walk the railroad tracks with [my father]," she said. "We used to walk the railroad tracks on Saturday mornings, just to talk. When my mother would go out of town, my father would say, 'What do you want to eat? I'll fix you something that Mom don't fix.' She didn't believe in dipped eggs, and all the things my grandmother used to fix when we lived there that I liked. My grandmother called them 'dippy eggs.' My mother didn't cook that kind of food. She said that's bad for you, greasy. So when she would go out of town I'd say, 'C'mon Dad, let's make those dippy eggs.'"

Greta's mother worked for the city newspaper. At first, she worked from home, selling and renewing newspaper subscriptions by telephone, but she was good at her work and was soon a supervisor, and traveled in her job. "After a while, [she] got higher up," Greta said, "and she was with the bosses. She used to go out to all these meetings and all. They didn't want her to stop doing that. She worked there until it folded." "I used to watch her work," Greta said. "I used to sit there and put the papers in order for her. I helped her. We knew our alphabet before we got to first grade because we used to sit there and put all the papers in order."

Julie also lived in a family that enjoyed a steady income provided by her father's job as a skilled tradesman. "He studied to gain an engineer's license," she said, "and ended up being the supervisor in his plant. And then he went onto another position as a supervisor and was the one who handled all the supervisory maintenance, but he also was the one who started the boilers up in the morning and did all the repair work. . . . Boilers were a big deal then; they did all hospital laundry. Hospitals did not have their own." Like Greta, Julie spent many contented hours with her father, talking and learning about his work:

Well, he talked a lot about the people he worked with. He talked about the kinds of things he did on his job because I was a really curious child. I was always asking questions. And so, he would talk to me about the kinds of things that he did. And as a matter of fact, once there was a repair job that needed to be done at home. He would repair all the home appliances as well, and I was always his sidekick on home appliance repair. And he would tell me about the kinds of things he did at work, so I could connect, by what he did on this little small appliance. And he was always collecting parts of things in case he needed them for a repair job. So he had boxes and drawers full of pieces of things [and] nobody knew what they were except him. Because he was always thinking, you know, "If I just need this little piece." Because you couldn't always go someplace and find parts to do repair work. It's kind of like working on a 1967 Mustang, now. Where would you ever find the pieces? Well, you go to the junkyard. Well, you could just go to my father's basement. I was always asking questions, and so he would talk to me about the kinds of things that he did.

"My mother was a constant," said Julie, "and both of my parents were involved in whatever I was doing or they were certainly available and interested. They were always asking questions, like when we came to a question about schoolwork, well they were both very interested. The fact that they were constant and the fact that they were always available and always interested probably influenced me more than anything."

Cindy's childhood was also happy and secure. Her father had left her family when she was three, but with a steady income from her mother's job as a secretary and the support of grandparents, they got by just fine. "I was raised in my grandparents' house," Cindy said. "[My father] was out of our lives and up until I was in the later elementary grades, I didn't realize there was anything unusual in our situation. I came home from school, my grandmother was there—my mom, of course, she had to work—so I just thought that was the way everybody was until I started having friendships outside the home. . . . I can't say it was a single-parent household. It seemed like I had, between my aunt and my grandmother and my mother, I really had three parents growing up. My grandmother . . . shared a lot of stories with us. It was really great to be raised with a grandmother."

The Other Side of the Coin: Poverty in a Time of Plenty

Greta, Julie, and Cindy were among the twenty-seven women who described their families' financial status as "somewhat short of money"; like many other families supported by good jobs, their families were working class, but not poor. "I'm sure that we had less money than most of the people in our neighborhood," said Julie. "But my father and mother were pretty good money managers. We as kids did not have as many things as most of the kids. . . . Everybody else had a bicycle, we didn't have one. That kind of thing . . . [but] everything we needed was there—the bills were paid, food was on the table, the clothes were on your back, but we didn't shop at some of the stores that some of the kids in our neighborhood shopped at." Other women, however, described families that were definitely poor; five women said that for some substantial length of time they were "very poor," and eleven said they were "quite poor." Among these sixteen women, eleven were the daughters of unskilled laborers, who were unable to command the good wages paid to skilled workers.

Sixteen women constitute one in four of the working-class women I interviewed, but I suspect even this proportion underestimates the true extent of the poverty they experienced; my reason for believing this is that in the unstructured part of the interview, four women described how their families' had needed food stamps, charitable food donations, or help with heating or rent, but then later said in response to questionnaire items that they were "often short of money," not "poor." There are at least two reasons women should hesitate to characterize their families as poor. The first is that they defined their own families' financial well-being relative to other families they knew, most of whom, in economically segregated neighborhoods, would have been no better off. As Phyllis said, "We might have been poor, but we didn't know it." The second is that, in our culture, poverty is stigmatized. As John Hartigan Jr. describes in a superb essay on white poverty, many people, especially people who are poor or living on the edge of poverty, are painfully aware of disparaging terms like "poor white trash"[4] that signify much more than an economic deficit. Doreen showed this awareness when she made a distinction between herself and her sisters who were—as she put it—"dirt poor." "My one sister," she said, "her kids look like—they look how they are—dirt poor! But they're not poor. She has, excuse my words, a son of a bitch for a boyfriend and she ain't half worth it. I mean she sneaks her bottle of whiskey and stuff." Doreen made a similar distinction when she described her childhood. "We got poor quite a few times," she said. "I mean not *poor* poor, but short of money." Being "short of money" lacks some of the pejorative meanings that "poor" can have; therefore it was probably much easier for women to describe their families' financial status this way—being "short of money" means being short of cash, not character.

The Ecological Context of Poverty

Most women, including women who described their families of origin as poor or short of money, came from families that provided a nurturing, supportive, and safe environment for their children. However, eleven of the sixteen women from poor families described family problems that were at best unsettling, at worst devastating: alcoholism, domestic violence, mental illness, and, in three cases, sexual abuse.[5] These are "psycho social ills" that occur more commonly among poor families. Why is this so?

Psychologists have always recognized poverty as a stressor with negative effects on children's development, but in the past they focused on children and parents in isolation from their social context. In the 1970s, however, the Harvard psychologist Uri Bronfenbrenner, known for his role in designing Head Start, proposed a theoretical perspective on human development that is sociological as well as psychological, and interprets individual human development in the context of a "total human ecology." His perspective provides a useful framework for understanding the causes and consequences of psychosocial ills, such as child abuse, and their relationship to poverty. It also suggests how children might be better protected, and how the adult consequences of mistreatment might be ameliorated. As the Surgeon General recently noted, the consequences of child abuse and neglect are often severe and long-lasting, but not all abused children suffer them; understanding this variability in consequences is "a major challenge to research."[6] A model of development that places the individual and family in a broader context can help us address that challenge.

In Bronfenbrenner's model, the individual is at the center of a social system with different layers. He describes it as a set of nested structures, like a set of Russian dolls. At the innermost level, surrounding the child, is the immediate setting—the family, school, and other groups in which the child directly participates; he calls this the "microsystem." At the next level is the relationship between these different structures—for example, the relationship between a child's home and school; he calls this the "mesosystem." At the next level are structures that are once-removed from the child—for example, parents' workplaces, and groups in the local community; this is the "exosystem." Finally, at the level most remote from the child is the "macrosystem," the overarching culture with its particular ideology, economy, and class system.[7]

Few researchers would make the claim that all parents are equally likely to become abusive; but parents whose temperaments make them vulnerable to abusing their children are more likely to do so if they are severely economically distressed and lack social support. Indeed, one recent study that compared neighborhoods in terms of the support systems they offered to residents found that the *potential* to maltreat children was more evenly distributed between neighborhoods than *actual* maltreatment. This finding is important because it suggests that "resources and controls in neighborhoods may prevent actual child maltreatment among populations that are similarly predisposed."[8]

Social supports are central to Bronfenbrenner's understanding of abuse; he believes that stresses occurring in any level of the "ecological context" can be ameliorated by social supports at that level or at others, and he predicts that child abuse is more likely to occur when stress levels are high and social supports are inadequate, and less likely to occur when stress levels are low and social supports are strong. Examples of support systems that reduce the risk of abuse are childcare facilities, educational opportunities for parents, and income supports. Note that these support systems involve larger social structures, not just the parent-child, or family-child microsystem.

Social support in the form of educational opportunities and income supports might have helped protect Liz and Laura, two of the women who were abused. Both women's fathers were poorly educated and worked in dead-end unskilled jobs that barely supported their families. Both men were at risk of becoming abusers: Laura's father was an alcoholic, and Liz's was abused as a child. "I actually don't think he had been to school," she said. "He told us stories; he was born in Arkansas in a covered wagon. Really! He was deaf in both ears, but after my mother died, he had an operation. Apparently when he was small, they used to stick the soap in their ears and this was what was causing the deafness." Judy, a daughter of an alcoholic, exemplifying Bronfenbrenner's ideas, explained her father's alcoholism and emotional abuse in terms of his dead-end job. "It was really strange," she said. "There's times I sit and I think about it. Even though he was an alcoholic, we always had a roof over our head. We was always fed, and we still had clothes on our back. And that was the amazing thing of it all. I mean, maybe he thought that was what he was entitled to. You know, because he worked long hours. But unfortunately it made him an alcoholic and that's why my parents got a divorce."

James Garbarino, another psychologist, was among the first to test the usefulness of Bronfenbrenner's model for understanding abuse. In a study based on macro-level data on the availability of resources in a New York community, he found that both "economic and educational resources" reduced the risk of abuse and that "economic distress" affected children not only by means of its effects on parents, but also on the neighborhoods and communities in which they lived. At highest risk were economically depressed parents "attempting to cope in isolation without adequate facilities and resources for their children."[9] Other studies have since found similar results.[10]

Childcare services are an important social support. As one abuse researcher noted: "No mother should be expected to care for her children around the clock, 365 days a year. Substitute care mechanisms should be routinely available to offer mothers opportunities for carefree rest and recreation."[11] Extended family members are important support systems, and, in fact, when we talked, Laura was grieving the recent loss of her mother's support. Her mother had just moved from the city to a rural county. "One thing that's stressful with me is my mom," she said. "My mom has always been there for me and for [my daughters]. Now that she's up in Cecil County it's like she's forgotten that she's got other children and grandchildren. She basically is around my youngest sister and her baby, and takes care of her mother. It's hard because my mom—it hurts to see that she has made freedom for herself."

Conditions of life in poverty can indirectly contribute to child abuse by placing stresses on parents, but they can have a direct effect in and of themselves.[12] For example, mothers who are poor cannot afford appropriate childcare for their children and may be forced to leave them with adults who are not reliable, thus increasing their children's risk of abuse. Overcrowded housing also increases risk. Nina, the third woman who was sexually abused, grew up in a small house with nine siblings, her grandfather, and at times, an uncle, who was disabled. Because the family could not afford nursing care for her uncle, Nina was often charged with his physical care, and this was the context in which his abuse of her took place.

An advantage of Bronfenbrenner's model is that it takes into account individual and family vulnerability, and the availability of social supports, but also social structures such as work and the overarching ideology of the culture in which abuse occurs. Examining different levels of the social structure that produces abusive parents and the different levels of support available to them gives us a better perspective on the problem and suggests better interventions. Families living in poverty face multiple stressors in their homes, neighborhoods, schools, and workplaces, and they do so in a culture that values material and occupational success and despises failure. Intervention at the level of the microsystem can be helpful to individual families, but to be helpful to all families at risk, it must take place at the level of the social and economic structures in which families live and work.

Poverty

I turn now to five women's experiences to illustrate the life conditions that may accompany poverty, and the sometimes long-lasting effects of these conditions. Four of the five women were poor as children, and one became poor as an adult; three of the four women who were poor as children—Liz, Laura, and Nina—were also sexually abused; most poor families were not abusive, but child abuse and neglect are more common in conditions of poverty. This was so for two of the three women. Poverty that begins in adulthood may be less psychologically destructive but even so, as Ruth's story shows, it imposes multiple stresses on women and their families. With Bronfenbrenner's model as a tool, I will explore these women's stories with a view to understanding them in their ecological context.

Sonya

Sonya had been poor for most of her life. She lived with her mother, husband, and son in a tiny, tumble-down, semirural cottage, on a winding lane obviously long ignored by the city snow-clearing teams. Her mother sat with us at the kitchen table during our interview, her frayed bathrobe and missing teeth evidence of the family's poverty. The kitchen was divided from the rest of the house by a thin curtain; Sonya said her grandson and teenage son were sleeping in one of the four curtained-off rooms. She was worried about this son because he stayed in his room all the time, and he was not in school. "I'm waiting on it now, for a decision," she said, "to see if he can go back to school. He got kicked out of school last year."

A mother at sixteen, Sonya was still only in her mid-thirties but she looked careworn. She had grown up mostly in this same house, with her factory worker father, her mother, five brothers, and two sisters. For five years, however, from the age of nine until she dropped out of school at fourteen, she had lived with an old couple across the street. "It was because they had cookies," she explained. "They had cookies and ice cream and all that good stuff that I didn't have. They was giving me everything, cookies, cakes. I had cookies every day, candies every day. See, they talked to my mother, my mother had what, four, five other kids, so my mother said, 'No problem,' you know. I lived there for five years." Sonya told me her mother didn't want her when she was born, a fact to which her mother cheerfully agreed. "She didn't want me because I was female," said Sonya.

Sonya quit school during seventh grade, but even now she had no regrets: "I got kicked out. You know, I was a smart mouth. I was the one [who would] decorate the bathrooms, set [them] on fire. That was me. I was really bad, a whole lot." She still talked tough: "I don't need nobody. I have a very hard shell to get through. You don't get close to me without me letting you. And then you'll only get so far, and I'll block it."

The veteran of two unhappy marriages, and now in her third, Sonya spent many years struggling to support her four sons on welfare before she took her first job at thirty-two, packing fruit in a factory. About a year before our interview, she had landed her present job when her husband left it for a job that paid more:

It's a barber's school. Normally, a routine day is inventory the warehouse. I order what I need of the equipment—shampoos, cutting material I need. I have to grade tests. See I don't like the nine-to-five jobs. Same thing every day. Like cutting hair. Cutting hair, every day, same day. See, with my job, I'm not sure what I'm gonna be doing from one day to the next. Now like Tuesday, I have equipment sales [people] coming in. I have, like, four or five people coming in. They come in [and] they want to open up a barber shop. I tell them the chairs they need, the shampoos, sinks, I tell them where to get the license, how to get the license, what they need to open a shop. Stuff like that. . . . And then I have to do the inventory. And then like Wednesday, I probably won't have hardly nothing to do but you know, odds and ends and all.

Sonya seemed to enjoy most things about her job—except the pay. "It's always different," she said. "New things happen. It's not like a nine-to-five, forty-hour-a-week job." But she liked work less now than before: "Because I realize all the work I do, the eight hours I'm working, you know, how long I'm working and stuff, and how less I'm getting paid. That has a lot to do with it." She made only the minimum wage, but couldn't count on her boss to pay her even that meager amount on time. Her husband was trying to talk her into quitting, but she took the job in the first place because she couldn't trust him to bring money home, so she wasn't about to quit. She had seen a psychiatrist for depression, and she stayed home from work sometimes because she felt too depressed to go in. How long had she been depressed? "All my years," she said. "All the time."

Sonya had been isolated from social institutions for much of her life. One of eight children, she grew up in a poor family with parents whose education went no further than elementary school. Expelled from school at fourteen, pregnant with her first child at sixteen, she had stayed at home for many years (except for one brief job). Since she started working, however, she had made an important discovery: she was able to do the same job as her husband and she enjoyed it. However, unlike some women, who had no basis for comparison, she knew full well she was underpaid—after all, her husband quit the same job because of the money. But what could she do? With a seventh grade education, no job training, and few skills to trade on the labor market, her chances of finding a better paid job were slim.

There were severe stresses in Sonya's life, and she was not being helped to deal with them. The most stressful aspect of her work was her low pay and the fact that her employer was not regular in his payments. Clearly, this situation would not arise in a unionized or "primary labor market" job, but as a casual worker, Sonya had few protections, and because she liked her job, she didn't want to make a fuss and risk being fired. Her relationship with her husband was stressful—she felt she could not depend on him to share his resources—and she was concerned about her son, who was obviously quite severely depressed. He had been suspended from school for an indefinite period and stayed in his room all the time. "It drives me crazy," Sonya said.

Ironically, Sonya had better access to social support when she was on AFDC. As a "welfare mom" she had been able to see psychiatrists for her depression, but now the weekly cost of a typical dose of depression medication, combined with a psychiatric visit, would cost more than her take-home pay. With no health benefits, professional help was now out of the question.

Sonya's predicament was common; sometimes she felt so depressed she could not go in to work, but if she missed too much work, she would lose her job. She had a job, but she was unable to afford the medical care that would help her keep it. It is hard to see how any action she could take as an individual would significantly change her life; such decisions—about job training, health care, and minimum wages—can be made only by macro-level institutions, not by individual women.

Ruth

Endowed with the misleading title of assistant manager, Ruth worked in a sub shop; like Sonya, she worked in a minimum-wage job without health benefits—a real problem because her husband was unemployed, and they were both in bad health. In some ways she was worse off than Sonya because there was little about her job she liked; like Sonya, however, she had no choice. Her face drawn and weary, she looked at me and sighed, "With my income being the only income right now, I had to take this job, even though I'm not satisfied with it."

I interviewed Ruth at ten o'clock on a weekday morning. Her home was a two-bedroom apartment in a large development several miles from the city, which she shared with her husband, her younger daughter, Faye, and—for the time being at least—her elder daughter, Tammy. Tammy's husband, and their two small daughters were also living there. Children's toys were strewn over the living-room floor and Ruth's husband, Roy, sat nearby watching television. While we talked, Tess, one of her granddaughters, miserable with a cold, sat in a high chair at the table with us, protesting loudly whenever one of us tried to wipe her nose. Trudy, Ruth's other grand-daughter, was playing nearby, and came over from time to time for some attention and reassurance. During the interview, Tammy, the children's mother, emerged from a bedroom with her husband, asked for some money, and announced she was going out. Ruth objected that she couldn't babysit the children because of our interview, but Tammy left anyway. Just before slamming the front door, she yelled over her shoulder that Faye, her younger sister, should get out of bed and take care of the kids. Faye, though, had her own ideas. She'd been working nights, and the last thing she wanted to do was get up and help—and who could blame her? Roy, apparently oblivious to the rowdy dispute, continued to watch television with dogged determination.

Ruth grew up in a family of five children. Her father, a "real nervous person," was a cook for the military who retired when she was ten. She enjoyed school, but was eager to leave home because she and her mother fought a lot; being "hardheaded," she ignored her mother's objections, quit school at sixteen, and was the mother of two children within as many years.

Soon after Tammy was born, Ruth started working evenings in one of the many waitressing jobs she would hold down over the years, most of them at fast-food places. When Faye, her younger daughter, was two, Ruth and her husband split up, and she and Roy moved to Florida, where she worked for a time in a tavern. Soon back in Maryland, they both drove cabs for the Yellow Cab Company; Ruth also filled in as a dispatcher, and worked part-time running a lottery machine at a bar. Then they had two major setbacks:

> After we had been in the [cab] company for about two years, they decided to sell permits for individuals. And we went with that [and bought a permit], but finally business just started getting really bad, and they just decided to sell out altogether. By that time, it was a lot of expense getting the cab running. I have a lot of leg problems, and it got to the point I couldn't drive as much as I'd like to. . . . So when the company decided to sell out, I just sold the permit.
>
> With me and my husband, when we were both driving, we were fine. We didn't have to worry; we'd have a weekend driver so we could take the weekend off. But then when I started having a lot of problems, we couldn't find a night driver half the time. They wouldn't show up, or some of them just—they didn't take care of the car at all. And, I mean, if they didn't take care of the car, it cost us money. So I just [quit]. It was getting to be a real headache. [Then] I went to work for Local Limousine. I worked in the office there. I think I was there not quite a year. And I had to go in and have some surgery done and I decided not to go back to work at that point. Basically I wasn't working for a year.

Ruth and Roy had done well driving the cab, but when business declined and her health deteriorated, they had no financial backup to help them through the crisis. As soon as she was—literally—back on her feet, she had no choice but to take the first available job; this was her job at the sub and pizza parlor where she still worked as a cashier and short-order cook. She hated it. The minimum wage and lack of benefits was one reason, but her boss's appalling behavior was another. She gave me this example: when $100 was stolen from another worker's cash drawer, he withheld it from the woman's paycheck, even though all the staff knew someone else had committed the theft. As Ruth said, "It's senseless to try to talk with this man. So you really get disgusted with it." She had been trying to convince her boss to give her a raise, but she'd about given up: "I mean, me and him's been arguing back and forth about my raise. He keeps expecting me to do more and more, but he don't want to give me any more money."

Her responsibilities at home were an added stress; she was concerned about her two daughters, unhappy with the way they seemed to be turning out, and disturbed by the parallels she saw between her own life and theirs:

> With me and my first husband, he was like Tammy's husband, he worked when he felt like it. It was always, "Well, we can go to your mother. Your mother will give us [what we need]. Your mother will do this. Your mother will do that." And I mean, I was so embarrassed to have to keep going to my mother. We got kicked out of so many places because we couldn't afford to pay the rent. And I just can't help but see that Tammy's doing the same thing. They've been together three years and I mean, I couldn't count the number of places they've lived, the amount of money I've given them to bail them out, the amount of money his parents have given them to bail them out. And it's like, I can see it happening and if I say anything, it's like, [she says], "No, no, no," [and won't listen]. Many times when we lived in the apartment across from them, they'd have their gas and electric cut off. I'd run an extension cord across to at least have the refrigerator plugged in. And I don't want to see that for them.

In another reprise of her own life, Ruth said Tammy had gotten pregnant when she was very young (fourteen), and she was afraid Faye would soon follow in her sister's footsteps. Faye also worked at Sam's Subs. "Overall, she's a good kid," Ruth said, "but she has a nasty attitude—basically only directed toward me. I mean if we have problems, just say we couldn't make the rent and we had to move or something, it's always my fault. It's not shared, it's not like me and her father's and her fault, it's my fault." And, again following in Tammy's footsteps, Faye refused to listen to her mother:

> Before she started dating, she would have money left from paycheck to paycheck. Now, I mean, we get paid on Saturdays, by Mondays she's broke! And I keep trying to tell her, I mean, she'll say, "Well I put gas in Joe's truck, me and Joe went for lunch, me and Joe went to this," and she gets aggravated when I say to her, "Well, you're not supposed to be the one that's buying all the time. Faye, you can't hold on to someone just by using money. You know, you don't know if he really cares for you, or [it's] because you keep spending on him all the time." So we argue a lot over that. And then I always get, "Well it's my money. I can do what I want with my money."
> [Does Faye contribute to the household expenses?] She buys her own makeup, her own shampoo, and this kind of stuff. If I need it, I'll say, "Faye, I need twenty-five dollars this week to go toward the electric bill." If she has it, she don't mind. But it's like, anything that goes wrong, it's like blame's always put on me. No one else.

Faye kept promising to go back to school, but Ruth hadn't been able to take her to the family planning clinic and feared that she would become pregnant: "My problem is right now, a lot of times, with transportation. And then, with mine and Faye's schedule, we're working different shifts most of the time, and it's like trying to get an appointment and then making sure we have a way [to get] there and . . . I've been giving it a lot more thought. We've discussed it and talked about it and everything, and she said she would like to go ahead and go on [the pill]. It's just getting down there."

Ruth had tried to improve her job skills by enrolling in a home-study course to train as a medical secretary; she believed that she would really enjoy secretarial work. The home-study school sent her test booklets, and a study course, and at the end of each booklet, there was a test that she mailed in to be graded. But it was by no means certain that physicians would accept this certificate as a qualification—she hadn't been taught typing and other office procedures, nor had she been advised to obtain a GED (General Equivalency Diploma). In any event, with no typing skills, no high school diploma, no transportation, no job on the horizon for Roy, and not a penny to spare, Ruth had no choice but to stay in her job. "I have to work to make things meet and [get the] bills paid, you know," she said.

Ruth had worked off and on for most of her life, and, even now, she and Roy would probably be managing financially but for his ill health. He had suffered a heart attack, but was ineligible for SSI because he was judged to be fit enough for light work; since his heart attack, though, he had suffered such severe anxiety that he was afraid to work. And—notice the similarity with Sonya's situation—even if he agreed to it, they could not afford treatment for his anxiety because they had no health benefits. They were caught up in a common predicament: bad health meant bad job or no job; bad job or no job meant bad health. This was a catch-22.

Because Ruth was poor and in bad health, other problems piled up. She knew her daughter was having sex, but with no car, and both of them working shifts, it was difficult to make it to the Planned Parenthood clinic. Lack of a car and ill health also made it harder for her to find a better job; she was limited by public transport, which was virtually nonexistent in her suburb. And because she lived quite a distance from her mother's house, she was no longer able to depend on her mother for support. The apartment complex was sprawling and faceless, lacking any sense of community or permanence, and Ruth had no friends there. All of these circumstances combined to make Ruth's life unhappy and highly stressed.

Alcoholism, Domestic Violence, and Child Abuse

Alcoholism and heavy drinking were the most often mentioned childhood family problems. Alcohol abuse is widespread in the population at large; according to the National Center for Health Statistics, for the period 1994 to 1996, 7 percent of people between the ages of twenty-five and sixty-four drank "very heavily," and an even higher proportion, 19 percent, drank "heavily." ("Very heavily" and "heavily" are defined in terms of the number of times in the last month a person drank at least five drinks in one session. "Very heavy" use, which is considered abusive, is a five-drink session at least five times in the last month; "heavy" use is a five-drink session at least once in the last month.) Rates of abuse are much higher, however, among men similar to many of these women's fathers—that is, men with no high school diploma who work in low-paid laboring jobs. In fact, men without a high school diploma report "very heavy" use of alcohol almost three times as often as men with a college degree, and "heavy" use almost twice as often;[13] the rate is almost one in three for men without a diploma, one in five for men with a degree.[14]

Alcohol abuse has consequences for working-class men's health; class differences in cirrhosis mortality and liver disease are so large that one leading researcher has suggested the need for "social and public health policies and interventions that target . . . the socially isolated, and the poor."[15] Alcoholism also has serious consequences for families. One of these consequences is financial hardship; when the family breadwinner is an alcoholic, the economic consequences can be devastating. "When you have an alcoholic, very little gets to the family," said Helen, now an accountant. "Back then social service would not provide for families when there was a man living in the home. It was hard when he was living to get any support. [When] he died, he hadn't worked for a whole year." "My mother had it very rough," she continued. "There was times she had to go to the Red Cross. And then they would send a policewoman to the home and check the refrigerator to see if anything was in there. We had times when we went without electricity. Back then they didn't have food stamps, they had food they gave out. We got the butter and the flour, and stuff like that."

Another consequence of alcohol abuse is its effect on parenting; several women described fathers who were violent when they were drunk—or, like Judy's father, just plain mean. "I remember right after I got married," Judy said, "my husband and I were talking, and I said, 'My father was an alcoholic and he used to think he was King Kong.' . . . He was a very nasty person. Because he would go down to the corner and buy pizza and then bring it home and sit it in the middle of the coffee table and literally dare us to touch it. You know . . . I always said I would never marry an alcoholic." Neither she did.

Judy's mother divorced her father because of his alcoholism, and, to Judy's relief, she had not forced her children to visit him after the divorce. Financially and emotionally, the divorce improved their lives; her mother was able to receive welfare, and when her father was awarded disability, she was also able to get SSI. Judy remained grateful to her mother for leaving the marriage.

Not all women were so lucky, however, and some women witnessed violence throughout their entire childhood. Kay described what this was like for her: "I had such a nasty childhood. The fact that we were poor didn't bother me at all, because I still shop in the cheapest places—for myself, but not my daughter. But just the arguments and stuff like that. They literally fought, I mean they didn't argue, they fought.

It was abusive. It was very abusive. And I made up my mind right then and there, when I grew up, I wasn't going to live like that, I wasn't going to put my kids through that. And so far so good."

Many studies have shown that alcohol is frequently involved in domestic and other violence. One study, for example, found that 30 to 40 percent of men who perpetrated violence against their partners were drinking at the time;[16] another found that sexual abuse occurred more often in families with a history of alcoholism;[17] a third found that alcohol was involved in at least 50 percent of homicides and assaults,[18] and a fourth found that an alcoholic father increases a girl's risk of sexual abuse by a family member, while an alcoholic or mentally ill mother increases her risk of abuse by someone outside the family.[19] Alcohol was a factor in Laura's abuse by her father, and in a number of cases of domestic violence.

Domestic violence is a leading cause of serious injury and death to women ages 15 to 44,[20] but it is also a form of child maltreatment; many children who witness it suffer acute and long-term emotional disturbances that include nightmares, depression, learning difficulties, and aggressive behavior.[21] This, and other forms of child maltreatment, are disturbingly common. Even if the most conservative estimates are used, based on cases referred to Child Protective Services agencies in each state, the number of children who are victims of maltreatment approaches one million—presumably, the actual numbers run higher. According to the Protective Services official data, neglect is the most common form of maltreatment; in 1998, about 53 percent of the million child victims of maltreatment suffered neglect, 22 percent physical abuse, 12 percent sexual abuse, 6 percent emotional maltreatment, 2 percent medical neglect, and 25 percent other forms of maltreatment.[22] Many children suffer more than one type of maltreatment. Of course, these rates exclude cases that are not formally reported to the authorities.

For sexual abuse, which was particularly devastating for the women in this study who suffered it, epidemiological studies of adults have found different rates, but they are all disturbingly high. One study reported that 15 to 33 percent of females and 13 to 16 percent of males were sexually abused in childhood. Another study, using a narrower definition of abuse, reported rates of 12.8 percent for females and 4.3 percent for males.[23]

The long-term consequences of sexual abuse include depression, anxiety, low self-esteem, and problems with social functioning and adult interpersonal relationships; post-traumatic stress disorder occurs in 33 to 86 percent of adult survivors.[24] Other long-term effects include self-destructive behavior, social isolation, poor sexual adjustment, substance abuse, and increased risk of revictimization.[25]

The three women I interviewed who were sexually abused were all abused by family members; Liz was abused by her stepfather, Laura by her father, and Nina by several male relatives: her grandfather, her uncle, and one of her brothers. (National data show that in more than a quarter of cases, abuse is committed by a parent or parent substitute and most often begins when children are between seven and nine years old.[26]) Consistent with research findings that mothers' mental illness is a risk factor for abuse, all three women were daughters of mentally ill mothers, and Laura's parents were both alcoholics.

Liz

Liz recalled her abuse: "I just came back from a foster home. [My mother] was at my aunt's—at the time she was still able to get into a cab and she had taken a cab to my aunt's—and I had came home from babysitting and was going to change my clothes, and my stepfather was behind the door and attacked me. After he tore my clothes off, I was finally able to get away from him, and I ran to this corner and told the people I knew, and the boys went back and beat him up. After that, [my mother] didn't want nothing to do with me because he decided he wasn't going to work and give her any money, so I told her I was going to get pregnant and get out of the house. In a couple months I had succeeded."

Liz's mother was mentally ill, desperately depressed. "I don't ever recall my mother being happy," Liz said, tears streaming down her cheeks. "She was always very depressed. She had spells where she would sit and cry for days. She would stand on the front street when she could get on the porch and she would rip her clothes off her back and scream and cry." Her mother became extremely obese (590 pounds when she died, at forty-one), and she was given to rages. "I mean we would be eating dinner, and she'd flip the table," Liz continued. "There were a lot of weeks that my brother spent home from school, because she would get [the buckle]. We got the razor strap that belonged to our grandparents and after that, it was the belt, and she didn't care if the buckle hit or not. So he would have to stay at home because he was bruised." At the time, Liz was unable to talk to anyone about the abuse. "Those were different times," she said.

> After my mother died, I talked to my [grandparents] about it, you know, because they had no idea what was going on all those years. But it was like, I could remember when I was a little girl—she married [my stepfather] when I was six—and I'd wake up and he would be, you know. I didn't understand it. Why he wanted to dry me after my bath. But then when I started getting a little size to me, it was, "Come sit on my lap, let me touch your—you know. It wasn't until I actually was like ten or eleven that I realized, this man should not be doing what he is doing. And my mother and him would have fights, and then I would be the bad guy. So it was easier to get preg-nant and get out of the home.
>
> I can actually see though, I can understand, and I can see how kids can grow up in a house where they're being abused, and don't know. I mean I can . . . understand this and how they could keep quiet. I knew that every time I told there was a fight,

everybody was unhappy, so it was easier just to keep my mouth shut, and he actually wasn't doing anything but fondling or fingering, or, you know. [It was better] just to keep my mouth shut and be quiet, but just to stay away from him.

Liz had suffered some of the consequences that are reported for survivors of child abuse. She had been severely depressed when her children were young. "For years . . . I was like totally depressed," she explained. "I had more suicide attempts . . . poor Joe [Liz's son], the last time I tried to do that, Joe was five years old. My suicide attempt really affected him. For days after I came home from the hospital, he just kept rubbing my wrists where I had slit my wrists. He just kept rubbing my wrist and [saying], 'Don't leave me Mom.'" But now, Liz said, she was doing much better: "Most of the time, if the blue comes on, I can usually pull myself out of it. You know, think of something else, or do something else." Because she "liked to feel her feelings," Liz had stopped taking antidepressants, but she still had anxiety attacks:

There's only one thing I dislike about my job and that's that I have to ride an elevator to go to the restroom. I'm terrified of elevators. I guess you would say I'm claustrophobic. I can't sit in a movie theater if it's crowded. There used to be concerts over at Robert E. Lee Park, and we used to go, but when the people started getting [there], I had to leave because I couldn't breathe. When I get in an elevator, I break out in a sweat, I have the shakes, and I'm only going one floor up, so that's the part I hate about my job.

In her first marriage, Liz was a victim of abuse, but when she married a second time, she was careful not to repeat her mistake. "I knew what marriage was like," she said. "In my first marriage, I unfortunately got one that liked to drink and beat, and was jealous of babies. He would kick the bassinet over. [He] threw [my baby] up against the bassinet, and I had to go to the hospital to have the paint picked out of the baby's eyes. And Friday and Saturday night the police would come take him away. . . . I'd seen this and I was never going to go through that again." By contrast, her second husband, she said, waited on her hand and foot, and "spoil[ed] [her] rotten."

Fortunately, Liz remembered some good times from her childhood, from before the death of her birth father:

He laughed all the time, he was a good man. My aunt keeps him alive [for us]. He was a tolerant person, and he loved the kids. I mean, every picture we've ever got of him is with either my brother or me, and he's always laughing, and doing something. And I can remember the rides. I don't care how old I was when he died, I can remember. His favorite [food] was scrambled eggs and rice—and I remember Saturday morning eating scrambled eggs and rice and going for a ride in his car, because it didn't have a roof! I remember this. But that's about all I do remember. That, and I can remember waiting at the door, him coming home for sugar.

Unlike her mother, who became more isolated over the course of her life, and steadily grew more obese and depressed, Liz had ventured into the world and was now able to deal with the public all day on her job. Although she still suffered from depression and anxiety, and was very distressed about her son, she had social support from her husband, and also from friends she had made on her previous job—in fact, she had found out about her present job through one of these friends.

As an adult, Liz had been desperately poor only once, after her first husband walked out. Her second husband had a good job with health benefits—as a foreman—so since she met him she had been able to avoid poverty, and also get psychiatric treatment for her depression. But, in these hard times, no job is really secure, and for a while recently, when her husband lost his factory job, they were forced to live on the minimum wage:

> The first fifteen years we were together he worked in a factory. He was a foreman of a factory. And he lost his job. And then he went to the video store [where I worked]. And then he got in an argument after I got laid off, and lost his job. And then he went to work for the guy that I'm working for. And it was like the total pits, because you can't survive on five dollars an hour. I don't care who you are or where you live. You can't live off of five dollars an hour. So we really struggled there.

With her husband earning a good wage again, the danger of falling into poverty was past—for now, at least. "He likes this and the money's good," she said, "and he has insurance, and in a couple of months we'll be back on the even keel again." Now, she could laugh. "I mean, what would life be if you didn't have to struggle," she said. "It would be awful boring. I'll find out some day."

When we talked, Liz was sad, but she was still able to laugh and feel some hope for the future; her job was boring, but even that had a good side because she loved to read, and she could often read a novel a day. Even though, as she said, no one else might like her job, for now, it suited her just fine. Laura, on the other hand, whose story follows, was miserable in her job, and at home. She could recall no happy childhood memories, and her fundamental self-esteem seemed more damaged than Liz's.

Laura

We talked in the living-dining room of Laura's apartment, which was in a large complex just inside the beltway. Her younger daughter, Michelle, a pert ten-year-old, was glued to the television. Later, when Michelle was engrossed in a sitcom, a somber Laura told me how her father had abused her.

He was a well driller, but Laura didn't know too much more about him because she had not seen much of him since her parents divorced. In her eyes, he was "dead and gone. The reason for my mother and him being divorced is because of me," she explained. "I was sexually molested. He made me perform the acts on him. That's why they were divorced. When I was three, four, five." She remembered it all. "I can remember inch for inch each piece of furniture [that] sat in there," she said. "I mean, I remember everything. And it took me until I was eighteen, pregnant with [my first child] to confront him, and he told me I was retarded, I dreamed it all up. That's why I have nothing to do with him."

I asked if at any time she had talked to her mother about the abuse. "I didn't in the beginning," she explained. "It was my older brother that told her. [Then] she left to do her normal routine of going shopping on a Friday night and came back and caught him. And she immediately just grabbed us all up and left. And he denied it. He denied it. He'll deny it to this day. He still denies it. . . . I asked my mother why—why was it me? And she told me it was because I was the type child that—anybody that reached for me, I went."

Only five years or so before our interview, Laura had talked to her grandparents—her father's parents—about what happened. "And when I told them, it was, it was hard for them to stomach it," she said, "but then again, because it was [his mother's] own child, she tried to defend him by saying that he got hurt on the job one time, he got hit on the head, and ever since then that's why he became an alcoholic, and may have did what he did. She wasn't going to take up for him for what he did, but [she said] I'd have to look at [it] from his side. But I said no one can change my mind on that. Nobody can change it. This is the way I feel about him, and I'll always feel this way about him." As well as sexually abusing Laura, her father physically abused her mother; many times, when he was in an alcoholic rage, she saw him put her mother's head through a wall.

A few years earlier, realizing she needed help, Laura went for counseling to a rape crisis center; she was advised to confront her father, but refused:

> I said, [if I] do that, I'm not going to be responsible for what I'm going to do to him.
> I said, because, to me, you know, I can never forgive him for it. No. And my brother
> and sisters became a little bit upset with me about it and all, but I told them that,
> until the day that man dies, I won't feel no relief. The day he does die, my family will
> disown me, because I will go to the funeral home, and I'm going to spit in his face.
> That's just the way I feel. He never seen his granddaughter till she was about two
> years old and my brother snuck her down there to see him. Then again when she was
> eight. And then when she was eight, and he pranced around in front of her in his
> underwear, and I found out, I said, 'Oh! No! No! No! No! No! Uh-uh.'

After her parents divorced, Laura, her mother, and three siblings went to live with

Laura's grandmother; their mother worked for a time as a waitress, then got by on public assistance. In the beginning, Laura liked it when her mother worked, "but she started having a lot of stress, a lot of anxiety attacks, and she turned to the bottle herself, and she became an alcoholic." The family lived in the city, which was where Laura went to school; in school, she was a "slow learner," and, ultimately, as she bluntly put it, "a ninth grade dropout":

> To be honest with you, city schools do not teach the children. Your teachers are petrified. They are petrified now even more so. But even when I was in school, the teachers had no control over us students at all. We ran the school. Same way now. And every one of us in my mom's—every one of my mom's kids was somewhat of a slow learner. You can't sit something in front of us and say, "Do it." You have to show it to us, at least once, and go step by step. And explain it to us. Don't set something in front of me and say, "Do it," because that makes you lose your courage, it makes you get very frustrated with it, and you just toss it to the side, or you just mark anything you want to mark.
>
> And to me, I wasn't getting the proper education I should have been getting, where my oldest brother, he went to a county school and he graduated. He's the only one of my mother's children that graduated. I got very frustrated. . . . Back then, I didn't get no special help. I'm the type person that I get very discouraged easy. I don't give myself enough credit where I should have credit. And I just [say], "Forget it. I can't do it." I just feel I'm a loser all the time so I won't try it.

Laura had very little work experience, so she lacked a history of success that might have boosted her self-esteem. Before this, she had worked in only one "real" job, which was housekeeping at a motel soon after she quit school. That was a disastrous experience. After only two months on the job, she had walked into a room one day and found an aborted fetus in a pool of blood on a bed; the coroner was called, and when he left, she was told to go ahead and make the bed. She refused to do it and was fired. After this brief encounter with work, she stayed home, and two years later, had her first daughter and went on public assistance.

Later still, she met and married her second daughter's father. They were divorced after three years, and for several years Laura supported her family on public assistance. She was eventually remarried, to Sam, her present husband. Sam worked as a groundskeeper at a golf club; he was an alcoholic, and very moody, so much so that Laura was fed up with him and sometimes felt her head was "about ready to explode." "To be honest with you," she said, "I've got a lot of hate in me for men. Sure. And the woman at the rape crisis center, and even my doctor told me, I'm a walking time bomb. . . . And when the day comes! There better not be males around me because I'll hit 'em. I'll hurt 'em."

Laura said Sam was good with her kids, and that he was "okay" sometimes, but when she came home from work, he was unable to give her the support she needed. "There is no communication between me and him," she said. She would like to separate from him, but she knew she could never afford the rent on her own. As far as she could see, there was only one solution: she would quit her job and babysit. Then she could care for her daughter's child and also take in some neighborhood children for a fee. "I don't want to do it," she said, "but I'm gonna attempt to pay the small bills off that I can pay off, and I'm quitting. I'm not going to go back. I'll take on a few babysitting jobs around here."

Some years earlier, with her daughter about to enter school, Laura was summoned into the welfare office and told to look for a job—or else. "The guy looked at me," she said, still fuming at the memory, "and he said, 'You'll never accomplish nothing in your life because you're'—I was a dropout, I was a ninth grade dropout—'you'll never accomplish nothing but cleaning rooms.' I looked at him and I said, 'Bet me!' And I just made up my mind that I wasn't going to let him prove that I was going to be that type of person."

Determined to prove she could do more than clean rooms, and aware that her lack of education was holding her back, Laura enrolled in a job-training course: "I knew I could do it. It was just that—what was stopping me from getting a good-paying job was the fact that I had no education behind me. But a lot of the work, common sense will tell you how to do it!"

> I went to New York Career Institute. It was only supposed to be a six-month program, but I started out [training as an] office assistant and was there for three months [but] I couldn't handle the way they were doing it, and I switched over to computers. It was nice in the beginning. What it is is part of your grant you get— what they call a guaranteed student loan. That has to be paid back. . . . The other part that paid for it was what they called a Pell grant, which the state paid for, and I didn't have to pay for that. But it came out to be where I owed [the Career Institute] like—well, it's about, well it's five years and it's not paid off yet because I went into debt. It think it's like about fifteen hundred [dollars] I had to pay back to the New York Career Institute place.

Trained, but in debt, Laura had landed her present warehouse job. She took orders over the phone and keyed them into a computer. She was expected to work fast and stay on top of a mass of detail, and she was finding her job very stressful. But it was not always like this. Before her factory was taken over by a new company, she had liked her job and could cope with the work. Now, she had multiple symptoms of stress: anxiety attacks, fatigue, depression, rage:

I have a tendency when I'm depressed—I guess you could say I tune everybody out.
I'm very quiet when I'm that way. I basically really shouldn't work when I'm in a
depressed mood because I don't want no one around me. And I get these—I call
them—I feel when I'm ready to go into an anxiety attack or a depression. Because
my hands tingle and all's I want to do is just sit there and just do this to them
[clenching fists] because I feel like I gotta break something.

She had insomnia. "It's been happening quite frequently for the past year," she
said, "and basically when I feel it, I feel like I'm falling. If I try to go to sleep and I close
my eyes, I can actually feel myself falling. And then I get tense, so I get up and I'll walk
around." Her anxiety was so severe that Laura sometimes thought she was having a
heart attack. At times, she also had suicidal thoughts. "I have my days," she said, "when
I just feel like just ending it all. Thinking Christine would be better off with somebody
else, Roxanne'd be better off with her father, and . . . I have my days." In the past, Laura
had turned to Parents Anonymous for help, but "most of the time I just keep it in
myself," she said. "I'm a screamer. I'll scream at [the kids] first before I swing or hit
them or anything. It helps to talk about it at them meetings, but the feelings just come
back again. I'm a very, very depressive person, very depressive." It was easier now her
daughters were older, but still, Laura said, she was unable to feel like a mother to them.
Now, she said, "I feel more like a best friend."

Laura was dissatisfied with her job, with her marriage, and also with her *self*, so
much so that her low self-esteem, depression, and anxiety were casting a shadow over
every facet of her life. Her strong dissatisfaction with a job she had previously liked
seemed, at least in part, as much a result of anxiety and low self-esteem as its cause. "I
never get told, 'You've done a good job,'" she said. "You just don't get it. You don't get
no feedback. . . . And it's like nobody gives you recognition. You need that to bring
your self-esteem up." Her anxiety spiraled: not acknowledged by the new owners in
her factory, she became anxious and frustrated; then because she was anxious and
frustrated, she felt unable to cope with the demands of the job, and felt she was a
"loser."

It appears that, all other things being equal, workers with low self-esteem are more
vulnerable to job dissatisfaction. Timothy Judge, Edwin Locke, Cathy Durham, and
Avraham Kluger, four psychologists who have extensively studied job—and life—satisfaction, found both kinds of satisfaction to be related to people's "core evaluations." By
core evaluations they mean self-esteem, self-efficacy, and "locus of control"—defined in
the following way. Self-esteem is "the basic appraisal people make of themselves; it is the
overall value that one places on oneself as a person." Self-efficacy is "one's estimates of
one's capabilities to mobilize the motivation, cognitive resources, and courses of action
needed to exercise general control over events in one's life."[27] Locus of control is "the

degree to which individuals believe that they control events in their lives (internal locus of control) or believe that the environment or fate controls events (external locus of control)."[28] In other words, people with high self-esteem feel they are good, capable, strong, and lovable; people with high self-efficacy feel they can summon the energy to change their lives; and people with an internal locus of control feel they are in charge of their own lives, not helplessly dependent on fate.

The authors argued—as have many social theorists—that how we judge the external world is influenced not only by its objective attributes but how we perceive them. They add, however, that how we judge the world is also influenced by how we perceive *ourselves* and our ability to cope. We filter the world "out there" through a set of deep assumptions we hold about ourselves, other people, and the world. Examples they give are assumptions such as "I am weak," "Other people will hurt me," or "The world is a dangerous place." Alternatives would be "I can handle life's exigencies," "Others can bring me happiness," and "Life is an adventure." Remarkably, they found that self-esteem *assessed in childhood* was related to adults' life and job satisfaction in their middle years.

All the women needed to feel respected on the job, but Laura's need ran deep. She was suffering severe anxiety attacks and was considering quitting her job, leaving the security of a better-than-average paycheck and health benefits for an uncertain future. My guess is that her rock-bottom self-esteem made her especially vulnerable to feelings of disrespect; after a lifetime of feeling like a failure, she needed a great deal of reassurance, encouragement, and support to be able to do her challenging work well—but these were the very conditions that were no longer available on her job.

The Consequences of Abuse: The Role of Social Support

Laura's depression, anxiety, and low self-esteem were a textbook example of the consequences of child abuse; she was also self-destructive and socially isolated, and had the problems with social functioning and adult interpersonal relationships that are also reported as common in adult abuse survivors. Nina, on the other hand, had been depressed in the past, but when I interviewed her, she was happy and fulfilled, satisfied with her work and with her family life. How can we understand these differences in well-being? For clues to the answer, I will explore Nina's experience in some detail, making some conjectures about what socially supportive conditions in her life might have helped her achieve her apparent sense of well-being.

As a child, Nina had one parent with whom she felt secure and loved, and, unlike Liz's, her father stayed in her life throughout her childhood. Her mother was verbally abusive, but her father seems to have been an exceptionally loving and gentle man, who spent as much time with his children as he could. He even took them to work with him whenever possible. He had wanted to be a priest, Nina said, but became a boat builder:

Oh he loved his work! He used to take us to the ship christenings, and I can remember sitting on his shoulders because I couldn't see, and he hiked me on his shoulders so that when they broke the champagne bottle I could see it, and we'd holler. And he used to take us on to big executive ships, into the dining rooms, into the captain's dining rooms, and we'd see all the beautiful silverware and glassware, and we loved it. We looked forward to it. We fantasized a lot, him and I.

As a child, Nina had also experienced community support when the Catholic church gave her family food and clothing; "the Catholic church tries to take care of at least their own people of their religion," she said. So Nina knew that, beyond her immediate family, a support structure existed that, at the very least, would not let her starve. As an adult, she would turn to this support structure:

For a long, long time I thought I didn't need anybody or anything else really. I could handle all the problems myself. And I know this is not supposed to be a religious conversation, but this really hit me profoundly. Like I said, I thought I could handle [everything], you know, [that] I didn't need anybody else—God, the Lord, or whoever you want to call it—as the person I went to.

One night, she went to a group that dabbled in "white magic," and was frightened by the experience. "I don't know if you'd call it evil or the devil—I know this is gonna sound crazy, but this is the truth. I could see like, I mean not really see it as in 'Here it is,' but I sensed it and in my mind at least I saw it." She felt "something that wasn't good," she said. "I knew that it wasn't good. I could feel it. . . . I was scared. I was scared. I really felt like the devil was really right there. . . . And it was like, that was when I had hit the bottom and I knew that there really wasn't any place but up."

And so I called on, I called the Catholic church up there and I had not gone to the church ever since we had been here. And I talked to Father X, and he gave me the number of a priest who was involved with having people work with the occult. And I went to a meeting, and it was like—like I said, ever since I had gotten away from the home I might go to church once in great while to have the kids baptized, or something like that, but it was just a facade I guess.

But, I went to that service, and it was a healing service, and they said, "Will somebody bring up the offerings?" And there must have been a thousand people in that church, it was like, "I'll do it." [I said to myself], "You said that Nina? I can't believe you said that!" So I did, I took up the offerings, which is the host and the wine, and then they needed people to—I mean it was really a healing service, you know how the priest lays the hands on. I always thought it was a bunch of bull! I'm still like, "Nah, this is not really true." And then they said they needed catchers, which meant, you know, that's what they were doing, they were catching people when they fell. I was so surprised I said I'd do it! I said, "Will you say that again? I can't believe it, it was really crazy!" So, I'm still, "No, this isn't really true." And as many people as I caught, I kept telling myself, "They're just doing that to make everybody think—and I'm telling myself, because I was the last person [to believe in it]." I thought, "I don't need a catcher, because I thought there was no way, no way!" The priest put his hands on me, and I just went like pshew, and I said to myself, "You will not go down, you will not go down."

And so now, I mean I know that a lot of it is just a farce, but I was so surprised that it made me realize that there is somebody who does care for us, and as many times as we do things that we are not supposed to do, and say things and all kinds of things, that no matter what, he forgives us. And sometimes I can't imagine why he keeps forgiving us, but he does. But it was really weird, because I kept saying, "There ain't no way you're going to go down." I could have died. And I laid on the floor!

So then I started going to church and I would go to church, and I don't know what religion you are, but there's mass in the Catholic church every day. So I started going to church in the morning and one day the priest came after mass—I was standing in back of the church, and he came and he spoke to me, and I started crying. And it was like everything just washed away, all the things just washed away, and he listens, he listens, and he doesn't tell you you're a terrible person or an angelic person. . . . He treats you like a person—he doesn't try to be "holy holy" because he is in his own way. He's had a great effect on everybody in this family. And I would say everybody in this community. He's a really good person. You know, if he doesn't go to heaven, none of us do.

Nina's solution would not work for everyone, but it serves as a model of the kind of support that might be helpful to other women. The church was a familiar, trusted community that was accessible and readily available. As a child, Nina had seen it give support and succor to her family, so it was easy and natural for her to turn to the same source; as she said, "I think my dad being a very religious person did, in the long run, affect me." She felt comfortable with the people in the church, perhaps in part because the priest was not a professional worker handing out advice, but was a man with his own problems—like her, he came from a large, poor family, and he had a drinking problem. He wasn't "holy holy," Nina said. Because they had so much in common, they developed a genuine friendship, and she went along with him to AA meetings, encouraged him to stick with the program, and chided him when he worked himself to exhaustion. As well as making her feel comfortable with him, the priest's problem allowed her to be a caregiver as well as receiver, and the reciprocity in their relationship meant that she was empowered as well as supported.

Nina had sources of self-esteem and stability that were not available to Laura. Her work was intrinsically meaningful, and she enjoyed it. Her religion gave her comfort, and her relationship with the priest was rewarding. She had lived in the same community all her life, and was well-known and well-liked. She knew she was making a difference in the life of her foster son, and she had a caring, loving relationship with her husband.

Are these women who were abused victims or survivors? Both. The long-term effects of child sexual abuse include fear, anxiety, depression, anger, hostility, poor self-esteem, self-sabotage, and difficulty with close relationships; Laura had suffered more of these consequences[29] than the other two women who were sexually abused, but they too had been depressed, and Liz was still very anxious. Sonya, though not, as far as I know, abused, was depressed, and she, Laura, and Liz were also dealing with teenage children with quite serious problems.

Laura and Ruth had tried to follow the American dream and get ahead; both women had taken training to increase their marketable skills. But they lacked the tools that would have helped them evaluate schools and scrutinize their claims, and both were vulnerable to the false promises made by proprietary schools that guaranteed their graduates fat paychecks and fascinating careers—even without a high school diploma. Ruth, with no diploma, was enrolled in a school that claimed it would train her to be a medical secretary but offered no computer or typing training. And the New York Career Institute had enrolled Laura for an officework course, not GED training, which would have given her a better chance of success; a year later, the school was still collecting its money, and Laura was still paying off her debt.

Had appropriate social supports been available, these women's efforts might have brought them more rewards. What stood between them and achieving their goal was neither lack of initiative nor laziness; it was lack of accessible information and guidance about community resources such as free GED-training programs, career advice centers, and labor unions. All these supportive structures are available but they are not easily accessible; very few women knew, for example, that there were centers where they could be tutored for a GED at no cost. Laura, in particular, needed warm, supportive counseling, not the hostile challenge that was thrown at her by the dismissive welfare man when he threatened to cut off her payments. She went to school, but no one helped her decide on appropriate training. Instead she made her decision partly to defy the man and prove her worth. Accessible community supports and counseling would have helped both Ruth and Laura make informed life decisions. And universal health benefits and a higher minimum wage—both of which I will return to in the last chapter—would have given them a wider margin of safety and security so they could make important life decisions free from the threat of destitution.

Laura, Sonya, and Liz had lived much of their lives isolated from mainstream institutions. They had little experience of school, having dropped out in middle school or at the beginning of high school, and little experience of work, with its access to social networks. After twenty years at home, Liz had worked in her first job three months before she could look people in the eye. "It was because I was heavy. I was afraid to go out or meet new people. After I got out, it didn't matter how big I was. It was just, I enjoy people."

Now, having left her isolation, Liz was determined not to return. "I'd be totally depressed. It's taken me so long to get any, I don't know, self-esteem, confidence, just to look someone in the eye. When I had broken my ankle, I was out of work three months. I was in one room for three months actually. When I went back to work, it was like starting all over again. I couldn't look people in the eye. I didn't have that—I can't explain it to you—not being able to look somebody in the face when you're talking to them. I don't know what it was, I just didn't have it in me. I didn't have enough courage to look up and see who I was speaking to. But I noticed after I went back to work after having my broken ankle that I had to go through all that again. It was like knots in my chest. I could talk to them but I just couldn't look at them. I don't want to crawl back into a shell."

Laura had also been isolated during the many years she was on welfare. Her job had boosted her self-esteem, and although, right now, she was unhappy, still, she knew it was better to work. If she did not work, she said, "I would probably have more pity on myself. I would probably sit in this apartment, and get more depressed."

We have come full circle, back to work. Work had brought positive change into these women's lives. But work in itself was not positive unless it was "good" work in a job that was rewarding or, if not rewarding, at least sufficiently well paid that it would lift women and their families out of poverty. Work could be empowering, but it could also be exploitative. Women who were vulnerable were easy targets for the worst forms of exploitation. These women were vulnerable, not because they had exploited the system as the poor are sometimes accused of doing—if anything, they knew too little about the system. They were vulnerable because they were the flotsam and jetsam of a social and economic system that rewards the rich and punishes the poor, that sees them as faceless numbers, not individual sisters and brothers struggling for a small piece of the pie. They were vulnerable because we see them, not as "us," but as "them." To borrow the words of Michael Harrington, that most eloquent of spokespersons for the poor: "Our eyes are so totally controlled by the stereotypes in our minds that we cannot see what we see."[30]

9.
Dropping
O u t

My personal opinion now, being an adult, is that I saw escape. I got married to
escape. Also I had been raped in the neighborhood, and the boy that had raped
me was giving me a [hard time]. So, to get married I was moving out of state,
and it was getting me away from everything. He threatened to kill my mother.
He shot me, so I knew what it was like, but it only skimmed my leg. So I think
that's why I left school. Then I didn't think so, but now I do.

—Sally

Now, as adults, with a perspective that was not available to them as teenagers, three in every four of the women I spoke with, regardless of their education level, wished it was higher; women who quit high school wished they had graduated, women who graduated from high school wished they had gone on to college, and the six women who graduated from college wished they had done a different degree. What prevented these women from getting the education they now wished they had? A simple rule gives us the answer. It is this: the further the women's families were from the urgencies of material need, the more education they attained. This rule operated at every educational stage. But because the dynamics and the consequences were a little different as the urgency of material need receded, I begin by discussing why women dropped out of high school. In the next chapter, I will address why high school and college graduates left school when they did—at a level of attainment they now wish was higher.

Causes of Dropout

Many sociologists of education look for the "causes" of dropout in characteristics of individuals or families. At the individual level, they find that students who fail, who have below average reading and math skills, or who are held back in a grade are more likely to drop out; so too are students who avoid extracurricular activities, are truant, or have a history of problems with the school authority structure.[1] Females who become mothers, or males who have families to support, are also more likely to drop out.[2] At the family level, parents who set rules for their children, expect them to achieve, help them with homework, and monitor their school progress all reduce the probability that they will drop out. The probability is increased, however, for children who come from one-parent families, from families that move frequently, and from families in which parents have not themselves completed a high school diploma.[3]

As state institutions, schools are (or should be) amenable to intervention, thus many sociologists choose to concentrate their research attention on schools and how they are organized, rather than on individuals and families. One of the first to do this was the sociologist Arthur Stinchcombe; in the 1960s, Stinchcombe argued that even rebellious students would persist in school if they saw some future benefit:

> High school students can be motivated to perform by paying them in the realistic coin of adult advantages. Except, perhaps, for pathological cases, any student can be made to conform if the school can realistically promise something valuable to him as a reward for working hard. But for a large part of the population, especially the adolescents who will enter the male working class or the female candidates for early marriage, the school has nothing to promise.[4]

Since then, researchers have found high dropout rates for schools that are large and anonymous or are located in neighborhoods with high rates of poverty, crime, and unemployment, and also for schools whose teachers emphasize control rather than teaching, whose teachers and school administrators are not cooperative, and whose rules are perceived by students to be unfair. Schools with these characteristics are less likely to hold students' interest, foster their motivation, and prevent them from dropping out.

Whatever the role of all these factors, however, they pale in comparison to one other: students are more likely to drop out when their parents are low in socioeconomic status or poor. In 2000, for example, for children from low-income families, the dropout rate was 10 percent, for middle-income families, it was 5.2 percent, but for high-income families, it was a minuscule 1.6 percent.[5] This strong relationship between income and educational attainment was just as sturdy in the 1950s and 1960s; among the twenty-three women I interviewed who dropped out, eighteen were either poor or short of money as children, and all twenty-three were daughters of manual laborers, men in the lowest-paid sector of the workforce.

Dropping Out: Reasons and Causes

When women and men who have dropped out are asked to give their reasons, they rarely cite the causes sociologists believe to be important. They never, for example, say they dropped out because their school was badly organized, or because their family was low in social status. Instead, they say they dropped out because they didn't like school, or because they were pregnant. As Marx observed, social class works behind our backs to foreordain certain choices; thus, in the general population, working-class women "choose" to become nurses, while middle-class women "choose" to become pediatricians. Max Weber made a similar point; our conscious motives, he stated, "may conceal the various motives and repressions which constitute the real driving force" of our actions. Thus, (subjective) reasons may not be the same as (objective) causes— and where social class is concerned, this is the rule, not the exception.

Reasons are important in their own right because they tell us how individual women and men construct meaning in their worlds. But they are also important because they tell us how the material conditions and "unconscious motives" that are the true causes come to be translated within individual consciousness into reasons, and, ultimately, intentions and actions. In the following section, therefore, I will explore women's stated reasons for dropping out and discuss them in the context of what researchers believe to be its objective "causes." As we will see, both gender and class shaped women's educational choices—choices that were made for different conscious reasons, but reflected similar underlying causes.

Reasons: Bad Times, Boredom, and Babies

Most of the women said they quit school for one of the following reasons: they were failing and had been held back, they wanted to get away from home, they became pregnant or got married, they wanted to avoid racial conflict in the schools, or they wanted, simply, to get on with "real" life.

Doreen dropped out because she was failing and had been held back—one of the most common reasons. "Tenth grade!" she snorted with disgust when I asked her why she left school.

I had failed two years and I was back into my third year and just didn't go. They weren't getting me out of there. I was just sitting there. I was just telling the kids about this the other day. They say things about school and I said, "Yeah, how would you like to be in school and have to go to a special reading class where there's maybe ten desks in there, the room is real little like the bathroom, and people walk by and laugh at you because you're [in] the special class?" And they still didn't do nothing.

I left elementary school a third grade reader. I went to Suburban, and they just pushed me through. You know, when you start out in one seat in a classroom and you're not doing nothing wrong, and next thing you know you're pushed all the way back in the corner, you know, [you wonder], "Why am I moved back here?"

I mean I can do my work, but I just couldn't keep up. I'm not stupid or nothing, but it's just that when the teacher would call on me to read, she would have to help me, or maybe she'd get disgusted because it was taking me so long.

[At the end of junior high], they called me to the office and told me I couldn't graduate off the stage because of my reading, and they sent me home. And then I went to Parkley [High]. I started over again. I did fine in science, all them classes. They had no problem with me taking any courses over there. I took typing, I took home economics, I took cars, and I took mechanical drawing, and I took wood shop. They had no problem putting me in no classes.

Laura left school for the same reason as Doreen. "I wasn't getting the proper education I should have been getting," she said. "I got very frustrated. I didn't get no special help. I'm the type person that I get very discouraged easy. I don't give myself enough credit where I should have credit. And I just [say], 'Forget it. I can't do it.'"

Carol left because her learning problems earned her the wrath of her teachers. She was terrorized—thrown in the cloakroom, hit, and castigated. "I had a horrible time with math," she said, "and [the nun] would have little flash cards, and I still, I couldn't do it. I'd get hit. You couldn't say one word. . . . The discipline was tough. If you were a child that was struggling, it was because you didn't study, so they would hit you. Hit you! That was the answer. [They'd say], 'Go sit in the back of the classroom.' 'Why don't you know your facts?' 'Why can't you do this?' 'You can't do it because you didn't study.' 'You were not listening.'"

If asked at the time why they quit school, Doreen, Laura, and Carol would probably have said, quite honestly, that they chose to drop out because they didn't like school. We can see, however—as could they, as adults—that their choices were not true choices. Laura now saw her dropout in terms of the school's failure, not her own; she observed that the only person in her entire family to graduate from high school attended a school in the suburbs not the city. "To be honest with you," she said, "city schools do not teach the children. Your teachers are petrified. They are petrified now even more so. But even when I was in school, the teachers had no control over us students at all. We ran the school. Same way now." Because it was the "same way now," Laura had rented an apartment in the suburbs and sent her children to school there, hoping they would avoid feeling, as she had, "very frustrated" and "very discouraged."

As an adult, Carol also blamed the school; she had no regrets about leaving school because she recognized that she had no choice. "Now that I have kids," she said, "and I worked with kids, and with my own children. [I know] I didn't need to repeat the grade. I needed a little help." Then, however, she was tired of being shouted at, hit by the nuns, and made to stand in the back of the room. She had no regrets about leaving school but regretted that school was such a bad experience. "I guess I wish it was different for me," she said. "I wish it would have been different. . . . I would be depressed if I still felt the same about myself as I did in school. I would be very depressed. I can't imagine growing up and being an adult who thinks that you're stupid." "Stupid" was still a scary word for Carol; she said she didn't want to "sit [t]here and feel stupid talking" on the job, for example, and she liked to be well prepared "because if a person comes back and if they have a question for you and you don't have the answer to it, it makes you feel kind of stupid." And, when she left school, she knew she "wasn't stupid, just wasn't real bright."

Typically, at the time, Doreen's reason for leaving school was an individual one; she was tired of failing, tired of humiliation, and tired of being laughed at. Now, however, she too blamed the school, and because she believed that little had improved since she was a student, she had enrolled her own children in the suburbs, not in their local city school. Their illegal status meant she had to drive them to school and pick them up each day, which was a major inconvenience, but she was determined to protect them from a school experience like her own. Rhetorically, she asked the children, "How would you like to be in school and have to go to a special reading class where there's maybe ten desks in there, the room is real little like the bathroom, and people walk by and laugh at you because you're [in] the special class?"

For a number of the women, pregnancy was the reason for dropping out, and sometimes—when it caused them to be expelled from school against their wishes—it was also the objective cause. In the middle to late sixties, the development of the contraceptive pill began to loosen up middle-class sexual attitudes, but the sexual revolution stopped short of the working-class neighborhoods in which these young women lived; there, pill or no pill, sex was still forbidden fruit, to be indulged in when necessary, but not talked about—much less enjoyed. Fewer than half the women remembered either of their parents ever mentioning sex, much less pregnancy; in fact, the topic was so taboo that several women laughed out loud when I asked them about it. "Oh God! Nobody talked about it back then," they said. Nice working-class girls didn't go "all the way," and if they did, they disappeared for a few months or were hastily married.[6] Pregnancy was so shameful that until the seventies, girls who became pregnant were required to leave their regular high schools.

Some of the women spoke in wonder about their parents' attitudes toward sex; Nina's mother called her a whore and screamed at her when she asked about a condom she had found on the street. Judy said her mother never so much as mentioned sex or pregnancy until Judy herself became pregnant. Only then could her mother talk about her own pregnancy. Judy recalled her story. "She was, like, about six months pregnant. She was laying on the couch, and her mother was sitting in front of her and [her mother] felt this funny kick, and that's when she found out. [My mother] said she couldn't [tell her]. . . . [I]t makes you stop and think, 'Well, no wonder my mother was like that. Because my grandmother never talked about that.'"

The silence around sex was not confined to working-class families. Margaret, a middle-class daughter, recalled the first time her father mentioned pregnancy. "Pregnancy!" she said. "My father mentioned it on the way to college. He said, 'If you ever get pregnant, don't come home.' That was pretty amazing. I didn't have a boyfriend, nobody serious. That was such a terrible time, about abortions and stuff. It had a very big effect on me. I moved out of the dorm because there were so many abortions." By the late sixties, when Margaret was in school, most states had legalized abortion,[7] but, as Kristin Luker points out in her history of the abortion reform movement, choice was less enthusiastically embraced by working-class women.[8] Even among middle-class women, attitudes were ambivalent; in 1965, for example, around 60 percent of respondents in a national survey thought abortion was acceptable when the reason was rape or risk to maternal health, but only 20 percent were in favor when the reason was family limitation, financial problems, unmarried status, or fetal defect. Clearly then, Margaret's reaction to the abortions among her college roommates was not unusual; abortion was legal, but it was still unacceptable to many women—even those who could afford it.

Although sex was unmentionable and nice girls didn't *do it*, according to government statistics, 69 percent of women who married between 1965 and 1975 (when most of these women married) had already had first intercourse. Clearly then, a lot of nice girls *did* do it.[9] A school for pregnant girls was established in 1966, but white girls rarely attended. Childbearing outside marriage was less acceptable for them than for black girls; between 1965 and 1974, a mere 12 percent of births to white women aged between fifteen and thirty-four were outside marriage compared with 56 percent of births to black women in the same age group.[10] Not that white girls waited until their wedding day to have sex—white and black girls had about the same rate of premarital conceptions, but, for white girls, a "shotgun" marriage more often came between conception and birth. Thus, 18 percent of first births to white women between 1965 and 1975 were the result of premarital conception but post-marital delivery, but for black women a much larger percentage—56 percent—were born as well as conceived premaritally.[11]

For all these reasons, when Rachael found herself pregnant, there was not much choice about what happened next; for her, pregnancy was definitely the cause of dropping out:

> I was going to go back to school in September, but back then they wouldn't allow you to go to school pregnant. I could have went to school. I was a straight A student when I got to ninth grade, but they wouldn't let me in. I could have lied, I guess. I have a sister-in-law now, who, she was in her last year of school, and they didn't know she was pregnant, they had no idea. With me it would have been a little different because I was so thin.

It was also the cause for Cora:

> I got pregnant in '71. It was very rare when I was growing up. If you got pregnant, you tried to hide it. It was such a bad thing, then, you know. I estimated that I was only about a month pregnant when I graduated [from middle school]. In September

I wasn't showing, but if I would have went, they would have made me leave school and I would have been embarrassed and I didn't want to go through that. I called, I did call, because I wanted to finish my education. But when they told me I had to go to school Number One, it was like, in the boondocks. It was a school for pregnant women. I can't even remember where it was, but it wasn't in a very good neighborhood. And I would have had to catch buses to get there, and I thought, "I'm not going to put myself through this."

Greta wasn't pregnant but even marriage broke the school rules:

They wouldn't let me back in school. They told me I was a bad influence on the girls, I knew too much. They knew more than me! And even though [my husband] went to Vietnam, they still wouldn't let me back in school. That wasn't fair, because I wasn't pregnant. So I figured I should be able to go back to school, but they said once you get married, you cannot be in school. See now they do it, but then they didn't. So I had to quit school.

One woman, Valerie, was able to stay in school because her parents could afford to send her to a Catholic home for pregnant girls, where she completed high school. But for daughters of parents with no cash to spare—and that was most of the women's parents—pregnancy meant dropping out.[12]

These young women liked school and left because they had to, not because they wanted to. For Liz and Sally, however, it was different—becoming pregnant offered a welcome escape. Escape from her abusive home was Liz's goal. "It was easier to get pregnant and get out of the home," she said. For Sally, it was escape from a violent neighborhood and an alcoholic father who was emotionally abusive and cold. She described his "negativity" toward her: "I remember coming home with an honor roll report card and he said, 'That can't compare to your sister's.' And he said I would never succeed." Later, when Sally and her two children were on the edge of starvation, searching dumpsters for food, she went to her family for help. "They were very desperate times," she said, "when I was on my own. That's when I learned not to depend on family. I went to my family for bread and milk, and [my father] said, 'You made your bed, now lie in it.'" For Liz and Sally, then, pregnancy may have been the reason they dropped out, but misery was the true cause.

Misery was the cause for Phyllis, too, but misery at school, not at home. A confident, outgoing woman, Phyllis laughed ruefully as she recalled the shy, nervous, young girl she used to be, unable to cope with a rowdy, intimidating school environment:

I didn't particularly care for school. People find this hard to believe, but when I was young, I was a very shy person, and if the teacher called on me in school, I wanted to throw up. You know what I mean? I was smart, and I did real good in elementary school. And then when I went to [middle school], it was like being in another country almost. It was so wild. It was, it's not a very nice neighborhood.

I was so distraught about going up there that I actually spent the whole summer . . . [being] sick. I had the shingles, and they said it was from stress. They asked my mother what was going on in my life and she said, "Well, she's going to junior high." I started school in September and I found out that I was pregnant with [my daughter] and I quit. That was the excuse I needed.

Pregnancy was one of the ways gender interacted with class to the detriment of these young working-class girls' schooling. There were others. Daughters whose mothers worked were often responsible for a heavy load of domestic and childcare duties, and among the women I interviewed, this particular consequence of gender was limited to working-class women. Amanda, for example, took over dinner duty when her mother started working the graveyard shift in a local factory. Then, when Amanda was in the twelfth grade, and her mother became seriously ill, she managed all the household work. "I stayed home," she said, "plus, you know . . . did the washing and ironing and cleaned. And made sure [my brothers and sisters] went to school." Her brothers were still grateful for her hard work and devotion—but Amanda never did finish high school.

Amanda's situation was not unusual. Regardless of how old the sons in a family were, the domestic burden fell on the eldest daughter still at home—in fact, according to Nina, her older sister dropped out of school, took a job, and left home for the sole purpose of avoiding this burden of domesticity. As soon as her sister escaped, the domestic torch was passed to Nina. When Marlene's mother worked, Marlene "got stuck with everything," she said. "I was the second, but the oldest was a boy. It was my brother Jack, then myself, then my sister Peggy, and then we had a younger brother Billy who I just about raised. I had to come right home from school and fix the dinner and laundry and clean and you know, so I've always done it." And Helen, whose father dubbed her his "little mother," still resented the fact that she missed out on after-school activities because she had to rush home each day to care for her younger siblings; she now believed that one of the reasons she got married in her senior year was to escape these burdensome domestic and childcare responsibilities.[13]

Race: A Reason or a Cause?

Phyllis had dreaded going to high school because it was not in a "very nice" neighborhood, and Cora didn't want to attend the school for pregnant girls because it was in the boondocks. Both women's feelings, I suspect, reflect a prevailing anxiety among whites living in inner-city Baltimore in the sixties. Baltimore was one of the first school systems in the "border" states—states that bordered the South—to integrate its schools. According to a 1967 Johns Hopkins study, however, desegregation never fully extended to elementary schools. The reason was that elementary schools are neighborhood schools, and neighborhoods in Baltimore were then (and still are) highly segregated; thus in 1955, when desegregation got under way, 80 percent of white elementary students attended a segregated school, and even ten years later, this proportion was still 60 percent.

Between 1960 and 1966, 12 percent of whites left the city; according to the Hopkins report, "whites who can afford the extra expense of moving into surrounding counties do so, and . . . new white immigrants enter the suburbs. These are families of better economic standing." Families of "better economic standing" also sent their children to private schools, with the result that, as the report observed, "the economically disadvantaged families are the ones whose children will be attending the city school system. They are the Negroes and whites whose socioeconomic status is so low that it prevents them escaping the worsening conditions of city living. The problem is one of a declining level of education for both the Negroes and whites remaining in the city school system."[14]

Because of busing, desegregation was more successful in senior high schools. This meant that both poor white and poor black students attended segregated neighborhood elementary schools, then moved on to desegregated senior highs—and they made this transition during a developmental period that is stressful, and in an historical period that was unusually tense.

For most of the sixties, Baltimore was a powder keg waiting to explode. As affluent whites continued to flee the city, black inner-city residents were increasingly asserting their rights, demanding better housing, fair prices, higher standards of public health, and freedom from discrimination. Finally, with the assassination of Dr. King on April 6, 1968, the city's black neighborhoods erupted in riots. In response, Governor Agnew placed the National Guard and city police on alert, and declared a curfew. Then, following reports of window smashing, looting, sniping, and fires, he called in 5,000 federal troops and declared a state of civil emergency. Not surprisingly, given this dramatic reaction, "some white people believed that a black invasion of white neighborhoods was imminent . . . [and] radio talk shows during and after the disorders were full of panicky fears that they were about to hit the suburbs."[15] A report compiled for the American Friends Service Committee after the riots noted that "the disorders express black rage against white power. In the post-disorder period, the rage still lives and so does its threat against white security in the status quo."[16] (Ironically, the whites who lived closest to the tumult had the least power to effect change.) Julie, now a teacher, gives us her impressions of these turbulent times:

> Things really changed then. It was a very difficult time. It was a very difficult time to be in school, to be a student, to be a youngster. Prior to that period, when I was in

elementary school, there was not a child of any other race except the white in my elementary school. When I went to junior high school, [it] drew from a little bit broader area, which is typical. Then we began to see, "Oh my goodness, there are people who don't look like us!" That was the very first time. When I went to high school, that was the year that they made the shift and decided to integrate fully. And I had a tremendously large high school class; there were 1,350 girls in the freshman class. They could not fit all of us in the building, so we had to go in shifts. We went from eight in the morning till twelve-thirty. You only got your academic subjects; there was none of this extra foolishness. You had to go extra time one afternoon to take physical education because that was a requirement. They couldn't squeeze it in.

On top of all that, we had about a sixty-forty racial mix of 60 percent white to 40 percent black, which was a tremendously different situation than any of us had ever been in, for both races. In the girls' school that I was in, which was City Senior High School, it turned out to be a real positive experience. I wouldn't have given it up for anything. It's unfortunate that we were on shifts and that there were so many of us, because had we been able to be there the whole day, have regular subjects, have the after-school kinds of activities that you normally do, there would have been more interaction and probably the transition would have been smoother.

Unfortunately it was not smooth. The boys' school was located across the street. They had more trouble than you can shake a stick at, and there were instances where gangs of kids would literally go after an individual kid. It was a very terrifying experience for many students, because we had miles to go to get home, and so you had to really rely on your wits in order to get from place to place. In our environment in the girls' school, things went fairly smoothly. There were individuals, I'm sure, [who] had altercations, but that wasn't anywhere near as blown out of proportion as it was for the boys. The boys found it much more difficult to make the adjustment. They were a lot more physical. There was more conflict.

It happened a lot. It was a real thing to overcome during those years when you were supposed to be buckling down and studying. It was [difficult] for everyone. [We are talking about] 1963 to 1967. So it was during the period when Martin Luther King was coming out, and Malcolm X was coming, and I mean all these [things] were happening. We were sitting in front of the television screen trying to find out what was happening in our world every night. It was a real dynamic time, in the Kennedy era, and [then] the assassination, and it was just a real rough period for us historically. It was a time when a lot of students were trying to keep grades up, and trying to do the regular adolescent kinds of things, the adjusting that you have to do during the adolescent period, and I just think that all made it more difficult. There were riots here in the city during that time.

An alternative perspective, this time from the other side of the racial divide, comes from the experience of Assata Shakur, who was at the time the only black girl in her classes at the school she attended in Queens. In her book, *Assata*,[17] she describes her school experience:

> My relationship with white kids deteriorated even more. They made it pretty evident that they didn't care too much for me, and I made it clear right back that I didn't care for them. The thing I most disliked about them was their assumptions about me. For one thing, they automatically assumed I was stupid, and they would really act surprised when I showed I had some brains. One of the biggest fights I had was when this kid in my class couldn't find some pen his father had given him and accused me of stealing it.

Assata was so angry she "jumped" the boy and shocked her teachers. No doubt, there were many stories just like hers in black communities in Baltimore during those years, just as there were in white communities, as teenagers faced each other in mutual distrust, fear, anxiety, and anger.

Were these difficulties a cause of dropping out? I suspect not, although they were, without a doubt, a reason. Reports at the time indicate that even whites living at a "safe" middle-class distance in the suburbs felt threatened; presumably whites in the city felt even more threatened, because they were more vulnerable. In this atmosphere, everyday conflicts in schools must have taken on a menacing aspect that, for students who would prefer not to be in school anyway, provided a good reason to quit. Thus it was women like Terry, who was already experiencing academic difficulties in school, who said racial problems were the reason she left:

> They combined schools. . . .They were putting the black children into schools with the white children. The school was just out of control. And I didn't agree with it. See . . . I had an incident, I had an incident with a black boy and I got suspended from school on account of I defended myself. He put his hands on me. And he tried to pull me in the bathroom with a knife, and I pushed him down the steps. He broke his arm, and I got suspended from school. So . . . we went to the principal, and he gave my mom a hard time. So she said when I turned sixteen, she was going to sign me out of school. So that's why I quit.

For some women, the reason for dropping out was simple—they just couldn't see the point of more schooling and were anxious to get on with "real" life. As Stinchcombe noted, many schools were unable to show students why education was worthwhile. This was true for Darlene. She "couldn't stand" school so at the end of junior year, she just never went back. "I wouldn't know any more now if I'd stayed," she said. Who could argue? Of course, what Darlene could not know, as a young girl of sixteen or so, was that part of the reason for staying in school an extra year was to gain a credential that would prove useful later in life.

If schools were not effectively motivating students such as Darlene, it was up to parents, but not all parents were equipped to do so. The fathers of all but one of the twenty-three women who dropped out and the mothers of all but three had not themselves completed high school, and many of these women and men—seventeen fathers and fifteen mothers—had dropped out having completed no more than ninth grade; these parents, with little personal experience of the education system, nor of the benefits of an education, were not in a good position to convince their children of the need for a high school diploma. Judy said, "My mom always used to say, 'You need to go to school.' But she never told me why I needed to go to school. That was the strangest part." Harriet said, "Most of my family didn't finish and so I said: 'I guess I won't either.' I guess I didn't have the right attitude. I liked it but I didn't have a positive attitude toward it. I went to work." And as soon as their children moved beyond their own education level—which was sometimes as low as fourth grade—it was difficult for many parents to help with homework or take a detailed interest in what their children were doing in school. Monica's father, for example, always said, "I didn't go to school. I didn't finish school, so I can't help you do anything."

Not only were these parents strangers to the world of education, they were also poor. Being poor meant they were unable to buy their daughters the records they listened to on the Top 40, or the clothes and makeup they saw in glossy magazines like *Seventeen*. Most young girls craved these things, and were encouraged in their craving by a seductive and increasingly powerful advertising industry, but working-class girls had to work if they were to enter this magical world, dangled so deliciously before them. As Sheila said, "My parents were low income, so I had to work so I could have." She had been able to earn money working in her high school office and so was able to buy her "things" and also graduate; many other young women, however, had to choose between working for "things" and working for school.

The GED: A Second Chance

Luckily, these teenage decisions need not have life-long consequences. The General Equivalency Diploma (GED) gives women and men who drop out a second chance to gain a high school diploma, and seven of the women I interviewed had taken advantage of this opportunity. Others had tried, or still intended to. Terry, for example, had signed up for GED classes at a commercial computer school; unfortunately, she lost her tuition when the school went broke. Anna planned on taking the test as soon as she felt ready; she worked in a school cafeteria, and one of the teachers was willing to help. Sally even attended a regular high school for a year. "I sat there with all the kids," she said. Finding a better job was a strong motivation to gain the diploma, but so was a desire for personal satisfaction. Cheryl, for example, "just want[ed] to have it"; for

Cheryl and a number of other women, schooling was unfinished business, an old wound that had never quite healed. They were reminded of it every time they missed out on a job or were unable to help their children on a homework project. In fact, as we saw in the last chapter, it was this strong desire for more education that made many women vulnerable to exploitation by commercial schools.

The GED doubled in popularity during the first six years of the 1990s, going from almost 5 percent of graduating students in 1990 to almost 10 percent in 1996; during the same period, the percentage of people holding regular diplomas decreased by the same amount, suggesting that for some people it is a more attractive option than a regular high school diploma. This was true for Marlene; she enjoyed learning, but not being told what to do. The GED was perfect, because it allowed her to study at her own pace in her own way. For the women who had it, the diploma brought obvious benefits. Marlene, for example, was able to become a licensed day-care provider, and Wanda was able to apply for training as a licensed practical nurse. But perhaps the most dramatic example of its benefits was Lisa, who not only passed the GED, but used it as a springboard for vocational training and a nursing degree.

Lisa

We talked in Lisa's dining room, a warm, inviting room painted a soft peach, with family pictures on the mantle and a dog curled up by the fire. At first blush, Lisa seemed too young to be the mother of two teenage girls, but it soon became obvious that underneath the pretty, youthful surface was a mature, thoughtful woman who was planning her life with deliberation and parenting her daughters with skill. Her husband worked at home, she explained, but he was out and her daughters were in school, so we had the house to ourselves. I started off by saying I was interested in women's work experiences. "Oh boy!" Lisa said. "We'll have fun then. Because I'm in the middle of trying to change professions."

Lisa had "always wanted to do something," and both her parents had wanted her to go to college and have "an important job." She had hoped to become a nurse, but, finding herself pregnant in the eleventh grade, she dropped out to get married; eight weeks after her daughter's birth, she took a job as a clerk for the state government. During this time, her mother gave her all the help and support she could hope for. She helped out financially—for example, she used to look in the young couple's refrigerator and then buy them whatever grocery items they needed—and she took care of the baby while Lisa worked. "I think that's probably why Becky turned out so well," Lisa said with a wry smile.

When her daughter was about eighteen months old, Lisa quit her job, and stayed home for about six years, doing home day care for the last two:

The first summer, I had six children including my own. I mean I love kids. I love to do that sort of thing, but that's when I said, "No!" It was too much. Because sometimes the first one was dropped off at 6:30 A.M. and the last one wouldn't leave until 7 P.M. They were with me all day! It was pretty hectic. And then my own children were beginning to resent it because it was summertime and we couldn't go anywhere. It wasn't really worth it.

Being with children all the time began to pall, and Lisa felt ready for a challenge, so she took the GED test, then began evening classes at a commercial vocational school, training as a dental technician. "I wanted to be a nurse," she said, "but I wasn't sure—I wasn't self-confident that I would be able to do it because I'd been out of school so long." So she finished the dental technician's training, and took a job with a children's dentist for a time, until she felt ready to go to community college to train as a nurse at last. "When I saw that I could," she said, "I was gaining in self-confidence and I saw I could do the study. And it was very easy. And the grades came very easy for me. So I thought, 'Just go for it.'"

By the time we talked, Lisa had fulfilled all her requirements, and had just started the first actual nursing course. The training would consist of two days a week and two weekends a month. While she trained, she planned on staying in her dental technician job part time—even though she didn't like it. "I have to say that I'm not too satisfied," she said, "because of the fact that you don't move on. There's no way to advance. It's just a repetitive job." Her dissatisfaction was an added motivation, as was her boss's rudeness to her and his disgruntled, disappointed attitude to his work. "A lot of dentists are burned out," she said. "Like the man I work for. He's an older man and there are days when I can tell—I could say, 'You just hate this, don't you?' . . . He is known in the office as the grouch, and other names."

Lisa's husband was supportive, and because he was self-employed, his job was flexible. "He gets the children off to school," she said. "It's almost like we have reversed roles. My job is not flexible as far as just leaving when I want to, but he can, so if something would happen, if one of the girls would get sick, he can go and pick them up. We've worked it out. Now if he had a job where he had to work [for someone else], I don't know how we would have managed—you know, if he had to punch time clocks."

In many ways, Lisa is a perfect example of why women need a second chance at education. At first, she had enjoyed being a full-time mother, but she soon realized she also needed a rewarding career. "I was young," she said. "I was just content being home. I think as I got older—around the time Maggie was born—I thought, 'I don't want to keep staying home and having children.' . . . I enjoyed it very much but I didn't realize, because I was so young, the amount of time that's required—the fact that, pretty much, your life goes on hold. I guess I didn't stop and think about that." Now, like many other women, she cared more about work, and she was ready to invest her considerable energies in education and job training. "When I was young," she said, "I know I looked at it as a chore. Now it's something I want to do." But now, too, she knew it was hard to do it her way, and she hoped her daughters would choose an easier route. "I would like them to pursue careers before they start families," she said. "Simply for the fact that they'd always have something to fall back on that they could take care of themselves, not having to rely on a man to take care of them. I worry about Becky . . . I want her to go to college, I really do, before she gets into any type of serious relationship. I don't want her to follow in my footsteps. I want her to go to school, go to college, because she is intelligent. She gets very good grades. I don't want her to throw it away. . . . I'm really just so worried that . . . [her] grades will slip and that when it's time to go to college, when she's out of high school, she'll say, 'We've decided to get married!' You know, that sort of thing I'm worried about."

If doing the GED was so easy for Lisa and its benefits so tangible, why did so few women take advantage of the second chance it offered? There were several reasons. As a child and as an adult, Lisa had a number of advantages many other women lacked. Her father was a skilled machinist in a government job whose pay could support his family in comfort, and both her parents had high school diplomas. Her family, therefore, was relatively rich in economic and cultural capital. Her parents also had confidence in her and encouraged her to pursue education—even now, she said, they were proud of what she was doing. Furthermore, she was a capable student who liked school and had only dropped out because she became pregnant—she had no reason to fear failure if she returned to school. Like her parents, her husband supported her efforts, both emotionally and practically, and his occupation allowed him to pull his weight with housework and childcare. Also, his good income allowed Lisa to begin working less than full-time now that she had begun nurse's training.

Lisa was an emotionally sturdy person who was academically successful in high school, but even she doubted her ability to succeed in school, and she took small steps until she regained confidence. For women who failed in school, the prospect of taking a test—any test—was intimidating, so intimidating that only nine women had tried. Seven succeeded, one (Laura) failed, and one, Amanda, gave up when she found the test too grueling. "I had to take five tests," she said, "and on the Saturday, I was there all day long. I took three tests, [from] something like eight to four. And I was supposed to go back the following weekend to take the other two, [but] I said to my husband, 'It's so brain wracking, you know.'" Even Wanda, who quite liked school and quit only because she was pregnant, put off taking the test for years. "I just got my GED," she said. "It took [my husband] all these years to get me to go take it. But in order to be trained as a [medical] tech, you need to be a high school graduate. And you have to carry a current CPR (cardio-pulmonary resuscitation) card. [My husband] sent in the card and the check. He bought me the GED book, and I sat there and got so frustrated. I said, 'You've gotta be kidding me!' He said, 'Don't study for it.' He said, 'Just go ahead.'" Wanda went ahead, and she passed the test.

Phyllis seemed to be self-confident, but she too had resisted taking the test:

> My mother-in-law used to ride me constantly that I should get my GED because [she said] if something happened to [my husband], at least I would have that. Back then, [if you had] a high school diploma, you could get in just about anywhere. So she babysat so I could take my classes two nights a week. And then my mother-in-law got real ill, and she passed away, and then about six months after she passed away, I decided, "Oh shit! I'm just gonna go do it." And I did.

What is involved in taking the GED that made it too grueling for Amanda, too difficult for Laura, and so intimidating that both Wanda and Phyllis had to be nagged into doing it? I obtained the following information from the Maryland Department of Education. Anyone interested in taking the test must find out how to apply and where to send a payment of $45 (which she must have to spare). Then, she must find out where and when the tests are administered. At most centers, testing is conducted on the second Saturday of every month, and on that Saturday morning, applicants need to arrive at 8 A.M. sharp, ready to spend the day. (The test can also be taken in two consecutive half-day sessions, but in Maryland this option is available at only five regional test centers and only during certain months.)

The test, which has five different components, takes seven hours and thirty-five minutes to complete. With the exception of one essay, all the questions are multiple choice with five possible answers. The questions are described as ranging from easy to hard and cover a wide range of subjects.

The rather daunting list of subtests follows: 1)writing skills, in two parts, comprises a grammar section of fifty-five questions to be completed in seventy-five minutes and an essay to be completed in forty-five minutes; 2) social studies comprises sixty-four questions on history, economics, political science, geography, and behavioral sciences to be completed in eighty-five minutes; 3) science comprises sixty-six questions, half on life science, half on physical science, to be completed in ninety-five minutes; 4) interpreting literature and the arts comprises forty-five questions, 50 percent on popular literature, 25 percent on classical literature, and 25 percent on "commentary on literature and the arts," to be completed in sixty-five minutes; 5) mathematics has fifty-six questions, 50 percent arithmetic, 30 percent algebra, and 20 percent geometry, to be completed in ninety minutes.

As you can see, the test *is* intimidating, especially for women and men for whom tests represent bad memories. This may be why almost 14,500 people in Maryland sent their $45 deposits to take the test in 1999, but almost three thousand backed out before testing day; two-thirds of those who actually took the test were under twenty-five years of age, much younger and closer to school days than these women. Even so, in an average year, only two-thirds of those who take the test pass it.[18]

Clearly, for most women (and men) who drop out, it is not enough that the GED be available. As Lisa's experience shows, some women can face it fearlessly and pass it with ease, but many cannot; these women (and men) need help to learn new skills and overcome past experiences of failure.[19] And the help needs to be both free and accessible. Terry lost her hard-earned money when she paid a school for GED classes, and many women could not afford to pay fees—let alone lose them. I will postpone, until the concluding chapter, a fuller discussion of how adult education might be made more accessible to working-class women like Terry, Amanda, and Laura, but note here that because many women lack confidence, the test is not truly accessible unless no-cost tutoring and support are freely available and well advertised.

When to leave school was one of the most important life decisions these women would ever make, yet they made it when they were little more than children. Women who persisted in school still reaped benefits decades later, while women who dropped out still suffered negative consequences. The most obvious consequence was in job quality; in terms of both income and job satisfaction, women who dropped out were disadvantaged, and women who dropped out early in their school career were most disadvantaged of all. Yet these women, unlike Lisa, were least likely to regret dropping out and least likely to want to return to school. Only half the women who dropped out "early" said they would return to school if they could, compared with 86 percent of "late" dropouts and 72 percent of high school graduates. Clearly, women who left school as soon as they could had little confidence that school would be any better the second time around. We can only imagine what school must have been like the first time.

There were many reasons for dropping out, but, as we saw, only a few causes, many of them associated with the conditions of living in poverty. Most of these causes—abusive homes, unsympathetic schools, dangerous neighborhoods, severe learning problems—were not within the power of young girls to change, yet many had carried a sense of failure and inferiority into their mature adult years. It was they, however, who were failed, their society that was inferior; it had failed them by not supporting families and protecting the children who live in them, by viewing school success as the responsibility of individual children and families, and by allowing the quality of children's schooling to depend on the depth of their parents' pockets.

But as I will argue more fully in the concluding chapter, these women and the thousands of other women and men who still drop out of school were (are) ultimately failed by the gross inequalities in income they suffer as a consequence of their youthful act. The U.S. dropout rate is roughly comparable to or better than that of other "developed" countries; in 1992, for example, the United States was second only to Germany and Norway in the percentage of the population aged 25 to 34 with a high school diploma (87 percent, compared with 88 percent for Germany and Norway).

But there are two important differences. First, compared with similar countries, women and men in the United States who do not complete high school suffer a much larger earnings deficit; here, female dropouts earn only 65 percent of the earnings of high school graduates, and males earn only 66 percent. By contrast, female dropouts in Australia earn 90 percent of high school graduates' earnings, in Sweden, 92 percent, and in Germany, 84 percent.[20] Second, the distribution of high school completion in the United States is uneven. Most dropouts are concentrated in poor urban or rural areas; in Baltimore, for example, some estimates place the percentage of high school dropouts as high as 60 percent. This means that the 1967 Hopkins report on desegregation I referred to earlier was disturbingly prescient when it predicted that "the problem is one of [a] declining level of education for both the Negroes and whites remaining in the city school system."[21] Clustered together in low-rent districts, no longer breaking the law and causing trouble the way their teenage counterparts are wont to do, adult dropouts are out of sight and out of mind, no longer a social problem, therefore easily forgotten.

What Will I
B e ?

I think if I'd had a different environment and a different way of growing up,
(that) wasn't more or less poverty stricken, I think I would have turned out
much different—probably would have stayed in school, probably would have
been a nurse by now.

—Laura

"I never had the desire [to go to college] because I figured I wouldn't have the money," said Helen, almost precisely echoing the words of Marx, who said, "If I have no money for travel, I have no need, i.e. no real and self-realizing need, to travel. If I have a vocation to study, but no money for it, I have no vocation for study, i.e., no real, true vocation."[1] Marx might, in turn, have been quoting Hume: "We are no sooner acquainted with the impossibility of satisfying any desire, than the desire itself vanishes."[2] Thus Helen never had the desire to go to college, and for the very few women who did, the desire quickly "vanished." And Loretta said she had thought about college, but knew "deep down" that it would be impossible for her bricklayer father and her homemaker mother to send her. "I dreamed about going to college and all that kind of thing," she said, "but I knew I would never afford it. I always knew in the back of my mind it was just a dream."

As Marx saw a century and a half ago, different economic roles—factory owner, landless laborer, or small shop owner—determine different belief systems, ways of thinking about and seeing the world, and ideas about how life should be lived—different ways of being that, all things being equal, are passed on from one generation to the next. As he put it, we make our own history but it's not of our choosing;[3] instead, different ways of living, grounded in the material realities of daily life, become taken for granted as not only the best way to live, but the only way. Children absorb their parents' understanding of what is suitable or unsuitable, desirable or undesirable, so that eventually they want only what they can have.[4]

The Habitus: Why We Choose What We Need to Choose

The brilliant French sociologist and anthropologist Pierre Bourdieu can help us understand how working-class children come to understand what is possible, and what is not, and how they come to choose what they need to choose. Bourdieu described the class-structured ways of thinking and being we all learn as children as the *habitus*, a taken-for-granted structure of ideas, sayings, and beliefs that reinforces economic boundaries, and makes some ways of living and being seem right or wrong, familiar or foreign: "[We] bring into play a whole body of wisdom, sayings, commonplaces, ethical precepts ('that's not for the likes of us') and, at a deeper level, the unconscious principles of the ethos which, being the product of a learning process dominated by . . . objective realities, determines 'reasonable' and 'unreasonable' conduct for every agent subject to those regularities."[5] Put simply, the process of learning who we are and where we belong is both conscious and unconscious. We learn sayings, customs, and beliefs that make sense of our particular life circumstances and that make the behavior of our social group or class seem most natural. We develop different ways of seeing the world, or at least the world as we know it, which assume the status of "common sense." Common sense determines what is real, and what is fantasy. Thus, "reality" was Harriet's response when I asked why she had left school. "I knew I wasn't going to college, if I made it through high school," she said. "I went to work." Work was Harriet's reality just as college was Eileen's; as Bourdieu tells us, our sense of reality matches the objective circumstances of our lives.

> Every established order tends to produce (to very different degrees and with very different means) the naturalization of its own arbitrariness. Of all the mechanisms tending to produce this effect, the most important and the best concealed is undoubtedly the dialectic of the objective chances and the agents' aspirations, out of which arises the *sense of limits*, commonly called the *sense of reality*, i.e. the correspondence between the objective classes and the internalized classes, social structures and mental structures, which is the basis of the most ineradicable adherence to the established order.[6]

Harriet liked school, but it was irrelevant. Her father worked as a furnace cleaner, and her mother did not work; they had very little money, and she realized as early as seventh grade that she would not be going to college, so what was the point of staying in school? As Darlene, who "couldn't stand high school," said about quitting school at the end of junior year: "If I had gone back, I wouldn't know any more now."

The notion of habitus is Bourdieu's attempt to explain why, in spite of its rapid expansion in the latter part of the twentieth century and its relatively greater accessibility to working-class students, the education system—in several European countries as well as in the United States—has not ruptured class boundaries but has reproduced them. The habitus is powerful because it is the grammar of life we learn as infants and young children; we learn it the way a child first learns language—not with explicit rules spelled out in formal lessons, but incidentally, as we go about the business of daily life. Our native language feels more natural to us than the language we learn in the classroom; so too does our original class habitus.

By the time children attend school, they have learned the grammar of their native language and the "rules" of their habitus. Because of the material and social conditions of working-class life, a working-class habitus tends to value the practical, specific, concrete skills that are necessary for survival and success in a working-class context. It is natural for middle-class parents, whose work is "mental," not manual, who manipulate thoughts or words, not concrete things, to pass on—unconsciously and consciously— a habitus that values working with thoughts and words, not with things. Similarly, it is natural for working-class parents, whose work is manual, who predominantly manipulate things, to pass on a habitus that values working with the material world of things. If the middle-class habitus values academic knowledge, the working-class habitus values common sense.

Common sense is not nonsense. It was common sense in the post-war era for working-class parents to limit their educational ambitions for their children to a high school diploma. They developed their own habitus as children of the Great Depression, before the upswing in public education. In 1930, for example, only about one in five adults had a high school diploma. Even a generation later, when their children—the women I interviewed—were teenagers, fewer than half the population in the United States had completed high school. In Baltimore city, as recently as 1968, only 28 percent of adults twenty-five and over had completed high school, and 38 percent of the population still had only an elementary school education.[7] In the normal course of events, therefore, given their time and place, these women's parents' common sense led them to hope that their children would gain a high school diploma and get a good job. Having survived the Depression, they knew the value of being able to stand on one's own two feet. "They really just encouraged us to be independent," Dorothy said, "to take care of ourselves. We were never pushed in any direction." Thus only thirteen working-class daughters recalled their parents encouraging them in any particular vocational direction.[8] What they had learned was that, as Dorothy said, "you have to get out there and support yourself."

And it was common sense for young working-class girls to reject an education they believed to be irrelevant and of no use for getting by in the world—at least in the world as they and their parents knew it. Schools are more successful, Bourdieu correctly says, when they teach what children are already predisposed to learn; the more distant the curriculum content is from children's already formed habitus, the less likely they are to see the point. For many working-class children, the distance between a commonsense home-learned habitus and academic school learning was too wide. Ethel's situation was typical: her high school teachers all wanted her to go to college, and her language teacher encouraged her to take a third year of Latin as preparation.

But she was not interested. "I'd had two years of Latin," she said. "I wasn't interested in no more Latin." When the question came up at home, her mother gave her daughter some advice that was based on her own life experience; she had taken the academic track in high school, but, she said, it was a complete waste of time. "Now look," she said, "I work in a tailor shop." So for Ethel, knowing that money "was a problem," the choice was simple. She thought to herself, "'Well, there's no point in making more of a burden financially,' so I said, 'Well, I can earn some money and then if I want to go to school I will.'" But she didn't.

It was easier for all concerned if daughters learned not to want what they could not have. In fact, Polly was the only woman who made it to the end of high school still hoping to attend college—the consequence for her was disappointment and hard feelings. "When I graduated from high school," she said, "my parents more or less hit me then with, 'We can't afford to send you to college, so you're gonna have to work and go part-time.'" Both Polly and Ethel took jobs but neither one ever made it to college. Polly "worked, but I didn't work long enough to go back to school. Then I got pregnant." And Ethel married "and then I thought, well, I still didn't have the money. Once I had the children, well then you don't have the time. So I could've went. If I would've gone back, I think I would've went back when I started back to work. But I chose at that point [not] to. We needed the money. So I thought, 'I'm just going to do the practical thing.'"

Polly's and Ethel's families were not exactly "poor," but they had no money to spare for luxuries. And when their daughters could expect to find a good job with a high school diploma, education was a luxury, so they did the right thing—the practical thing—and went to work. It was only common sense.

Schools: Teaching What Needs to Be Learned

With the exception of a few students who were considered "college material," the schools trained young working-class women for jobs. And because their practical habitus was already well-established, this was usually what the young women themselves wanted. Jill, for example, said her favorite course was typing. "I had all business in high school," she recalled. "I didn't have to take any other subject, other than business. It was the same class all day, and it was all business. It was nice. It was a good program, because we didn't have to take all of these classes that you didn't really want and you weren't interested in." Betsy, like Jill, a secretary, did not regret her mostly vocational courses: "My typing teacher thought I was marvelous, and she always recommended me for my work study. I remember a German teacher who was quite upset with me because she knew that I was not fulfilling my potential. But I said, 'I'm not going to use this stuff.' I wound up with A's in her class."

Neither Betsy nor Jill regretted the path they had taken. Nina, though, with hindsight, said she might have made more effort, but "nobody really ever said, you know, 'If you get better grades . . . ' The counselors really didn't—they were only for the ones who had the super high scores and that's all they really cared about then. Sometimes it's like that now too." Julie—one of the six women who went to college—said that, even in her magnet high school, there was little guidance: "I asked and really didn't get good enough answers. I don't think that the advice that I was given about colleges or careers was worth anything. There was nothing that you could actually hold on to— nothing you could do anything with—no direction given. There was not even any advice. As a matter of fact, they didn't have application forms. It was just pitiful."

Middle-class young women had a very different experience. Their schools were excellent. Margaret went to school in one of the more affluent Washington suburbs: "The high school that I went to was one of the top-rated schools in the country. I think I had an excellent education. And we all knew that. And all the kids came from all over because the government was always changing." Eileen went to a private girls' school: "I think one of the most interesting pieces of it was that I went to all girls' Catholic schools, and they were very encouraging. Sixth grade through high school and college, it was all-female education. The message the nuns gave was, 'You can be whatever you want to be.'"

For Margaret, Eileen, and other middle-class daughters, college was taken for granted. "They certainly encouraged me to do anything I wanted," said Marie, a professor's daughter, "and I wouldn't say that my mother ever was limiting or felt that there were any limits or constraints. And they definitely encouraged me to go to college, and my father encouraged me to go to the best college possible." Had they both encouraged her to stay in school? "Oh, yes. But it was not necessarily the kind of thing that was stated as such; it was implied, and there was never any question, on the part of any of us, that any of the children wouldn't finish college."[9]

To be sure, middle-class daughters were affected by gender-based norms. Their parents usually recommended traditionally female careers such as teaching—something their daughters could "fall back on"—or they focused on college as an end in itself rather than a means of training for a career, but even these expectations, gendered though they were, helped their daughters gain access to higher incomes and more interesting jobs later in life.

Cultural Capital

Much of what middle-class parents pass on to their children is what Bourdieu calls "cultural capital." All parents pass on cultural "goods" —pieces of information, lore, rules for life—to their children that are part of the cultural world they inhabit. But only cultural goods that are valued by the dominant culture are cultural capital, because only they can be traded for other valued goods—especially economic capital. Part of the cultural capital possessed by parents of the middle-class women I interviewed was the absolute certainty that without an advanced education (and marriage to a man with a prestigious occupation) their daughters would not live the good life. This absolute certainty meant that, for their daughters, going to college was the path of least resistance, the path that, for working-class girls, was getting a job.

But cultural capital is more than parents' aspirations for their daughters; it is also knowing the "right" thing to do, say, wear, and like, and the "right" places to go—preferences, tastes, and values that include the "right" people and exclude the wrong. Liz and Greta were both confronted with this hard truth when they were still young, and they recoiled in hurt surprise to discover that there was an entire world from which they were excluded.

Liz was the daughter of poor parents, but she had been given a fairy-tale chance to do better. Her aunt, a single working woman with no children of her own, offered to pay her tuition at a prestigious private girls' school that sent almost all its graduates to college. But, as Liz found out, she didn't belong: "Well, see, my aunt had put me in Roland Park Country School, and they wore little blue dresses, and I just loved that. I didn't dislike school. I disliked the fact that all of the girls—when you got to junior high—you noticed everybody had things. When you don't [have things], you notice it even more and there's fun poked. You know, [they said], 'She has fish heads on.' And it still goes on today." Greta had a similar experience. Greta's mother encouraged her to be socially ambitious:

> I went out with a rich boy, but I didn't marry him. Do you know what happened? I met this boy. He lived in Roland Park and he had a lot of money. My mother said, "He's great, why don't you marry him?" His family was very rich. His first name was Carter. The only problem was, we went out on a boat one day—he had a yacht—and I wore this nice pretty dress on the yacht, but I had worn the dress about a week before that at their home up in Roland Park, and their mother said to me, "Oh, didn't you wear that dress up at my house two weeks ago?" And I said, "Yes, I did."
>
> And that's all she said to me, and I went home and I started crying. And my mother said, "What's the matter?" And I said, "I don't want to see him, I don't want to marry him. Don't you try to get me with these rich people!" [His mother] got all upset, just because I had this same dress on that I wore two weeks ago. Just because she wears a new dress every day, I can't afford new clothes every day! And I figured nobody would know it, because I figured if we was going to be on the yacht, they wouldn't be the same people that had been at his home. But she opened her mouth and said, "You've got the same dress on." It was very rude. She was real snotty Roland Park, a rich lady up there. And she hurt my feelings. I would never say nothing like that. It was a clean dress. I said to my mother, "No, I don't want nobody like that."

Liz and Greta both lived (and still do) in Hampden, a working-class suburb that abuts Roland Park, an "old money" area whose huge Victorian houses share the streets with private schools, tennis courts, and mature shade trees. The customs and cultural codes of the two neighborhoods could hardly be more different. Greta's pretty best dress, so right in her eyes for any special occasion, was a neon light signaling to Carter's mother that Greta was not "one of us." For most working-class girls, college and prestigious careers were as remote and foreign as sailing a yacht; they were for rich folk from Roland Park, not ordinary folk from Hampden.

Muriel

Muriel's story illustrates how economic and cultural capital functioned for the middle-class daughters. The wife of a partner in a prominent law firm, Muriel lived a high-status life; her rambling Victorian house was in one of the city's most prestigious neighborhoods, whose wage-earners were doctors, lawyers, and businessmen, and whose children were students in private schools. She was simply but elegantly dressed for our interview, in a plaid wool skirt and red lambswool sweater, gold earrings just visible under her stylishly cut auburn hair.

Muriel worked part-time as a secretary for a foundation. It quickly became clear, however, that hers was not a typical secretary's job, because she had the kind of autonomy usually associated with a more prestigious occupation: "We all can do everything, and we all do each other's job. It's really nice. When my boss is out every winter with terrible bronchitis for at least two weeks, then I run the office. When she comes back, I step back into my other position, and she runs the office. People aren't touchy about titles or, 'Well, this is my job, this is hers. I'm not going to do that.' It's really wonderful. We are all equal."

The only secretary who worked in such a collegial atmosphere, she was on at least an equal social footing with the other foundation employees—and board members—and was treated more as an equal than working-class women in similar jobs. Her upbringing had prepared her well:

> My mother was home. I remember her being in slacks and a turtleneck, having routines every day. And then about three-thirty, she'd start the dinner. She would then go take a bath, put on stockings, a skirt, and a cashmere sweater, and heels and pearls and come down and greet my father like that. She did this five nights a week. She never served a hamburger in that house! My father was always home by five-thirty. We always had a formal family dinner. He was brought up very formally, and that continued. We had no bathrobes, no rollers, even on prom night, and we sat at the table. There were candles. There were courses served. We had discussions. [Father] is a "fourth." OK? That tells you. Grandfather was a congressman, the whole bit.[10]

At first, Muriel had neither liked nor excelled in school, but her experience was very different from that of working-class daughters who were not successful students:

In elementary school, I was scared all the time. I was one of those children who wanted to please adults, and for some reason, I didn't do particularly well all the time, and so I didn't think I was pleasing them, so I was always scared. . . . [But] there's a course I remember making me realize I wasn't stupid. I somehow lucked into an honors history course and there was a very erudite teacher. I had to look up half of all the words he said. I felt wonderful about myself, being in there and doing well. That's when the light started to dawn: maybe I wasn't dumb after all.

Like so many other young women, Muriel was confused about her career goals, but her parents had stepped in and solved her problem:

I didn't know what to do. I didn't know where to go to school, and my parents thought I shouldn't go to a four-year school because they didn't know if I could finish. So my mother had a friend who had gone to a junior college in Massachusetts. So they put me in the car one day, and drove me up there to look at it. It looked fine to me, so that's where I signed up. And then when we went down for the first day, all of the department heads were sitting in the library at tables. And you walked around and met them, and I said to my father, "I don't know what to major in," and we walked around and he said, "Well, let's major in retailing. He seems like a nice man." And so that's what I did. It turned out I was very good at it.

After junior college came a job with Bergdorf Goodman, where Muriel worked until she was married.

Who Muriel was and how she looked had allowed her to fit in easily at Bergdorf's and also at the foundation.[11] Working in the office of a philanthropic organization, dealing with wealthy and powerful benefactors and board members, it was essential that she looked and acted as though she belonged, and she did:

We all have to be dressed. We have lots of very rich people who support us. We call them the big guys, and they come in and out of the office all the time, and they can be in a sweatsuit but we have to present this [gesturing to her clothes] image.

Muriel was an exception, the only woman from an upper middle-class background who was not the graduate of a four-year college, and the only one who worked as a secretary. But her less than upper-middle-class education and occupation had no effect on her upper-middle-class style of life, because her social class origins had bequeathed her a secure place in the upper-middle-class world. By contrast, women from working-class origins, not bearing the imprimatur of high status, needed to earn their place in that world by following what has been men's traditional route to prestige—ambition, advanced education, and a professional-managerial occupation.

Moving between Worlds: Social Mobility

Most of the working-class daughters in the study had built lives that mirrored their parents': their own and their husbands' occupations had about the same social ranking as their fathers', and their style of life was similar to their parents'. The exceptions were six working-class daughters who had gone to college and entered professions. All six of these women were daughters of parents who as high school graduates were better educated than most working-class parents at the time.[12] Their fathers were all skilled workers: Beth's father was a butcher then a liquor store manager; Dawn's was a mechanic; Julie's was a skilled maintenance supervisor; Pam's was a dental technician; Connie's was a foreman in a textile factory; and Lillian's was a supervisor and crane operator in a steelyard. And—unusually for that time—four of the women's mothers had worked full time and consistently during their daughters' childhoods.

But they had even more in common. As a group—though admittedly too small to permit grand generalizations—all six women described their parents as motivated by a firm desire to "get ahead," and to see their children get ahead. (Two parents were immigrants and another was the child of immigrants.) Lillian described her father, the son of immigrants from Eastern Europe:

> He always had the same occupation. He worked in a steel company, but he was the manager of the steelyard. He really was a crane operator and then he later began managing, so he moved up, I guess. It was a small company; it got bigger. He still ran the crane, but he managed other people to run it. But he was a workman, he really was a workman. He wore one of those blue work suits and he took a shower before he came home in steel shoes.
>
> He graduated, but it was embarrassing for him that it was a vocational high school. . . . He was always embarrassed that he didn't know anything. They were Jewish. Their parents came over, both my parents were born in the United States. But they did not speak English, their parents, so it was a very important thing. That's why college was pushed on us.

Beth's parents were also ambitious, for their children and for themselves. Although her father was out of a job for a time and money was tight, Beth said she had never doubted she would go to college. Like Lillian's father, Beth's had moved up occupationally, and her mother worked as a secretary:

> I think that my position being the first child was probably very important to both of [my parents]. Not that they put it that I was the first, but it was clearly important to them. I don't remember being given the opportunity to say that I would not go to college. It was just assumed that I would go. Did our parents want our lives to be different from theirs? Absolutely, and they were different. They were the first generation

in this country; they were from Russia, Poland.

I think that I would be a very boring person to my family if I didn't work. I don't view women who sit at home very positively. And I don't know how much of that was my mother working. Most of my friends' parents worked.

Connie's father had also encouraged his children to continue in school, and she and her siblings all shared their parents' achievement orientation:

My father often [encouraged us]. He really walked us down that road and was very instrumental in guiding us toward what he felt were good habits. My brother is now a controller for a hospital. My sister never did go to college, but has a real strong work ethic and has worked herself into a high administrative-secretarial kind of position. [Do we all have this orientation to work?] We really do. When the families are together, the spouses will talk about how we are all too work oriented.

It would be foolish to attribute these women's social mobility entirely to their parents' encouragement or ambition. Yet it would be equally foolish to ignore it. Without exception, their parents were achievement oriented for themselves, and for their children. They valued education and pushed their daughters to continue in school. They set an example of hard work and "getting ahead," and by a combination of hard work, ambition, and opportunity they had gained some measure of economic security. They were unable to offer sophisticated career guidance, but, as far as they were able, whether through example, shared endowment, expectations, or encouragement, they had been able to give their daughters the opportunities they so highly valued.

Common Sense: The Tyranny of the Practical

But even the working-class daughters who were college graduates, like other working-class women, were limited by financial constraints—less confining than those faced by daughters from poor families, to be sure, but no less real. They too were hamstrung by the practicality and common sense that working-class women and men need to get by. Their parents had been able to gain some distance from the urgencies of material need, but not enough to feel they could encourage their daughters to throw caution to the wind and major in literature, anthropology, art history, or some other "impractical" subject. They encouraged them to choose a field that was safe, secure, and would guarantee survival—in other words, to use their common sense.

Beth

Beth's career choice was an example of common sense in action. Beth was head of the Social Work Department in a large hospital, and I met her there. Before we started, she handed me her résumé, which included a very impressive list of publications, but, as she pointed out, no Ph.D. Her husband had done his, she said, as an adult, but she had chosen not to. "The question is what would it get me if I went back to school at this point?" she asked. "At this point in my life I don't think it's worth all the hoops that I'd have to jump through. I would at this point rather come home and spend time with the kids as they're getting ready to leave rather than spend time writing papers and buried in the library having to jump through the hoops."

The daughter of immigrants from Russia and Poland, Beth was the first generation in her family to attend college. Her parents had both worked. Her father, a high school graduate, was a butcher when she was small, then later managed a liquor store, and her mother began working as a secretary when Beth and her sister were in elementary school. When Beth was in high school, her father was laid off for a time. "I know it was hard," she said, "and there were talks about [how to pay for] college." From these talks, and from witnessing this difficult period in her parents' life, Beth learned a lesson: "Knowing that they were not wealthy, and seeing them both working hard, I went into a field where I could sustain myself, whether I married or had children or whatever. There was a time in college when I thought I might go into art history, and absolutely loved it, but [I] never chose it as a major once I was there, because I just didn't think I could make a living at it. So those things probably formed me, that I knew that I had to make a living at what I did."

Beth was not a woman to bemoan her choices, but she wanted to give her own two children more choice: "I've told my kids, I often say to them, 'We're in a financial position where we can help you. If you want to get a Ph.D. and you know what you want to get it in, do it up front.' Do I have regrets? I would say sometimes."

Dawn

Dawn's story was similar. A slender, elegantly dressed woman with sleekly coiffed dark hair, Dawn lived in a large, airy house in an affluent suburban development and worked as regional director for a large chain of nursing homes. She had taken a master's in administrative science, and "fine-tuned" her skills for just such a position: "I'm my own boss to a great extent. And again, a little further down the road, I will be making my own schedules so that flexibility was built in there. And I think it really pulls together a lot of the skills, and, I guess, training that I've had, all into this one job. Which was why I wanted it."

Dawn had spent an untroubled childhood in a rural township in the South, with parents who were determined that all their children would graduate from college. She went to an excellent high school: "In the school we were in, 95 percent of kids went to college. It was one of those unspoken things, it was just assumed that you would go. One way or the other, you were going. It was unusual for rural Tennessee. It was a really nice town. Parents were involved. There was an excellent music program that I was involved with. We were rated superior for the marching band, the concert band by the state. We went to tri-state contests for many years. It was a town that had a lot of pride. There were a number of well-educated parents."

Dawn knew she was headed for college, but she also knew she needed a practical career: "I guess, my first year in college, I was a journalism major, and I guess my idea then was, you know, writing for magazines . . . [but] I really became discouraged with that, just because the journalism would add another year of college, and I thought, 'That's not practical.' There have been many times that I really wish that I had stuck it out, because that was something I really enjoyed, English. I always enjoyed writing, all of that, and I really used to wish that I had continued. But that was that."

That was that, for Dawn, who had "too many brothers and sisters who had to go to school." Now she was making sure her own daughter would feel free to follow her dreams, no matter how impractical they might be. "I really hope that Katie feels she can do what she would like to do, and I think she does, because she's doing theater at school, because that's what she's really interested in. Whereas, until last year, she was pretty much straight science and math and stuff. I guess—and I think she's doing this—she had a little more, I guess, freedom to make choices as to what she wants to do by not being influenced so much by being realistic or too practical."

Bourdieu's work can help us understand the relationship between economics and the need to be "realistic" or "practical" that Beth, Dawn, and the other socially mobile women felt. Because their parents had moved one step away from the realm of material necessity in which most working-class parents lived, these young women were open to the possibilities of education. As Bourdieu put it:

> [Habitus] prepares that much better for secondary [schooling] based on explicit pedagogy when exerted within a class whose material conditions of existence allow them to stand more completely aside from practice, in other words to "neutralize" in imagination or reflection the vital urgencies which thrust a pragmatic disposition on the dominated classes.[13]

But although they were one step away from the "vital urgencies" of material need, these urgencies could not be forgotten; they had not yet faded over generations of family history. The next generation, their mothers hoped, as they worked in jobs that were not fully satisfying, would be at a safer remove, and would therefore be more free to discard the dictates of common sense.

Fragile Ambitions

It was startling how many women had dismissed their youthful ambitions as dreams, even when those ambitions were modest; the most common career aspiration among the working-class women were nurse (nineteen women), teacher (eleven women), and secretary (five women),[15] but only a handful of women actually worked in the careers they had imagined for themselves as children. Vocational psychologists can help us understand why, how, and when all these young women abandoned their early ambitions.[16] They describe how children adjust their occupational aspirations to fit their developing image of themselves, and their sense of where they belong in terms of gender, class, abilities, and interests. It is well known that very young children of all social classes choose occupations that are sex-typed; for young girls, nursing and teaching fit the bill, for young boys, police officer and firefighter. (Along with famous athletes, these occupations are both highly visible and familiar.) As their self-image develops, however, they begin to classify occupations in terms of sex and class "appropriateness," and to rule out those that fail on either count. Girls and boys and middle- and working-class children first rule out occupations that "belong" to the other gender, then those that "belong" to the other class until, eventually, girls aspire to "female" occupations, males to "male" occupations, and upper-class children aspire to high-prestige occupations, working-class children to low. Only then, when they have zeroed in on a set of occupations that "fit" in terms of gender and class, do young people take into account their individual vocational interests and abilities; they are more willing to settle for an occupation that is not exactly what interests them than one that seems inappropriate to their gender and class.

The earlier aspirations and current jobs of the women in the study conformed to this developmental progression. Compared with middle-class women, working-class women had aspired to and now worked in occupations that were lower in the occupational hierarchy, and, although they had aimed lower to begin with, most had ended up choosing an occupation even lower than their original choice. In fact, of the forty-four working-class daughters who could recall aspiring to a particular occupation, only six had ultimately worked in that same occupation or one with equal or higher status. The working-class women's final choice of occupation, therefore, came after a double downgrading; to begin with, they aimed lower than middle-class women, and they ended up lower still.

In an ideal world, an adolescent would choose her career at the end of a lengthy process. First, with the help of adults—guidance counselors, librarians, teachers, parents, and friends—she would become informed about different occupations. Second, again with help, she would assess her own interests and abilities. Third, she would explore different occupations that have been grouped and rated in terms of the abilities and qualifications they require and the kind of person they appeal to. Only then would she make a career choice, and that choice would be limited solely by her own personal aptitudes and interests.

But few, if any, women in the study followed these steps. Instead, without guidance, and largely unconsciously, most had discarded occupations that came to seem unattainable or unsuitable. How had they come to define the boundaries between attainable and unattainable so that occupations they had previously considered possible became impossible, those they had considered suitable became unsuitable? How was it that a number of women of obviously high ability had failed to pursue occupations they might have found more rewarding? Were they mistaken as to their abilities and interests? Were they misled as to the suitability of different occupations? Rhonda and Helen can suggest some answers to these questions.

Rhonda

On the face of things, Rhonda was successful in both her professional and private life. A cool, confident blonde in her early forties, she owned her own beauty salon, a medium-sized enterprise that could seat six clients at a time. In her private life, too, she was doing well; her second marriage was happy, and she was delighted with her daughter, an only child. (Her husband had been laid off recently, but life was looking up again now that he had found another job.) Like so many other women in the study, however, Rhonda was making do, making a good living and a good life, but not under circumstances she would have chosen: "I wanted to be a schoolteacher, but I didn't do that. I wanted to be a math teacher, but I didn't know anything about scholarships, and my mother wasn't—she didn't either. I mean, now they have assemblies in school, but then they didn't do that. I didn't know. I thought to get a scholarship you had to win one. I was a good student and I had perfect attendance for five years, for seventh, eighth, ninth, tenth, and twelfth [grades]. I missed twenty-four days in eleventh grade because I had my appendix out; otherwise I would have had six years of [perfect attendance]."

The first thing missing in Rhonda's real life story compared with the ideal career choice scenario I just outlined was help from her parents. Because her own experience of education and careers was limited, Rhonda's mother had been unable to help her explore careers that would make use of her math ability. "She worked all of her life as a counter girl," Rhonda explained. "She had no education. Counter girl, that was basically about it. I think maybe she completed fifth grade."

Neither could her father, a plumber, give her advice. Like her mother, he had little formal education and, in any case, he was not close to his children. In fact, Rhonda could find little positive to say about him or her mother. Her father "didn't like to work" she said, and her mother "was never there" when Rhonda was a child, because she was "always working." Her mother hated her own job "very strongly," and only did it to "make a living." Both her parents, who were divorced, were quite poor.

Nor was advice available at her city public school, from guidance counselors or teachers. Rhonda said she never saw a guidance counselor and, although a math teacher in junior high had encouraged her interest in math, none of her teachers ever gave her advice about scholarships or careers.

A profession may have been within the realm of objective possibility, but it had no subjective reality in Rhonda's day-to-day world. To find her way between her known world and the unknown world of a profession, she would have needed some signposts, but there were none to be found. But a beacon shone brightly on cosmetology, a tried and true working-class occupation: her working-class school area taught its girls this trade, and she "knew people who were hairdressers and they made money."

Rhonda was successful. She had not become a professional person but she ran a successful business and she claimed to be satisfied. It became clear, however, that her satisfaction involved a lot of compromise. She disliked "putting up with people. Putting up with so many different personalities in a day. You're putting up with people's wants, and their own personal body. We're beauticians, not magicians." And in spite of her professed satisfaction, she was determined that her beloved daughter would not follow in her footsteps; she told her that she "absolutely would not pay for her to do [hair]." Much to Rhonda's relief, her daughter had chosen "the accounting field."

Helen

Like Rhonda, Helen grew up in a poor family; she also shared Rhonda's aptitude for math. Unlike Rhonda, though, Helen had returned to school and, after almost ten long years of part-time study, had just finished an associate's diploma in accounting. Because of this hard-earned diploma, she could now move up from accounts associate to accountant, a promotion she had long awaited. As we talked, however, it became clear that neither her diploma nor her job as an accountant gave her much pleasure.

Helen had known early on that she liked math, but her aptitude, ability, and interest were considered unremarkable by her parents. Her mother believed that a woman's job was to "stay at home and look after the man," an ambition Helen said she had adopted as her own: "I wanted a dozen kids," she said. "That's all I wanted to be, a housewife with twelve children." And her father had wanted her to be a secretary. "Back then," she said, "there were only three careers for girls: secretary, teacher, or nurse." Her talent also went unnoticed and unnurtured at her working-class all-girls school:

> I was disappointed in high school, because I wasn't allowed to further my
> learning. . . . When I went to Milltown, in twelfth grade, all that was required was
> your general math. I didn't even get algebra. I had algebra in the ninth grade and I
> wasn't even offered it in high school. We just had to do our general math and know
> our fractions. I think back then they thought women didn't need the higher math.
> You know, Milltown was a school geared to secretaries. You know, you go to work;
> you go out and you get a job; you don't go to college. I never had anybody—I didn't
> feel that anybody encouraged me to go to college. I never had the desire because I
> figured I wouldn't have the money.

After-school activities might have been some compensation for boring classes, but as the eldest girl, Helen had to rush home every day as soon as classes were over to take care of her six younger brothers and sisters. In fact, she did such a good job of cooking and cleaning for them that her father used to call her "the little mother," and her youngest sister said she still thought of Helen more as a mother than a sister: "If my mother had to go somewhere or something, I always had to stay home. So it was like, you know, I always had to like put my life on the back burner."

In light of her home situation and the lack of academic encouragement at home and at school, it is surprising that Helen managed to graduate from high school. But she did graduate, even though she was already pregnant with her first child. She had married a soldier who was soon transferred overseas; when this happened, Helen and her baby moved back in with her mother, and she took a job as a file clerk in the large university where she still worked. She had planned on quitting her job to become a housewife as soon as she scraped together the down payment on a house, but this was not to be.

After a time, she became bored with her work as a clerk and took a position as a computer operator in one of the university labs. To her surprise, her outlook began to change, and staying at home as a housewife no longer seemed so inviting. "I started excelling in the lab, and getting promotions and taking on more responsibility on the outside, outside the home," she said. "I like doing systems design, going in to set something up. And I'm a more organized person. That's why I do so well in computers, because it's logic, step by step. And you can't get to the next step unless the last one's correct." She continued to take courses in computers, moved up to systems design, and was soon running the entire computer operation. She loved the job. Eventually, however, she was forced to give it up—she had to be on-call weekends and evenings, and her husband refused to help out at home.

It may seem that working as an accountant was a good choice for Helen, and presumably at one point she thought it would be; she had certainly worked long and hard for her job. But all along the way, and still, she had been searching for something she had still not found. Now, with her promotion in hand, she said she was still not "fulfilled inside":

> I can move up to a senior accountant. I mean, really, the promotion that I've gotten, it has not really changed my job. I mean I've been in the department, I've done the jobs many times before, it's just that it's going to be more my responsibility. I mean I felt I should have had this promotion before now, but it was always brought up to me that I didn't have the piece of paper that I need. I just thought it was very unfair if a person had the ability to do the job—but it didn't come about until I had the degree. So it doesn't really make any difference. I don't want to—I don't want to really stay in this job—I don't want to move to management level, especially not in

the field I'm in. I'd like to go back to school for computers. If I go back for my degree, a B.S., it will be for computers.

Helen's story contains themes that most women readers her age will recognize, whatever their class. The pull back and forth between wanting a career and wanting to "be a housewife with twelve children" is one. Giving up a demanding job when it interferes with family life is another. Familiar too is her confusion about what she wanted to be. During the interview she said she wanted to be a housewife, to study for a real estate license, and to study for computers. In many ways, she was still the young working-class girl who was faced with the "three things a girl could be: nurse, secretary, or teacher."

There was very little overlap between the worlds of working- and middle-class women and little movement between the two worlds; not one woman "fell" from a middle-class childhood to a working-class adulthood, and although several women from working-class backgrounds were living comfortably, as we saw, only six women gained reliable access to the middle class by completing a professional degree. This is consistent with the high level of "social reproduction" that is found time and again in sociological studies; these studies consistently find that the best predictor of a child's future social status is the status of her parents, especially her father. Yet few women commented on the role of social class in their lives. Why? What is it that makes us so willing to cut our hopes and dreams to fit the cloth of our social class?

Class segregation is, I believe, a large part of the answer; only when women penetrated a different world were the effects of class made transparent—for example, when Liz's aunt paid for her to attend the private school and she was teased mercilessly for being different; and when Greta dated the rich boy from Roland Park and was humiliated by his mother for wearing the wrong clothes. Both women felt out of place and chose to return to where they fit in, giving up ambitions that were "unrealistic," and "not for the likes of us." So it was that, in almost all cases, working-class girls became working-class women.

Getting By on the
M i n i m u m

Unequal Education

Earlier this century, in most western democracies, universal free education held out the promise of a new equality. No longer would education be the preserve of an aristocratic class, a form of symbolic capital reserved for those already rich in economic capital. No longer would social and economic position be handed down from one generation to the next. Now, education would guarantee that in each new generation differences in achievement would depend only on differences in motivation and talent. That was the dream. The reality is that, on the whole, the extent of children's schooling can still be predicted from their parents' social class, so much so that many sociologists refer to education as the main mechanism for the "reproduction" of social class, and a major subsection of the discipline studies why this is so.

How education reproduced social class among the women I interviewed varied with their distance from the urgencies of material need. As we saw, women who were poor dropped out for a number of reasons, most of which directly or indirectly stemmed from the material conditions of their lives; women whose families were poor were pushed by the conditions of life that often accompanied poverty into an early adulthood—in the form of a pregnancy (a new life) or a job (independence). Pregnancy was a way out of the childhood powerlessness that caused these young women such pain.

Some women had dropped out because they were unsuccessful in school or saw no point in further education. Yet even these "individual" reasons are not causes because the outcome of these aptitude differences differs by class. Dropping out is the logical outcome for working-class students who lack academic aptitude or interest. For middle-class students, dropping out is unthinkable; no matter how weak their aptitude or how tepid their interest, all middle-class students are "good students."

For women who completed high school but went no further, class was reproduced a little differently. Because their parents were further removed from the urgencies of material need, these young women were able to postpone adulthood for a little longer. But education was a luxury, not a necessity, and although their parents were typically not poor, they were very often short of money, and four years of college tuition, room, and board was beyond their means. For this reason, their daughters obeyed the dictates of "reality" and clipped their wings. As Bourdieu says, "individuals have hoped for nothing that they have not obtained and obtained nothing that they have not hoped for."[1]

As Jo's experience shows, reality was different for middle-class daughters. Jo, a middle-class daughter, started out life in the working class. Her father died before she was born, however, and when she was six her mother remarried, to an attorney from a prominent family. Before she remarried, Jo's mother had wanted her to do "something glamorous," perhaps work in a large local department store when she grew up; her stepfather, however, had other ideas:

> My stepfather, as far as education was concerned, was definitely the next step up. My mother's family all had high school educations, including my real father. She always wanted me to go to college, but then we had my stepfather's family where it was an expectation. His generation had all gone, including the women. His one sister has a Ph.D., so it was like "of course you will go!" I was the first one in my mother's family and my real father's family to have a college degree, but in my stepfather's family, it was expected.

Like many other working-class parents, Jo's mother *wanted* her to go to college, but her stepfather *expected* it. The difference between wanting and expecting is the difference between daydream and reality.

School is the workplace of childhood. Success in school means learning facts, skills, and techniques but also that learning is possible, rewarding, and worthwhile. At its (middle-class) best, the school experiences of the women I interviewed rewarded them with knowledge and skills, and an easy familiarity with the world of words, ideas, and information. It built their self-esteem, and made all things seem possible. At its (working-class) worst, it created a negative view of the world of learning and of the self. It confirmed what many working-class girls already knew—that school was not "for the likes of us."

Because school funding is based on local property taxes, there is a direct relationship between the size of parents' bank balances and the quality of their children's education; as a consequence, the children who most need generous school resources have least access to them. College is still out of the question for many working-class students. As Nicholas Lehman tells us in a *Time* magazine article, until the mid-seventies, most state colleges charged about one-tenth of the actual cost of tuition, but, toward the end of the decade, this proportion increased to a third, and "[s]ince 1980, the cost in most states has tripled or quadrupled. Today the price of a state university education is distinctly not nominal. The average total cost for a year of public higher education is $9,285."[2] This amount is about equal to some working-class women's annual take-home pay.

Unequal Work

The consequences of these differences in education for the women I interviewed were long lasting. In terms of job conditions and pay, the women without a college degree were worse off than college graduates; they earned less, were eligible for fewer benefits, had less autonomy and control on the job, and less flexibility. But the women without a high school diploma—especially women who dropped out at the beginning of high school or in middle school—were worse off still; not only were they paid much less, they were rarely eligible for health benefits or paid leave, and they were subject to harsh and arbitrary authority, especially when they worked in gray-collar factory and service jobs that lacked union protections—or even a middle-class veneer of politeness. Customer service and other counter workers were often treated with disrespect if not outright hostility by their customers as well as their bosses. Disrespect was a major source of distress for many of the women I spoke with, who told me, again and again, that being stripped of their dignity was far worse than hard work, low pay, or lack of benefits. Being humiliated in front of others, spoken to harshly, ridiculed, and treated with disdain—these were the truly distressing job conditions—and it was this disrespect rather than any other work condition that made them dissatisfied. Respect mattered, not deference—respect for the dignity of work, and for women's dignity as workers.

The low pay, lack of benefits, and disrespectful treatment these women were subjected to are disturbing, because jobs like theirs represent the future for thousands of women (and men) who lack the skills and educational credentials that bring access to better-paid jobs. In the past, the distribution of married women's work participation relative to their education has been shaped like an inverted U—that is, women with the least and the most education have participated at lower rates than women in the middle. The reason for this was that paid work was socially unacceptable and women who were highly educated were not forced to work by economic need. Women with the least education, on the other hand, experienced economic need, but they had few opportunities and could find only the most unpleasant jobs. With welfare-to-work reforms pushing women into the workforce, and men's wages no longer adequate to support a family, women with the fewest skills and lowest education now must work, but the jobs available to them are no better. Handicapped by limited education, they are vulnerable to the most callous exploitation.

But education alone does not bring equality; workers who upgrade their qualifications improve their own chances of finding a better job, but the structure of the labor market remains the same. For this reason, as well as making education more accessible, it is essential to address inequities and unfair practices in the labor market.

The "new economy" has split the working population into haves and have-nots. This split is not because all service jobs are low-wage; in fact, service jobs themselves fall into two extremes in terms of pay and conditions. Nationwide, the fastest-growing occupations are in retail and services—specifically business services, health services, and public and private education. With the exception of retail trade, whose wages are uniformly low, the demand for both highly paid skilled workers and low-wage workers is escalating in these service sectors. In business services, for example, systems analysts, general managers, and top executives are in demand, but so are office clerks and mail packagers. In health services, highly paid nurses, but also personal care and home health aides are sought after. In education, college teachers, but also teacher's assistants.

To some extent, Baltimore, where most of the women I interviewed live and work, mirrors this national picture; the service sector in Baltimore is growing, but expansion is disproportionately among low-wage jobs as salespersons, cashiers, waiters and waitresses, guards, janitors, and food preparation workers. The median annual wage (the pay level at which 50 percent of people earn less, and 50 percent earn more) for these jobs ranges from only $13,340 for waiters and waitresses to $18,580 for janitors. Even for Baltimore, whose median wage of $32,570 is lower than the national figure of $35,296, these are dismal wages; a janitor and a cashier together can earn less than the average wage for one person.[3]

But the story doesn't stop there. The fastest-growing sector in the local economy is the provision of business services, especially personnel supply services. Why personnel supply services? The Maryland Department of Labor can provide the answer: they tell us that personnel supply services are expanding rapidly because of "the outsourcing of tasks not related to a firm's core business and its need to reduce costs in the face of increasingly competitive global markets."[4] A number of the women I spoke with worked in jobs created by this outsourcing strategy; misnamed as temporary, their jobs were permanent as long as employers wanted them to be, but they provided none of the benefits of permanent jobs. Personnel supply services keep businesses supplied with a reserve army of these so-called temporary low-wage workers who can easily be discarded when no longer needed. Using a flesh and blood form of just-in-time inventory methods, employers thus have maximum flexibility—and employees have maximum insecurity. By employing many workers on a part-time or temporary basis, employers evade institutions that protect workers, such as strong unions and government regulation.

In a brilliant analysis of different class, gender, and racial patterns of inequality in five hundred U.S. local labor markets, Leslie McCall, an economic sociologist, shows that in labor markets such as Baltimore's that are low-wage and highly "casualized"— and in which unemployment is high (8 percent in Baltimore)—women who lack a high school diploma are particularly disadvantaged in relation to other women and to men; they "face a harsher labor market" and "are among the most vulnerable to new and deepening forms of flexibility and insecurity."[5] McCall notes, too, that "flexible labor market conditions [are] the most important factor in fostering high levels of inequality between college and non college educated women."[6] Thus highly paid managerial and professional women do well in low-wage local economies such as Baltimore's, but women with little education or formal job training do particularly badly.

One might expect that low unemployment would lead to better jobs as employers are forced to compete for workers, but there is a catch: working capital is more mobile than working-class families. Because many of the new service industries do the business of packaging, assembling, compiling, telephoning, and mailing—not producing goods—they are not hampered by heavy equipment or the need for a skilled workforce; they can all too easily pick up and move on if the local labor supply starts to dry up or demand higher wages. Working-class families, however, are often firmly attached to their home city or cannot afford to move. Low-wage areas such as Baltimore, with a captive poor population, therefore, are an asset to firms bent on maximizing profit.

Public Policy and Individual Responsibility

For the last three to four decades, legislation and public outcry have whittled away at race and gender discrimination, yet workplace and income inequality based on class has worsened. Why is this so? One reason is that there are few social policies explicitly aimed at equalizing income and mandating fair workplace conditions for every worker. In fact, workers in this country have fewer rights and protections than workers in any other comparable country. The major piece of legislation governing workers' rights is the Fair Labor Standards Act, which is one of the least protective pieces of labor legislation in the industrialized world; it fails to mandate sick leave, personal leave, or even vacation leave. Furthermore, it applies only to companies that do at least half a million dollars a year in business. The much heralded Family and Medical Leave Act of 1993 gives workers up to three months leave to deal with family matters or personal emergencies—but without pay. For most working-class women, who can scarcely afford a day without pay much less three months, this is a slap in the face; even if they could afford to take the leave—which they can't—the act applies only to employers with at least fifty workers, which immediately excludes large numbers of the workers who need it most. For these women, because it gives the appearance of progress when there is none, this piece of legislation is worse than nothing.

Legislators—and advocates—who tout legislation such as the FMLA as a major breakthrough for women forget about the working poor. Ironically, the United States—home of the Protestant work ethic—is one of the few countries in the world in which adults who work full-time can still be poor. In fact, according to the OECD, poverty rates for working single parents are higher in the United States than in any other major western industrialized country; close to 50 percent of the poor population in the United States live in families with one worker, but—even more startling—23 percent live in families with two adult workers.[7] The Earned Income Tax Credit Act, which was passed in 1996, has helped some of these working poor families by reimbursing a portion of their taxes, but still the United States lags behind most similar countries in reducing poverty by means of taxation and income transfers. In fact, the United States has the dubious honor of being the only country where income transfers are redistributed *from* lower to *higher* income earners in the form of benefits such as mortgage deductions.

Because the current prevailing political ideology is anti-"big government," it seems that the union movement is the last best hope for women such as those in this study. Women union members earn 31 percent more than non-members ($596 c.f. $436), and more often have health benefits.[8] Unfortunately, however, women have a lower rate of union membership than men (12 percent c.f. 17 percent) and only around 10 percent of service workers (outside protective services), and 5 percent of retail sales workers have union representation.[9] Thus the occupations in which women most need protection have a lower rate of union membership.

Moreover, even when women *are* union members, they tend to have lower rates of participation than men. In part, this is because unions in the past have not actively encouraged women's participation, and because women's family responsibilities limit their time and availability. But these two explanations tell only part of the story; the other part, it seems, is that "women [are] uncomfortable with the climate of union meetings and other aspects of 'male union culture.'"[10] Researchers have found that "families and other social networks provided more effective and satisfying sources of personal empowerment" for them. In the view of the authors of one study, if they are to attract women workers, particularly service workers, unions must change their style of decision-making to make it less confrontational and more decentralized, and they must also try to tap into women's extensive family and religious networks.[11]

Two of my interviews support this view. I did not specifically ask the women about union membership, but two women talked about their husbands' union activity. Ann said she was very frustrated with her husband's involvement in the union, because he had a powerful position and he "brought it home." And, in support of the research, Jill definitely saw her husband's role as a shop steward as confrontational. "He's been fighting with the boss," she said. "Every day I'll say, 'Well, did you fight today?'" Both women saw union activities as detracting from family life because they robbed men of family time and added to their load of stress. These perceptions, if widespread, present a challenge to union organizers.

There are other barriers to unionization. Women who work in low-paid service and other gray-collar jobs often have little formal education and work experience, and because their jobs are insecure, they have a realistic fear of losing them. Furthermore, many of these women work in relative isolation—in convenience stores, for example—with no opportunity to develop the group solidarity that fosters union membership. These factors must all be overcome if the women who most need it are to get union protection.

If for no other reason than their own self-esteem, women should be given opportunities throughout life for education and training. As it is, the waste of woman power—what economists call "human capital"—is truly tragic. Many of the women in this study, including a number of the women who had dropped out of high school, had volunteered in schools and hospitals, and had proven themselves to be competent, committed workers. They had acted as teacher substitutes, clerks, secretaries, and physical therapy assistants, performing a social service and gaining a sense of fulfillment and usefulness far beyond any they could find in paid work. It was hardly surprising that so many of these women said they would like to volunteer: only as volunteers could their real worth be recognized and their real abilities put to use.

Early educational intervention would remove some of the need for adult education, but although more guidance in schools, more humane educators, and more intensive enlightened assistance for students who struggle would all help, they will make a real difference only if young women and men from working-class backgrounds learn that school *is* for the likes of them. And it will be difficult for them to learn this as long as they not only live in different neighborhoods from middle-class students but are educated in different institutions. There is little cause for optimism that education will fundamentally change inequality as long as the elite classes—both conservative and liberal, Democrat and Republican—continue to shun the public schools. As long as elite children attend one school and poor and working-class children another, and elite children live in one neighborhood and poor and working-class children in another, a few working-class daughters (and sons) may cross class boundaries, but the boundaries will remain firmly in place.

The women who have the least—the least education, material resources, and skills—clean the houses and care for the children and parents of the women who have the most. They shampoo their hair, bag their groceries, and wipe up their spills. The needs of these women should now be at the forefront of middle-class women's advocacy agendas; until working-class women are treated fairly and policies that help them—such as an increased minimum wage, universal health insurance, and paid family leave—are implemented, women cannot truly be said to have made progress. The most pressing challenge for middle-class women now should be to help create workplaces that reward all workers fairly, female as well as male, unskilled as well as skilled, black as well as white.

Most of these suggestions involve greater government participation, which is, of course, bitterly opposed by political conservatives. More surprisingly, social policy attempts to remedy social injustice are also opposed by some Marxist theorists, who argue that such attempts merely tinker with the system and reproduce existing class societies. This is true if the tinkering is minor, but must it be minor? When states actively seek to equalize income and wealth, class inequalities are reduced. The new economy is ruthless: it chews up some workers and spits them out when they become superfluous; it richly rewards some, and punishes others. Real positive change can be accomplished through social policies aimed at taming this beast; as one author put it, "the welfare state is a mighty opponent to the economy's inegalitarian thrust."[12]

Unequal Opportunity

In spite of the expansion of public education, still around one-fourth of the female population of the United States has not completed high school; this represents about thirty million women. Among these millions of women, we can assume, are quite a number who—like Sonya and some of the other women I interviewed—have been shut out of mainstream society, as children whose suffering no one noticed, as students whose failure no one cared about, and as working women in jobs no one else wanted.

Some of these women might be described as "underclass." Is this description apt? If by this term we mean people who are swept under the carpet, who are invisible because they cause no trouble and make no demands, then, yes, it is; they are members of an underclass. If, on the other hand, we mean people whose behavior is so deviant they cannot participate in social institutions, then, no, it is not. If the term means people who are "slow learners" in a culture that worships the quick, the smart, the aggressive and upwardly mobile go-getter, yes they are an underclass. But if it means people who have given up on the American dream, then no, they are not. In fact, not one of these women had given up; in their forties, they still wanted an education, a job, a part of the good life, and they were prepared to work for it—they *were* working for it. To accomplish it, some, especially women who had been disadvantaged throughout their entire lives, needed social support. Others, however, needed no more than fair conditions and a just wage. Is that not the American way?

Notes

Chapter One: Introduction

1. Symbolic interactionism is a sociological approach that states that we can only understand human actions if we understand their meaning for the actor. It emphasizes that we learn meanings in the context of our interactions with others.

2. Herbert Blumer, *Symbolic Interactionism: Perspective and Method* (Berkeley: University of California Press, 1986), p. 36.

3. *Symbolic Interactionism*, p. 39.

4. Studs Terkel, *Working* (New York: Ballantine Books, 1972).

5. Barbara Ehrenreich, *Nickel and Dimed: On (Not) Getting By in America* (New York: Metropolitan Books, 2001).

6. bell hooks, *Where We Stand: Class Matters* (New York: Routledge, 2000).

Chapter Two: The Meaning of Work and Class

1. Karl Marx, *Economic and Philosophical Manuscripts of 1844*, trans. Martin Milligan (Moscow: Foreign Languages Publishing House, 1956).

2. Ronald Kutscher, "Historical Trends, 1950–92, and Current Uncertainties," *Monthly Labor Review* (November 1993): 3–10; Bureau of the Census, Census 2000, Table 11, pp. 178–183 (http://www.uscensus.gov).

3. Bureau of Labor Statistics, *Handbook of Labor Statistics—Bulletin 2340*, August 1989.

4. Census 2000, Table 11, pp. 178–183; U.S. Department of Labor, Women's Bureau, *Working Women Count! A Report to the Nation, 1994* (Washington, D.C.: Government Printing Office, 1994).

5. U.S. Department of Labor, Women's Bureau, *20 Leading Occupations of Employed Women, 2000 Annual Averages* (http://dol.gov/dol/wb).

6. Karl Marx and Friedrich Engels, *The Communist Manifesto*, in *Capital and Other Writings by Karl Marx*, ed. Max Eastman (New York: Random House, 1959), pp. 328–329.

7. Friedrich Engels, *The Condition of the Working Class in England* (Stanford: Stanford University Press, 1968), pp. 324, 333.

8. Wanda F. Neff, *Victorian Working Women* (New York: Columbia University Press, 1929), p. 42. Cited in Louise A. Tilly and Joan W. Scott, *Women, Work and Family,* (New York: Routledge, 1989), p. 64.

9. Report of the Special Assistant Poor Law Commissioners of the Commission on the Employment of Women and Children in Agriculture, 1843, p. 65. Cited in Eric Hopkins, *Childhood Transformed: Working-Class Children in Nineteenth Century England* (Manchester: Manchester University Press, 1994), p. 21.The following section owes much to this book, which is a superb example of historical scholarship.

10. *Childhood Transformed,* p. 24.

11. *Childhood Transformed,* p. 53.

12. Children's Employment Commission, 1840, First Report, Mines, p. 84. Cited in *Childhood Transformed.*

13. Parliamentary Reports (Hansard), third Series, vol. 63, p. 1351. Cited in *Childhood Transformed.*

14. Barbara Welter, "The Cult of True Womanhood, 1820–1860," *American Quarterly* 18 (1966): 151–174.

15. "The Cult of True Womanhood," p. 53.

16. "The Cult of True Womanhood," p. 160.

17. "The Cult of True Womanhood," p. 165. See also Alice Kessler Harris, *Women Have Always Worked: A Historical Overview* (New York: McGraw-Hill, 1981).

18. Viviana Zelizer, *Pricing the Priceless Child: The Changing Social Value of Children* (New York: Basic Books, 1985).

19. Virginia Yans-McLaughlin, *Family and Community: Italian Immigrants in Buffalo, 1880–1930* (Ithaca: Cornell University Press, 1971), p. 193. Cited in *Pricing the Priceless Child,* p. 69.

20. Karl Marx, *The German Ideology.* The exact quote is: "The ideas of the ruling class are in every epoch the ruling ideas, i.e. the class which is the ruling material force of society, is at the same time its ruling intellectual force. The class which has the means of material production at its disposal, has control at the same time over the means of mental production, so that thereby, generally speaking, the ideas of those who lack the means of mental production are subject to it." (Karl Marx and Frederick Engels, *The German Ideology,* ed. C. J. Arthur (New York: International Publishers, 1988), p. 64.

21. Elizabeth Fox-Genovese, "Difference, Diversity and Divisions in an Agenda for the Women's Movement," in *Color, Class and Country: Experiences of Gender,* ed. G. Young and B. Dickerson (London: Zed Books, 1994), p. 237; and Elizabeth Fox-Genovese, *Feminism Is Not the Story of My Life* (New York: Nan A. Talese, 1996).

22. Judith Rollins, *Between Women: Domestics and Their Employers* (Philadelphia: Temple University Press, 1985), p. 8.

23. Max Weber, *The Theory of Social and Economic Organization,* ed. Talcott Parsons (New York: Free Press, 1964), p. 97.

24. Talcott Parsons on page 93 of his translation (with A. M. Henderson) of *Social and Economic Organization* correctly criticizes Weber's implication that actions are meaningful only when they are interpretable as "rational means-end schema." Using this criterion limits meaningful action to only a small universe of human actions.

25. Weber, *The Theory of Social and Economic Organization*, p. 91.

26. Alfred Schutz, *The Phenomenology of the Social World*, trans. George Walsh and Frederick Lehnert (Chicago: Northwestern University Press, 1967), pp. 88, 91.

27. For example, Barbara Ehrenreich and John Ehrenreich, "The Professional-Managerial Class," *Radical America* 11, no. 2 (1971).

28. For example, Vilfredo Pareto, *The Mind and Society*, trans. A. Bongiorno and Arthur Livingston, ed. Arthur Livingston (New York: Harcourt, 1935). Cited in Gerhard Lenski, *Power and Privilege: A Theory of Social Stratification* (New York: McGraw-Hill, 1966). Although, as Lenski points out, Pareto does not exactly equate elite status with class, but with the upper echelon of a class or society. According to C. Wright Mills, the elite "feel themselves to be and are felt by others to be, the inner circle of 'the upper social classes.'" C. Wright Mills, *The Power Elite* (London: Oxford University Press, 1956), p. 11.

29. Ralph Dahrendorf, *Class and Class Conflict in Industrial Society* (Stanford: Stanford University Press, 1959). *Power and Privilege* (see note 28).

30. For readers who are interested in this debate, I recommend the following overview: Rosemary Crompton and Michael Mann, eds., *Gender and Stratification* (Cambridge: Polity Press, 1986). See also Heidi Hartmann, "The Family as a Locus of Gender, Class and Political Struggle: The Example of Housework," *Signs* 6, no. 3 (1981): 366–394; and "The Unhappy Marriage of Marxism and Feminism: Towards a More Progressive Union," in *Women and Revolution: A Discussion of the Unhappy Marriage of Marxism and Feminism*, Lydia Sargent, ed. (Boston: South End Press, 1981).

31. For example, Pierre Bourdieu, *Distinction: A Social Critique of the Judgement of Taste*, trans. Richard Nice (New York: Routledge and Kegan Paul, 1984).

32. Pierre Bourdieu, *Outline of a Theory of Practice* (Cambridge: Cambridge University Press, 1977), p. 506.

33. Bourdieu, *Distinction*, p. 70.

34. C. Wright Mills, *The Sociological Imagination* (New York: Oxford University Press, 1959), p. 6.

35. Anthony Giddens, *The Class Structure of the Advanced Societies*, 2nd ed. (London: Hutchinson, 1980).

36. See Peter Berger and Thomas Luckmann, *The Social Construction of Reality* (New York: Doubleday, 1967), as well as Alfred Schutz and Thomas Luckmann, *Structures of the Life World*, trans. Richard M. Zaner and H. Tristam Engelhardt Jr. (Evanston: Northwestern University Press, 1973).

37. However it is defined, the women's social class was strongly related to both their fathers' and their husbands'.

38. Richard Sennett and R. Cobb, *The Hidden Injuries of Class* (New York: Vintage Books, 1973). Lillian Breslow Rubin, *Worlds of Pain: Life in the Working-Class Family* (New York: Basic Books, 1976).

39. The Quality of Employment Survey, a national survey fielded in the 1970s, was helpful, as was Melvin Kohn's pathbreaking book *Work and Personality*. Robert P. Quinn and Linda J. Shepard, *The 1972–73 Quality of Employment Survey* (Ann Arbor: Institute of Social Research, University of Michigan, 1974); Melvin Kohn and Carmi Schooler, *Work and Personality: An Inquiry into the Impact of Social Stratification* (Norwood, N.J.: Ablex Publishing, 1983).

40. Mary Catherine Bateson, *Composing a Life* (New York: Atlantic Monthly Press, 1989).

41. Included as middle-class women are the six women of working-class origin who were college graduates. As a group, their work conditions were not significantly different from those of women from middle-class origins who worked in similar positions.

42. Erik Erickson, *Childhood and Society* (New York: Norton, 1963).

43. Arlie Hochschild, *The Second Shift: Working Parents and the Revolution at Home* (New York: Viking, 1989).

44. For a discussion of the rapid cycling of generations among African-American families, see Cynthia Merriwether-de-Vries et al., "Early Parenting and Intergenerational Family Relationships among African-American Families," in *Transitions Through Adulthood: Interpersonal Domains and Contexts*, Julia A. Gruber, Jeanne Brooks-Gunn, and Anne C. Petersen, eds. (New Jersey: Lawrence Erlbaum and Associates, 1996).

Chapter Three: Life on the Job

1. U.S. Department of Labor, Women's Bureau, *Women's Jobs, 1964–1997, Thirty Years of Progress* (Washington, D.C.: Government Printing Office, 1998). Eighteen of the twenty leading occupations for women published by the Department of Labor in 1997 were service jobs. U.S. Department of Labor, Women's Bureau, *Twenty Leading Occupations of Employed Women* (Washington, D.C.: Government Printing Office, 1997).

2. It's easy to lose sight of how dramatically things have changed; in 1950 only 3.4 percent of lawyers and 6.5 percent of physicians were female. *Statistical Abstracts of the United States* (Washington, D.C.: Government Printing Office, 1953), Table 198, p. 224.

3. U.S. Department of Labor, Women's Bureau, *Equal Pay: A Thirty-five Year Perspective* (Washington, D.C.: Government Printing Office, 1998).

4. Ruy Teixeira and Joel Rogers, *Why the White Working Class Still Matters: America's Forgotten Majority* (New York: Basic Books, 2000).

5. Michael C. Wolfson and Brian B. Murphy, "New Views on Inequality: Trends in Canada and the United States," *Monthly Labor Review* (April 1998): 3–23.

6. Christopher Jencks, Lauri Perlman, and Lee Rainwater, "What Is a Good Job? A New Measure of Labor Market Success," *American Journal of Sociology* 93, no. 6 (1988): 1322–1357.

7. Erik Olin Wright argues that job conditions can be seen as criteria of social class, not just as consequences. Specifically, he uses autonomy at work as a criterion for distinguishing between the proletariat and "semiautonomous employees." Erik Olin Wright, *Classes* (Thetford: Verso, 1985).

8. For example, Melvin Kohn and Carmi Schooler, *Work and Personality: An Inquiry into the Impact of Social Stratification* (Norwood, N.J.: Ablex Publishing, 1983).

9. A combination of low levels of job control and high levels of demand seems to be particularly harmful. In his extensive research on job conditions and health outcomes, Robert Karasek has found situations in which workers have low "job decision latitude," and high "job demands" to be stress-inducing and damaging to health. For example, Robert Karasek et al., "Job Decision Latitude, Job Demands, and Cardiovascular-Disease—A Prospective Study of Swedish Men," *American Journal of Public Health* 71, no. 7 (1981): 694–705; "Job Demands, Job Decision Latitude, and Mental Strain: Implications for Job Redesign," *Administrative Science Quarterly* 24 (1979): 285–309; "Work and Non-Work Correlates of Illness and Behavior for Male and Female Swedish White-Collar Workers," *Journal of Occupational Behavior* 8 (1987): 187–207.

10. In *Symbolic Interactionism: Perspective and Method* (Berkeley: University of California Press, 1969), p. 33, Blumer criticizes social science for avoiding firsthand experience of the real world. He notes, "The astonishing fact that the overwhelming proportion of key concepts have not been pinned down in their empirical reference in the proper sense that one can go to instances in the empirical world and say safely that this is an instance of the concept and that is not an instance." To be fair, this is much less true in 2002 than it was in 1969.

11. To avoid imposing predetermined categories before women had a chance to offer their own, I left these questions until the end of the interview.

12. For a review of the importance of social relationships with supervisors, see Reta Repetti, "The Effects of Workload and the Social Environment at Work on Health," in *Handbook of Stress: Theoretical and Clinical Aspects*, Leo Goldberger and Shlomo Breznitz, eds. (New York: The Free Press 1993), pp. 368–385. Louise Lamphere et al., in their study of Chicana factory workers, found that women liked their jobs when managers and supervisors were friendly. Louise Lamphere, Patricia Zavella, Felipe Gonzalez with Peter B. Evans, *Sunbelt Working Mothers: Reconciling Family and Factory* (Ithaca: Cornell University Press, 1993).

13. Jean Baker Miller, *Toward a New Psychology of Women* (Boston: Beacon Press, 1976), p. 83.

14. Carol Gilligan, *In a Different Voice: Psychological Theory and Women's Development* (Cambridge, Mass.: Harvard University Press, 1982), p. 171.

15. "Essentialism," the view that women are fundamentally different from men, is the "difference" side of a same/different dichotomy that divides feminist theorists. For an excellent discussion of this and other bones of contention within feminist theory, see Barbara Ryan's *Feminism and the Women's Movement: Dynamics of Change in Social Movement Ideology and Activism* (New York: Routledge, 1992).

16. None of the women in professional jobs (including those from both working-class and middle-class backgrounds) said that "liking the people" was the most important thing to have in a job; professional women were more likely to say that having interesting work was most important.

17. In a study of midlife women (based on a national data set), Ronald D'Amico found that women were about two-thirds as likely as men to supervise others, but only about one-third as likely to have any say over pay or promotion. Women with higher education and more extensive work experience were more likely to supervise than were other women. Ronald D'Amico, "Authority in the Workplace: Difference Among Mature Women," in *Midlife Women at Work: A Fifteen-Year Perspective*, Lois Banfill Shaw, ed. (Lexington, Mass.: Lexington Books, 1986), pp. 37–49.

18. Arlie Russell Hochschild describes the emotional work men and women do in jobs, but notes that, compared with men, women have a "weaker status shield against the displaced feelings of others." Nowhere was this more obvious than in customer-service jobs. See Arlie Russell Hochschild, *The Managed Heart: Commercialization of Human Feeling* (Berkeley: University of California Press, 1983), p. 163.

19. Sixteen of the twenty-nine women who supervised were daughters of entrepreneurs or supervisors, compared with only eleven of the fifty-two women who did not.

20. For a superb analysis of the experience of family day-care providers, see Margaret K. Nelson, *Negotiated Care: The Experience of Family Day Care Providers* (Philadelphia: Temple University Press, 1990).

21. These differences and the tensions they create are sometimes magnified by class differences in childrearing practices between providers and parents.

22. Center for Child Care Workforce, *Current Data on Child Care Salaries and Benefits in the United States*, March 2001, p. 3.

23. Erving Goffman was a pioneer in the exploration of shared assumptions and the consequences of their violation. See, for example, *The Presentation of Self in Everyday Life* (Woodstock, N.Y.: Overlook Press, 1973).

24. About half the women who worked in low-paid gray-collar jobs agreed their pay was "good," and only two said the pay was what they liked least about their job. About the same percentage of professional women (twelve of twenty-three) said they

had good pay.

25. Laura and Sonya both illustrated the importance of expectations: Laura's proprietary school had given her an inflated idea of what she would earn when she graduated, so she was disappointed in her pay, and Sonya took over her husband's job when he left it for better pay. With these two reference points, both women were dissatisfied with their pay, but they were exceptions.

26. For women in unskilled jobs, challenge often meant pressure. This is consistent with the research by Karasek and others (note 9), who are interested in the relationship between job control and health. Women in the worst jobs had a combination of high demands with little control, the very conditions that have been found to be most stressful.

27. In their extensive research on the relationship between work and personality, Melvin Kohn and his colleagues have identified closeness of supervision, the "substantive complexity of work," and "routinization" as the three job conditions that most affect workers' psychological functioning. Melvin L. Kohn, "Unresolved Issues in the Relationship between Work and Personality," in *The Nature of Work: Sociological Perspectives*, ed. Kai Erickson and Steven Vallas (New Haven: Yale University Press, 1990), pp. 36–68.

28. Usually women in professional jobs had more autonomy, but this was not so for teachers in the public school system. Because they were hamstrung by the bureaucracy—which they all complained about—public school teachers felt less autonomous than most other women, including women who worked in the school system as unskilled workers.

Chapter Four: Can't Get No Satisfaction

1. Although they have different connotations, "commitment" and "centrality" are often used interchangeably. A large amount of literature during the seventies and eighties looked at commitment and centrality, but, in fact, most of it looked at middle-class women's career commitment, not work commitment, and career motivation, not motivation to work.

2. This is a point that the sociologist Myra Marx Ferree has been making for some time. See in particular "Between Two Worlds: German Feminist Approaches to Working-Class Women and Work," *Signs* 10, no. 5 (1985): 517–536. And men's—especially working-class men's—ambivalence about work has probably been underestimated. Kornhauser, for example, noted that while "workers express predominantly favorable feelings toward their jobs . . . there are many important negative reactions; it is apparent that large numbers of men are not well satisfied and that their positive responses to general questions must be cautiously accepted and heavily discounted." A. Kornhauser, *Mental Health of the Industrial Worker: A Detroit Study* (New York: John Wiley and Sons, 1965), p. 9. Given the cultural ideology that men should be psycho-

logically invested in their job, it is likely that men are reluctant to admit to disaffection.

3. See Ferree, "Between Two Worlds," and also Karen Loscocco, "Reactions to Blue-Collar Work: A Comparison of Women and Men," *Work and Occupations* 17, no. 2 (1990): 152–177.

4. H. F. Moorhouse, "The 'Work' Ethic and 'Leisure' Activity: The Hot Rod in Post-War America," in *The Historical Meanings of Work*, ed. Patrick Joyce (Cambridge: Cambridge University Press, 1987), pp. 237–257.

5. This orientation to work—where "a job is just a job"—has been attributed to working-class men. As far as I know, the British sociologists John Goldthorpe, David Lockwood, Frank Bechhofer, and Jennifer Platt were the first to describe it as an "instrumental" approach to work—that is, an attitude that a job is a means to an end, not an end in itself. Their study was of male factory workers, so perhaps it should not be surprising that work was a means to an end, not an end in itself, but, nonetheless, their findings sparked a continuing debate. Sociologists of work clearly hold to the "central life interest" ideology, which I discuss more fully in the next chapter, because ascribing an instrumental orientation to working-class men is considered insulting to them when, in fact, viewing work as a means to an end, in the case of many jobs, seems eminently sensible. See John H. Goldthorpe, David Lockwood, Frank Bechhofer, and Jennifer Platt, *The Affluent Worker: Industrial Attitudes and Behavior* (Cambridge: Cambridge University Press, 1968).

6. Abraham Maslaw, *Motivation and Personality* (New York: Harper and Row, 1970), p. 46.

7. *Motivation and Personality*, p. 37.

8. *Motivation and Personality*, p. 46.

9. Mihaly Csiksentmihaly, *Flow: The Psychology of Optimal Experience* (New York: Harper Perennial, 1990), p. 67.

10. *Flow*, p. 69.

11. See Stanton Wheeler, "Double Lives," in *The Nature of Work: Sociological Perspectives*, ed. Kai Erickson and Steven Peter Vallas (New Haven: Yale University Press, 1990), pp. 141–148.

Chapter Five: What Work Means

1. Cotton Mather, *Two Brief Discourses: The One Offering Methods and Motives for Parents, The Other Offering Some Instructions for Children* (Boston, New England: Printed by T. Green for Benjamin Eliot, 1702).

2. D. Rodgers, *The Work Ethic in Industrial America, 1850–1920* (London: University of Chicago Press, 1978), p. 14.

3. A. Kornhauser, *Mental Health of the Industrial Worker: A Detroit Study* (New York: John Wiley and Sons, 1965).

4. As H. F. Moorhouse, a historian, points out in his analysis of the 1950s hot-rod subculture in the United States, the "central life interest" ideology especially trivializes leisure and other activities that are not "intellectual." H. F. Moorhouse, "The 'Work Ethic' and 'Leisure' Activity: The Hot-Rod in Post-War America," in *The Historical Meanings of Work*, ed. Patrick Joyce (Cambridge: Cambridge University Press, 1987), pp. 237–257.

5. There are very slight differences based on gender, race, and education, but overall levels of job satisfaction are high. In a study that looked at the relationship between job satisfaction and race, gender and occupation, Glenn Firebaugh and Brian Harley found white women to be more satisfied than African-American women, but they found virtually no race differences among men. Even among women the differences were quite small, leading the authors to conclude that the main result of their study was "the similarity of race and gender groups with regard to job satisfaction." Glenn Firebaugh and Brian Harley, "Trends in Job Satisfaction in the United States by Race, Gender and Type of Occupations," *Research in the Sociology of Work* 5 (1995): 87–104. For a study of the relationship between education and job satisfaction, see Jack C. Martin and Constance L. Shehan, "Education and Job Satisfaction: The Influences of Gender, Wage-Earning Status, and Job Values," *Work and Occupations* 16, no. 2 (1989): 184–199. These authors found that more highly educated workers were slightly more satisfied with their jobs, but the differences were small. In a study of blue-collar workers, however, Karen Loscocco found that education depressed job satisfaction; presumably this was because the more highly educated women in her study had higher expectations that were not being met. See Karyn A. Loscocco, "Reactions to Blue Collar Work: A Comparison of Women and Men," *Work and Occupations* 17, no. 2 (1990): 152–177. For two studies that explicitly ask why women are just as satisfied as men, see Jo Phelan, "The Paradox of the Contented Female Worker: An Assessment of Alternative Explanations," *Social Psychology Quarterly* 57, no. 2 (1994): 95–107. Asking why women are not dissatisfied even though they are paid less than men, Phelan found salary to be unrelated to satisfaction for both women and men in the organization she studied. Her dependent variable, however, was organizational satisfaction rather than job satisfaction specifically, and her sample was limited to one company. Her article includes a useful discussion of the different hypotheses that are advanced to explain the "paradox." See also Randy Hodson, "Gender Differences in Job Satisfaction: Why Aren't Women More Dissatisfied?" *The Sociological Quarterly* 30, no. 3 (1989): 385–399. Hodson concludes that two processes may explain women's high levels of satisfaction. First, women may use different comparison groups than men, comparing themselves with women who don't work and women who work in jobs similar to their own; second, men may be more willing to express dissatisfaction. Myra Marx Ferree also suggests that working-class women compare themselves to housewives. Myra Marx Ferree, "Class, Housework, and Happiness: Women's Work

and Life Satisfaction," *Sex Roles* 11/12 (1984): 1057–1074. Finally, for a literature review on gender and job satisfaction, see Joanne Miller, "Individual and Occupational Determinants of Job Satisfaction: A Focus on Gender Differences," *Sociology of Work and Occupations* 7, no. 3 (1980): 337–366. See also Wendy C. Wolf and Neil D. Fligstein, "Sex and Authority in the Workplace," *American Sociological Review* 44 (1979): 235–252; like Joanne Miller, these authors found that women seemed to value authority less than men.

6. General Social Survey, National Opinion Research Center, 1988.

7. See, for example, Arne Kalleberg, "Work Values and Job Rewards: A Theory of Job Satisfaction," *American Sociological Review* 42 (1977): 124–143. Also J. H. Goldthorpe, David Lockwood, F. Bechhofer, and Jennifer Platt, *The Affluent Worker: Industrial Attitudes and Behavior* (Cambridge: Cambridge University Press, 1968). Also Cecily C. Neil and William E. Snizek, "Gender as a Moderator of Job Satisfaction," *Work and Occupations* 15 2 (1988): 201–219.

8. See Joanne Miller article, note 5.

9. Different studies define and measure "commitment" differently, which makes comparison difficult. In any case, commitment is an ambiguous concept.

10. See, for example, H. Beynon and R. M. Blackburn, *Perceptions of Work: Variations within a Factory* (Cambridge: Cambridge University Press, 1972). For an excellent summary, see Michael Betz and Lenahan O'Connell, "Work Orientations of Males and Females: Exploring the Gender Socialization Approach," *Sociological Enquiry* 59 3 (1989): 318–330.

11. Jon Lorence, to cite just one example, found, in one of the few longitudinal studies, that work involvement varied in response to levels of job autonomy, but not to family life-cycle stage. Jon Lorence, "Work Experience and Occupational Value Socialization: A Longitudinal Study," *American Journal of Sociology* 84 (1979): 1361–1385.

12. For an excellent discussion of this issue, see Karen Loscocco, "The Instrumentally Oriented Factory Worker," *Work and Occupations* 16, no. 1 (1989): 3–25.

13. See Jo Phelan and Randy Hodson, note 5. For a fuller discussion of relative deprivation theory, see Faye Crosby, *Relative Deprivation and Working Women* (New York: Oxford University Press, 1982). Also Myra Marx Ferree, "Working Class Jobs: Housework and Paid Work as Sources of Satisfaction," *Social Problems* 23 (1976): 431–441. Also by Ferree, "Class, Work, and Happiness: Women's Work and Life Satisfaction," *Sex Roles* 11 11/12 (1984): 1057–1074.

14. The reliability of the scale for the entire sample, according to Cronbach's alpha, was .74.

15. Challenge was strongly correlated with autonomy only for women with a high school diploma; women such as Ethel, who worked for a prison superintendent, had

self-directed and challenging work. Autonomy was independent of challenge for professional women because it was part and parcel of being a professional; because it was uniformly high (except for teachers), it did not vary along with challenge. For working-class women without a diploma, in gray-collar disrespectful workplaces, the situation was different; challenge and autonomy were such scarce conditions they did not co-occur in enough workplaces to be related. Recognition, however, was more available to some women without a diploma and it was strongly related to challenge; in particular, the six women dropouts who worked in the school system and the two who were self-employed felt appreciated and considered their work challenging.

16. Working-class women with a diploma and middle-class women had virtually identical scores on a scale that combined a number of questions on the importance of work for identity. However, on the single, direct question—How important is work for your sense of identity, of who you are?—high school graduates were the group who most often said work was "strongly important."

17. C.f. Jean L. Potuchek's description of "reluctant providers," women who have no choice about being breadwinners. In interviews conducted in 1987/1988, Potuchek found that a small proportion of wives (only one in seven) and about one in four husbands reported that they shared the breadwinning role, and considered such sharing appropriate. Jean L. Potuchek, *Who Supports the Family? Gender and Breadwinning in Dual-earner Marriages* (Stanford: Stanford University Press, 1997).

18. In fact, women in this group who were more satisfied with their jobs were also most strongly involved with them; this was true also for women with education credentials but the relationship was not nearly so strong.

19. The origin of class differences in workers' psychological dispositions or orientations is unclear; there is obviously a chicken-and-egg problem here. If working-class women more often say they work for money, not personal fulfillment, for example, does this difference reflect personal qualities or abilities that make them not enjoy challenging, intrinsically meaningful work? Or does it reflect their more pressing need for money than for personal fulfillment? Or their acceptance that they have little hope of finding a personally fulfilling job? For reasons that I will go into more fully in later chapters on working-class childhood, working-class women were less likely to believe that paid work could be autonomous and personally fulfilling.

20. Grace Baruch, Rosalind Barnett, and Caryl Rivers, *Lifeprints: New Patterns of Life and Work for Today's Women* (New York: McGraw-Hill, 1983).

Chapter Six: Work (f)or Family

1. Constantina Safilios-Rothschild, "The Influence of Wife's Degree of Work Commitment upon Some Aspects of Family Organization and Dynamics," *Journal of Marriage and the Family* (November 1970): 681–687.

2. Denise Bielby and John Bielby, "Work Commitment, Sex-role Attitudes, and

Women's Employment," *American Sociological Review* 49 (1984): 234–247.

3. Kathleen Gerson in *Hard Choices: How Women Decide About Work, Career and Motherhood* (Berkeley: University of California Press, 1985).

4. *Hard Choices*, p. 106.

5. A possible explanation for the differences between this study and Gerson's is that all the women I spoke with were married. However, if anything, that should have given them more choice, not less.

6. Phyllis Moen, *Women's Two Roles: A Contemporary Dilemma* (New York: Auburn House. 1992), p. 54.

7. On average, women who worked off and on had three children, as did women who put off going to work. The women who deferred work started childbearing at a younger age than women who worked off and on—who, in turn, started earlier than women who worked continuously.

8. Using a national data set, Frank L. Mott and Lois Banfill Shaw found that white women who worked in the 1940s and 1950s—when they were mothers of small children—were more likely to work at midlife. For this earlier generation of women, working with young children was evidence of "unusual commitment to the workplace." Frank L. Mott and Lois Banfill Shaw, "The Employment Consequences of Different Fertility Behaviors," in *Midlife Women at Work: A Fifteen-Year Perspective*, ed. Lois B. Shaw (Lexington, Mass.: D.C. Heath and Company, 1986), pp. 23–36. The same may have been true for some of the women in my sample; for others who worked continuously, though, it was at least in part a matter of serendipity. Mary, for example, found that she was unable to have more children, and Helen felt too insecure in her marriage to feel confident giving up her income. The role of unpredictable life experiences in prodding women toward or away from a work (or family) orientation has been described by Kathleen Gerson in *Hard Choices: How Women Decide About Work, Career and Motherhood* (Berkeley: University of California Press, 1985). By finishing high school, Trudy, for example, had created a situation in which work was more likely to be an attractive option to staying home and having a larger family, but she was also prepared to limit her family size. Other women, such as Ann, on the other hand, were forced to give up work as more children came along.

9. Most women felt comfortable leaving their child with a family member, less so with "a stranger."

10. Vera, the other part-time worker, was a clinical psychologist who taught part-time at a local community college while she was completing her dissertation. After completing her Ph.D., she gave birth to her first child and switched to teaching part-time. After a time, she began counseling one evening a week, and when her second child was born, she gave up teaching and started a clinical practice in her home. Over the years, her hours had slowly built up, and she was now seeing patients about fifteen hours a week. She spent as many hours on paperwork.

Chapter Seven: The Work of Caring

1. Deborah Belle, "The Stress of Caring: Women as Providers of Social Support," in *Handbook of Stress: Theoretical and Clinical Aspects*, ed. Leo Goldberger and Shlomo Brezowitz (New York: The Free Press, 1982), pp. 496–505.

2. Nancy L. Marshall and Rosalind C. Barnett, "Race, Class and Multiple Role Strains and Gains Among Women Employed in the Service Sector," *Women and Health* 1, no. 17 (1991): 1–19.

3. Annie E. Casey Foundation, *City Kids Count: Data on the Well-Being of Children in Large Cities* (1997) (http:www.aecf.org/publications/#kidscount).

4. Ken Bryson and Lynne M. Casper, Coresident Grandparents and Grandchildren, Current Population Records P23-198, U.S. Bureau of the Census (Washington, D.C.: U.S. Government Printing Office, 1999).

5. Carol M. Musil, Susan Schrader, and John Mutikani, "Social Support, Stress, and Special Coping Tasks of Grandmother Caregivers," in *To Grandmother's House We Go and Stay: Perspectives on Custodial Grandparents*, Carole B. Cox, ed. (New York: Springer Publishing Company, 2000), pp. 56–70.

6. H. S. Kleiner, J. Hertzog, and D. B. Targ, "Background Information for Educators"; L. H. Towle, "Grandma, Where's Mommy?" *Carolina Parent*, 1997; also in *Grandmother's House*, p. 62. Grandparents Acting as Parents: http://www.nnfr.org.nnfr/igen/gaap.html.

7. Marshall and Barnett, "Race, Class and Multiple Role Strains and Gains," pp. 1–9.

8. American Association of Retired Persons, 1994, AARP Grandparent Information Center, cited in *To Grandmother's House*, p. 63.

9. J. A. Odulana, L. D. Camblin, and P. White, "Cultural Roles and Health Status of Contemporary African-American Young Grandmothers," *The Journal of Multicultural Nursing and Health* 2 (1996): 28–35.

10. Arlie Hochschild (with Anne Machung), *The Second Shift: Working Parents and the Revolution at Home* (New York: Viking, 1989).

11. Diemut Elisabet Bubeck, *Care, Gender and Justice* (Oxford: Clarendon Press, 1995), p. 25. In *Carework*, Francesca M. Cancian defines care more narrowly as "feelings of affection and responsibility, with actions that provide for an individual's personal needs or well-being in a face-to-face interaction." Francesca M. Cancian, "Paid Emotional Care," in *Care Work: Gender, Labor and Welfare States*, ed. Madonna Harrington Meyer (New York: Routledge, 2000), pp. 136–148.

12. Elizabeth Bott, *Family and Social Network: Roles, Norms, and External Relationships in Ordinary Urban Families* (New York: MacMillan, Free Press, 1971), p. 135.

13. The data in this paragraph are from Census 2000; see http://www/census.gov/main/www/cen2000.html.

14. Not all caring is devalued; physicians, for example, are among the highest-

paid professionals. However, among physicians, specialists whose work involves more direct patient care (these include a larger proportion of women), for example, psychiatry, pediatrics, general practice, are paid less than those in areas that are more remote and impersonal, such as radiology (where the person being cared for may not even be seen). Everett C. Hughes, in his classic *Men and Their Work*, notes that doctors seem to be an exception to the dirty-work-equals-low-status equation. In the same work, Hughes observes that "the delegation of dirty work to someone else is common among humans. . . . Delegation of dirty work is also part of the process of occupational mobility." Everett C. Hughes, *Men and Their Work* (Glencoe, Ill.: The Free Press, 1958). The reason for doctors' exemption may be that, as Paul Starr points out in his award-winning book, *The Social Transformation of American Medicine,* they have aggressively pursued and protected their status. Paul Starr, *The Social Transformation of American Medicine* (New York: Basic Books, 1982).

15. Census 2000 (see note 13).

16. Center for the Child Care Workforce, Current Data on Child Care Salaries and Benefits in the United States, Washington, D.C., March 2001.

Chapter Eight: Growing Up Poor in Postwar America

1. U.S. Union Membership 1998–2000, Labor Research Association, http://www.laborresearch.org/content3g.html.

2. Stephanie Coontz, *The Way We Never Were: American Families and the Nostalgia Trap* (New York: Basic Books, 1992).

3. Coontz, *The Way We Never Were.*

4. John Hartigan, "Name Calling," in *White Trash: Race and Class in America*, ed. Matt Wray and Annalee Newitz (New York: Routledge, 1997).

5. Some women who were not poor talked about their parents' alcoholism, but only women who were poor described family violence, abuse, and neglect.

6. Howard H. Goldman, Patricia Rye, and Paul Sirovatkaeds, eds., *Mental Health: A Report of the Surgeon General.* U.S. Public Health Service, 1999. Available from The Virtual Office of the Surgeon General, http://www.surgeongeneral.gov/library/reports.htm.

7. Uri Bronfenbrenner, *The Ecology of Human Development: Experiments by Nature and Design* (Cambridge, Mass.: Harvard University Press, 1979).

8. Claudia J. Coulton, Jill E. Korbin, and Marilyn Su, "Neighborhoods and Child Maltreatment: A Multi-Level Study," *Child Abuse and Neglect* 23, no. 11 (1999): 1019–1040.

9. James Garbarino, "A Preliminary Study of Some Ecological Correlates of Child Abuse: The Impact of Socioeconomic Stress on Mothers," *Child Development* 47 (1976): 178–185.

10. See, for example, James Garbarino and K. Kostelny, "Child Maltreatment as a

Community Problem," *Child Abuse and Neglect* 16 (1992): 455–464. James Garbarino and D. Sherman, "High Risk Neighborhoods and High Risk Families: The Human Ecology of Child Maltreatment," *Child Development* 51, no. 1 (1980): 188–198. R. Gelles, "Poverty and Violence towards Children," *American Behavioral Scientist* 35, no. 3 (1992): 258–274. A study by Brett Drake and Shanta Pandey found that neighborhood poverty is positively associated with three forms of child maltreatment, but to different degrees; compared with sexual abuse and physical abuse, child neglect was most powerfully associated with poverty status. Brett Drake and Shanta Pandey, "Understanding the Relationship Between Neighborhood Poverty and Specific Types of Child Maltreatment," *Child Abuse and Neglect* 20, no. 11 (1996): 1003–1018.

11. D. Gil, *Violence Against Children: Physical Child Abuse in the United States* (Cambridge, Mass.: Harvard University Press, 1970), p. 146, quoted by James Garbarino, "A Preliminary Study of Some Ecological Correlates of Child Abuse."

12. A British study found an association between mental illness and poor material standard of living—including overcrowding and structural housing problems (for example, a leaky roof)—independent of socioeconomic status. Scott Weich and Glyn Lewis, "Material Standard of Living, Social Class, and the Prevalence of the Common Mental Disorders in Great Britain," *Journal of Epidemiology and Community Health* 52, no. 8 (1998): 8–14.

13. The class differences were much less dramatic among women. For "heavy use," the rate for women without a high school diploma was 16.3 percent, for women with a degree 6.1 percent; for "very heavy use," the corresponding rates were 3.9 and 1.4 percent. National Center for Health Statistics, 1998.

14. National Center for Health Statistics, 1998. The strong relationship between alcohol abuse and social class is not unique to the United States. Studies in Britain have found an even stronger relationship among younger men. One study found that men aged twenty-five to thirty-nine in the "unskilled manual class" were ten to twenty times more likely to die from alcohol-related causes than those in the professional class. See L. Harrison and E. Gardiner, "Do the Rich Really Die Young? Alcohol-related Mortality and Social Class in Great Britain, 1988–94," *Addiction* 94, no. 12 (1999): 1871–1880. The class difference in mortality was significant, but not as dramatic, among older men. This is the case, too, in the United States and in several other countries, where the class difference is more pronounced for the more serious level of abuse.

15. American Indians and Hispanic Americans are also high-risk groups for cirrhosis. See G. K. Singh and D. L. Hoyert, "Social Epidemiology of Chronic Liver Disease and Cirrhosis Mortality in the United States, 1935–1997: Trends and Differentials by Ethnicity, Socioeconomic Status, and Alcohol Consumption," *Human Biology* 72, no. 5 (2000): 801–820.

16. Alcohol was also involved in 27 to 34 percent of incidents in which females

perpetrated violence against their male partners. See Raul Caetano, John Schafer, and Carol B. Cunradi, "Alcohol Related Intimate Violence Among White, Black and Hispanic Couples in the US," *Alcohol Research and Health* 25, no. 1 (2001): 58–65. Although the rate of female to male domestic violence as reported in national studies is higher than male to female violence, the consequences for women are more grave; more women than men are seriously injured or die as a result of domestic violence.

17. J. Fleming, P. Mullen, and G. Bammer, "A Study of Potential Risk Factors for Sexual Abuse in Childhood," *Child Abuse and Neglect* 21, no. 1 (1997): 49–58.

18. See, for example, D. Murdoch, R. O. Pihl, and D. Ross, "Alcohol and Crimes of Violence: Present Issues," *International Journal of the Addictions* 25, no. 9 (1990): 1065–1081.

19. Fleming et al., see note 17.

20. S. Wilt and S. Olson, "Prevalence of Domestic Violence in the United States," *Journal of the American Medical Women's Association* 51 (1996): 77–82.

21. G. el-Bayoumi, M. L. Borum, and Y. Haywood, "Domestic Violence in Women," *Medical Clinics of North America* 82 (1996): 391–401; Sisley et al., see note 16.

22. U.S. Department of Health and Human Services, *Child Maltreatment 1998: Reports from the States to the National Child Abuse and Neglect Data System* (Washington, D.C.: U.S. Government Printing Office, 1999). Data available from National Clearinghouse on Child Abuse and Neglect.

23. The higher rate is from M. A. Polusny and V. M. Follette, "Long-term Correlates of Child Sexual Abuse: Theory and Review of Empirical Literature," *Applied and Preventive Psychology* 4 (1995): 143–166. The lower rate is from H. L. MacMillan, J. E. Fleming, N. Trocme, M. H. Boyle, M. Wong, Y. A. Racine, W. R. Beardslee, and D. R. Offord, "Prevalence of child physical and sexual abuse in the community. Results from the Ontario Health Supplement," *Journal of the American Medical Association* 278 (1997): 131–135. Both cited in Howard H. Goldman, Patricia Rye, and Paul Sirovatka, eds., *Mental Health: A Report of the Surgeon General* (U.S. Public Health Service, 1999). Available from The Virtual Office of the Surgeon General, http://www.surgeon-general.gov/library/reports.htm.

24. Polusny and Follette, "Long-term Correlates of Child Sexual Abuse."

25. A. Browne and D. Finkelhor, "Impact of Child Sexual Abuse: A Review of the Research," *Psychological Bulletin* 99 (1986): 66–77; J. Briere, *Child Abuse Trauma: Theory and Treatment of the Lasting Effects* (Newbury Park, Calif.: Sage, 1992).

26. Polusny and Follette, "Long-term Correlates of Child Sexual Abuse." A. J. Sedlak and D. D. Broadhurst, *Executive Summary of the Third National Incidence Study of Child Abuse and Neglect* (Washington, D.C.: U.S. Department of Health and Human Services, Administration for Children and Families, National Center for Child Abuse and Neglect, 1996).

27. Timothy A. Judge, Edwin A. Locke, Cathy C. Durham, and Avraham N.

Kluger, "Dispositional Effects on Job and Life Satisfaction: The Role of Core Evaluations," *Journal of Applied Psychology* 83, no. 1(1998): 17–34.

28. Judge et al., see note 23, p. 19.

29. Laura's anger was healthy—but she was unable to direct it.

30. Michael Harrington, *The New American Poverty* (New York: Penguin, 1984), p. 209.

Chapter Nine: Dropping Out

1. Karl Alexander, Doris Entwisle, and Nader Kabbani, "The Dropout Process in Life-Course Perspective: Early Risk Factors and Home and School," *Teachers' College Record* 103, no. 5 (2001): 760–823.

2. For a very readable, nontechnical review and discussion of individual and school causes, see Robert F. Kronick and Charles B. Hargis, *Dropouts: Who Drops Out and Why? And the Recommended Action* (Springfield, Ill.: Charles Thomas, 1990). Also, for an article that suggests specific school reforms, see Edward L. McDill, Gary Natriello, and Aaron M. Pallas, "A Population at Risk: Potential Consequences of Tougher School Standards for Student Dropouts," *American Journal of Education* 94, no. 2 (1986): 135–181.

3. Results from the Baltimore Beginning School Study show a dropout rate of almost 60 percent for students in the bottom third of the socioeconomic status distribution of the sample (which is lower than average because Baltimore is predominantly low-income). This compares with a rate of about 33 percent for students in the middle third, and 17 percent for students in the top third.

4. Arthur Stinchcombe, *Rebellion in a High School* (Chicago: Chicago University Press, 1964).

5. U.S. Department of Education, *Dropout Rates in the United States, 2000* (Washington, D.C.: U.S. Government Printing Office, 2001).

6. Alice S. Rossi and Bhavani Sitaraman, "Abortion in Context: Historical Trends and Future Changes," *Family Planning Perspectives* 20, no. 6 (1988): 273–281.

7. Maryland, for example, repealed its anti-abortion statute in 1968.

8. Kristin Luker, *Abortion and the Politics of Motherhood* (Berkeley: University of California Press, 1984).

9. U.S. Census 2000, Historical Tables.

10. Explanations for this difference vary widely; they range from cultural explanations that suggest that extramarital births have their roots in slavery, to materialist explanations—for example, that black men are less likely to marry because they lack jobs that could support a family. Support for abortion was lower among blacks than whites, and rates of abortion were much higher for whites.

11. U.S. Census Bureau, *Trends in Premarital Childbearing: 1930–1994*, October 1999.

12. For a discussion that contrasts the options available for pregnant teenagers of different race, see Rickie Solinger, *Wake Up Little Susie* (New York: Routledge, 2000). Emphasizing the extent to which whites opted for giving birth in an institution that then arranged for adoption, Solinger's analysis, though possibly valid for the middle class, underestimates the extent to which working-class whites solved the pregnancy problem by marriage.

13. Unfortunately, girls are still given more of these responsibilities than boys, to the detriment of their studies. See T. Smith, "School Grades and Responsibility for Younger Siblings: An Empirical Study of the 'Teaching Function,'" *American Sociological Review* 49 (1984): 248–260.

14. Dollie Walker, Arthur L. Stinchcombe, and Mary S. McDill, *School Desegregation in Baltimore* (Center for the Study of the Social Organization of Schools, The Johns Hopkins University, Report Number 3, 1967), pp. 31–32.

15. Jane Motz, *Baltimore Civil Disorders, April 1968* (American Friends Service Committee, Middle Atlantic Region, 1968), p. 28.

16. Walker, Stinchcombe, and McDill, *School Desegregation in Baltimore*, pp. 31–32.

17. Assata Shakur, *Assata* (Chicago: Lawrence Hill Books, 1987). Cited in Wini Breines, *Young, White and Miserable: Growing up Female in the Fifties* (Boston: Beacon Press, 1992), p. 16.

18. Maryland Adult Literacy Resource Center, University of Maryland, Baltimore County, 2000.

19. There is now an alternative method of obtaining the equivalent of a high school diploma, the National External Diploma Program, which is less intimidating, but more time consuming. Applicants eighteen and older can work with an assessor to develop a portfolio that proves they have "essential" academic competencies and life skills. Academic skill areas include reading, writing, mathematics, oral communication, and critical thinking. Life skills relate to occupational, self, social, aesthetic, consumer, and scientific awareness. This method is less well known.

20. Michael J. Forster, assisted by Michelle Pellizsari, *Labor Market and Social Policy—Occasional Papers No. 42: Trends and Driving Factors in Income Distribution and Poverty in the OECD Area* (Directorate for Education, Employment, Labor and Social Affairs, OECD, 2000).

21. Walker, Stinchcombe, and McDill, *School Desegregation in Baltimore*, pp. 31–32.

Chapter Ten: What Will I Be?

1. Karl Marx, *Economic and Philosophic Manuscripts of 1844*, trans. Martin Milligan (Moscow: Foreign Languages Publishing House, 1959), p. 140.

2. Cited in Pierre Bourdieu, *Outline of a Theory of Practice* (Cambridge: Cambridge University Press, 1977), p. 77.

3. Karl Marx, *The Eighteenth Brumaire of Louis Napoleon* (New York: International Publishers, 1987), p. 15.

4. Of course, social mobility does occur, but the first generation to be socially mobile has not yet learned to take for granted its middle-class status and way of thinking; it has not yet acquired what Bourdieu (see later this page) calls the habitus of the middle class. For two sensitive portrayals of this, see Richard Sennett and J. Cobb, *The Hidden Injuries of Class* (New York: Vintage Books, 1973), and also J. Ryan and C. Sackrey, *Strangers in Paradise: Academics from the Working Class* (Boston: South End Press, 1984). In a perceptive article on how women in particular experience class mobility—and in Britain, where class markers are arguably more rigid than in the United States—Steph Lawler notes that taking on the markers of middle-class existence is particularly problematic for women because they run the risk of being labeled "pretentious": "There is a particular jeopardy for women who have been especially associated with desires for artefacts associated with bourgeois existence." Steph Lawler, "Getting Out and Getting Away: Women's Narratives of Class Mobility," *Feminist Review* 63 (1999): 3–24.

5. Bourdieu, *Outline of a Theory of Practice*, p. 77.

6. Bourdieu, *Outline of a Theory of Practice*, p. 164.

7. U.S. Census, Percent Distribution of Years of School Completed by Persons 25 Years and Older, by Race, for 30 Selected Standard Metropolitan Statistical Areas: 1968.

8. "Secretary" was the parental ambition women recalled most often. Thirteen of the eighteen middle-class daughters remembered parents' having an ambition on their behalf. The remaining five said they remembered that they were expected to finish college, but they had no recollection of discussing any particular career with their parents. Most working-class girls had to restrict their career choices to occupations that required no training, or very little training beyond high school. Cosmetology and secretarial work were suitable because training was provided in high school.

9. A number of middle-class women remembered being given guidance in school about college, but little guidance about specific careers.

10. Notice that Muriel let me know, casually, that her grandfather was a congressman, establishing beyond doubt her elite credentials while at the same time making light of them to show that she was not boasting—"the whole bit."

11. A study of the relationship between cultural capital and socioeconomic status found that cultural capital was most important for high-status females. The authors concluded that "cultural interests and activities were culturally prescribed for teenage girls, while for adolescent boys they were less strongly prescribed, perhaps even negatively sanctioned by peers. High cultural involvements may have been part of an identity kit that academically successful, high status girls, but not similar boys, possessed." P. DiMaggio and J. Mohr, "Cultural Capital, Educational Attainment and Marital Selection," *American Journal of Sociology* 90, no. 6 (1985): 1231–1261.

12. In 1940, for example—when the parents of the women in the study were in this age group—only 38 percent of the population aged between twenty-five and twenty-nine were high school graduates and only 6 percent were graduates of a four-year college. By 1980, when the women in the study were in the same twenty-five- to twenty-nine-year-old age group, both these percentages had approximately doubled; more than 16 percent of the population graduated from college and almost 74 percent completed high school. *Statistical Abstracts of the United States* (Washington, D.C.: Government Printing Office, 1991).

13. Pierre Bourdieu and Jean-Claude Passeron, *Reproduction in Education, Society and Culture,* 2nd ed. (Newbury Park: Sage, 1994), p. 49.

14. Bourdieu has studied the class origins of students in different majors and found that over 80 percent of art history students, but only 35 percent of geography students, enrolled in French universities were of upper-class origin. The more distant a discipline or sub-discipline is from the concrete material world, the more students' backgrounds also reflect distance from the "vital urgencies" of that material world. A consequence, of course, is that degrees in art history and similar disciplines become valuable symbols attesting to class origins.

15. Seventeen women were unable to remember any job ambition. All except one of the twelve middle-class women who remembered their early aspiration had ended up working in that career or one of equal status.

16. This discussion is largely based on an article by Linda Gottfredson: "Circumscription and Compromise: A Developmental Theory of Occupational Aspirations," *Journal of Counseling Psychology Monograph* 28 (1981): 545–579.

Chapter Eleven: Getting By on the Minimum

1. Pierre Bourdieu, *Outline of a Theory of Practice* (Cambridge: Cambridge University Press, 1977), p. 496.

2. Nicholas Lehmann, "With College for All," *Time,* vol. 147, no. 24 (June 10, 1996).

3. Maryland Department of Labor, *Maryland Occupational Wages: All Industries in Baltimore City,* September 2001.

4. Maryland Department of Labor, *Industry Outlook 1996–2006—Personnel Supply Services.* Available from Maryland Department of Labor.

5. Leslie McCall, *Complex Inequality* (New York: Routledge, 2001), p. 137. In these areas, too, she tells us gender wage inequality among the college educated is significantly lower than in more high-skill economies.

6. McCall, *Complex Inequality,* p. 170. Baltimore has relatively few immigrant workers.

7. Michael J. Forster, assisted by Michelle Pellizsari, *Labor Market and Social Policy—Occasional Papers No. 42: Trends and Driving Factors in Income Distribution*

and Poverty in the OECD Area (Directorate for Education, Employment, Labor and Social Affairs, OECD, 2000).

8. AFL-CIO, *Unions Raise Wages, Especially for Minorities and Women, and Union Workers Have Better Benefits* (www.aflcio.org/uniondifference/uniondiff4.htm).

9. U.S. Bureau of Labor Statistics, *Union Members in 1996*, http://www.bls.census.gov/cps/pub/union_96htm.

10. Barbara Thomas Coventry and Marietta Morrisey, "Unions' Empowerment of Working Class Women: A Case Study," *Sociological Spectrum* 18 3 (1998): 285–310.

11. Coventry and Morrisey, "Unions' Empowerment of Working Class Women."

12. Gosta Esping-Andersen, *The Three Worlds of Welfare Capitalism* (Cambridge: Polity Press, 1990).

Bibliography

Alexander, Karl, Doris R. Entwisle, and Nader Kabbani. 2001. "The Dropout Process in Life Course Perspective: Early Risk Factors at Home and School." *Teacher's College Record* 103 (5): 760–823.

Baruch, Grace, Rosalind Barnett, and Caryl Rivers. 1983. *Lifeprints: New Patterns of Life and Work for Today's Women.* New York: McGraw-Hill.

Bateson, Mary Catherine. 1989. *Composing a Life.* New York: Atlantic Monthly Press.

Benenson, Harold. 1984. "Women's Occupational and Family Achievement in the U.S. Class System: A Critique of the Dual-Career Family Analysis." *British Journal of Sociology* 35 (1): 19–41.

Berger, Peter and Thomas Luckmann. 1967. *The Social Construction of Reality.* New York: Doubleday.

Betz, Michael and Lenahan O'Connell. 1989. "Work Orientations of Males and Females: Exploring the Gender Socialization Approach." *Sociological Enquiry* 59 (3): 318–330.

Beynon, H. and R. M. Blackburn. 1972. *Perceptions of Work: Variations Within a Factory.* Cambridge: Cambridge University Press.

Bielby, Denise and John Bielby. 1984. "Work Commitment, Sex-role Attitudes, and Women's Employment." *American Sociological Review* 49: 234–247.

Blumer, Herbert. 1986. *Symbolic Interactionism: Perspective and Method.* Berkeley: University of California Press.

Bourdieu, Pierre. 1977. *Outline of a Theory of Practice.* Cambridge: Cambridge University Press.

Bourdieu, Pierre. 1984. *Distinction: A Social Critique of the Judgement of Taste.* Translated by Richard Nice. New York: Routledge and Kegan Paul.

Bourdieu, Pierre and Jean-Claude Passeron. 1994. *Reproduction in Education, Society and Culture.* Newbury Park: Sage.

Braverman, Harry. 1974. *Labor and Monopoly Capital.* New York: Monthly Labor Review Press.

Breines, Wini. 1992. *Young, White and Miserable: Growing up Female in the Fifties.* Boston: Beacon Press.

Briere, J. 1992. *Child Abuse Trauma: Theory and Treatment of the Lasting Effects.* Newbury Park, Calif.: Sage.

Bronfenbrenner, Uri. 1979. *The Ecology of Human Development: Experiments by Nature and Design.* Cambridge, Mass.: Harvard University Press.

Brown, George W. and Tirril Harris. 1978. *Social Origins of Depression: A Study of Psychiatric Disorder in Women.* London: Tavistock Publications.

Browne, A. and D. Finkelhor. 1986. "Impact of Child Sexual Abuse: A Review of the Research," *Psychological Bulletin* 99: 66–77.

Bubeck, Diemut Elisabet. 1995. *Care, Gender and Justice.* Oxford: Clarendon Press.

Burawoy, Michael. 1979. *Manufacturing Consent: Changes in the Labor Process under Monopoly Capitalism.* Chicago: Chicago University Press.

Burris, Beverly. 1991. "Employed Mothers: The Impact of Class and Marital Status on the Prioritizing of Family and Work." *Social Science Quarterly* 72: 50–66.

Cancian, Francesca M. 2000. "Paid Emotional Care." In *Care Work: Gender Labor and the Welfare State,* edited by Madonna Harrington Meyer. New York: Routledge.

Center for Child Care Workforce. March 2001. *Current Data on Child Care Salaries and Benefits in the United States.*

Challener, Daniel D. 1997. *Stories of Resilience in Childhood.* New York: Garland Publishing.

Coontz, Stephanie. 1992. *The Way We Never Were: American Families and the Nostalgia Trap.* New York: Basic Books.

Coulton, Claudia J., Jill E. Korbin, and Marilyn Su. 1999. "Neighborhoods and Child Maltreatment: A Multi-Level Study." *Child Abuse and Neglect* 23 (11): 1019–1040.

Council of Great City Schools. 1994. *National Urban Education Goals: 1992–93 Indicators Report.*

Coventry, Barbara Thomas and Marietta Morrisey. 1998. "Unions' Empowerment of Working Class Women: A Case Study." *Sociological Spectrum* 18 (3): 285–310.

Crompton, Rosemary and Michael Mann, eds. 1986. *Gender and Stratification.* Cambridge: Polity Press.

Crosby, Faye. 1982. *Relative Deprivation and Working Women.* New York: Oxford University Press.

D'Amico, Ronald. 1986. "Authority in the Workplace: Differences Among Mature Women." In *Midlife Women at Work: A Fifteen-Year Perspective,* edited by Lois Banfill Shaw. Lexington, Mass.: D.C. Heath and Company.

DiMaggio, P. and J. Mohr. 1985. "Cultural Capital, Educational Attainment and Marital Selection." *American Journal of Sociology* 90 (6): 1231–1261.

Drake, Brett and Shanta Pandey. 1996. "Understanding the Relationship Between Neighborhood Poverty and Specific Types of Child Maltreatment." *Child Abuse and Neglect* 20 (11): 1003–1018.

Egginton, E., R. Wells, D. Gaus, and M. Esselman. 1990. "Underlying Factors Associated with Dropping Out and Factors Impacting At-Risk Students' Attitudes towards School: A Comparison Study of Low-Income, White Females." Presented at the annual meeting of the American Educational Research Association, March 16, Boston, Mass.

Ehrenreich, Barbara. 2001. *Nickel and Dimed: On (Not) Getting By in America.* New York: Metropolitan Books.

Ehrenreich, Barbara and John Ehrenreich. 1971. "The Professional-Managerial Class." *Radical America* 11 (2).

el-Bayoumi, G., M. L. Borum, and Y. Haywood. 1996. "Domestic Violence in Women." *Medical Clinics of North America* 82: 391–401.

Elder, Glen J. 1974. *Children of the Great Depression: Social Change in Life Experience.* Chicago: The University of Chicago Press.

Engels, Friedrich. 1968. *The Condition of the Working Class in England.* Stanford: Stanford University Press.

Entwisle, Doris R., Karl L. Alexander, and Linda S. Olson. 1997. *Children, Schools and Inequality.* Boulder: Westview Press.

Erickson, Erik. 1963. *Childhood and Society.* New York: Norton.

Esping-Andersen, Gosta. 1990. *The Three Worlds of Welfare Capitalism.* Cambridge: Polity Press.

Ferree, Myra Marx. 1976. "Working-Class Jobs: Housework and Paid Work as Sources of Satisfaction." *Social Problems* 23: 431–441.

Ferree, Myra Marx. 1984. "Class, Housework, and Happiness: Women's Work and Life Satisfaction." *Sex Roles* 11 (11/12): 1057–1074.

Ferree, Myra Marx. 1985. "Between Two Worlds: German Feminist Approaches to Working-Class Women and Work." *Signs* 10 (3): 517–536.

Firebaugh, Glenn and Brian Harley. 1995. "Trends in Job Satisfaction in the United States By Race, Gender and Type of Occupations." *Research in the Sociology of Work* 5: 87–104.

Fleming, J., P. Mullen, and G. Bammer. 1997. "A Study of Potential Risk Factors for Sexual Abuse in Childhood." *Child Abuse and Neglect* 21 (1): 49–58.

Forster, Michael J., assisted by Michelle Pellizsari. 2000. *Labor Market and Social Policy—Occasional Papers No. 42: Trends and Driving Factors in Income Distribution and Poverty in the OECD Area.* Directorate for Education, Employment, Labor and Social Affairs, OECD.

Fox-Genovese, Elizabeth. 1994. "Difference, Diversity and Divisions in an Agenda for the Women's Movement." In *Color, Class and Country: Experiences of Gender,* edited by G. Young and B. Dickerson. London: Zed Books.

Fox-Genovese, Elizabeth. 1996. *Feminism Is Not the Story of My Life.* New York: Nan A. Talese.

Furstenberg, Frank F. Jr., Thomas D. Cook, Jacqueline Eccles, Glen H. Elder Jr., and Arnold Sameroff. 1999. *Managing to Make It: Urban Families and Adolescent Success.* Chicago: University of Chicago Press.

Garbarino, James. 1976. "A Preliminary Study of Some Ecological Correlates of Child Abuse: The Impact of Socioeconomic Stress on Mothers." *Child Development* 47: 178–185.

Garbarino, James and K. Kostelny. 1992. "Child Maltreatment as a Community Problem." *Child Abuse and Neglect* 16: 455–464.

Garbarino, James and D. Sherman 1980. "High Risk Neighborhoods and High Risk Families: The Human Ecology of Child Maltreatment." *Child Development* 51 (1): 188–198.

Garfinkle, Irwin and Sara S. McLanahan. 1986. *Single Mothers and Their Children: A New American Dilemma.* Washington, D.C.: Urban Institute Press.

Garmezy, Norman. 1993. "Children in Poverty: Resilience Despite Risk." *Psychiatry* 56: 127–136.

Gelles, R. 1992. "Poverty and Violence towards Children." *American Behavioral Scientist* 35 (3): 258–274.

General Social Survey. 1988. National Opinion Research Center.

Gerson, Kathleen. 1985. *Hard Choices: How Women Decide About Work, Career and Motherhood.* Berkeley: University of California Press.

Giddens, Anthony. 1980. *The Class Structure of the Advanced Societies.* 2d ed. London: Hutchinson.

Gil, D. 1970. *Violence Against Children: Physical Child Abuse in the United States.* Cambridge, Mass.: Harvard University Press.

Gilbert, L., C. Holahan, and L. Manning. 1981. "Coping with Conflict Between Professional and Maternal Roles." *Family Relations* 30: 419–426.

Gilligan, Carol. 1982. *In a Different Voice: Psychological Theory and Women's Development.* Cambridge, Mass.: Harvard University Press.

Glazer, Nona A. 1993. *Women's Paid and Unpaid Labor: The Work Transfer in Health Care and Retailing.* Philadelphia: Temple University Press.

Glenn, Evelyn and Rosalyn Feldberg. 1979. "Clerical Work: The Female Occupation." In *Women: A Feminist Perspective,* edited by J. Freeman. Palo Alto: Mayfield.

Goffman, Erving. 1973. *The Presentation of Self in Everyday Life.* Woodstock, N.Y.: Overlook Press.

Goldman, Howard H., Patricia Rye, and Paul Sirovatkaeds, eds. 1999. *Mental Health: A Report of the Surgeon General.* U.S. Public Health Service. Available from The Virtual Office of the Surgeon General, http://www.surgeongeneral.gov/library/reports.htm.

Goldthorpe, John H., David Lockwood, Frank Bechhofer, and Jennifer Platt. 1968. *The Affluent Worker: Industrial Attitudes and Behavior.* Cambridge: Cambridge University Press.

Gottfredson, Linda. 1981. "Circumscription and Compromise: A Developmental Theory of Occupational Aspirations." *Journal of Counseling Psychology Monograph* 28 (6): 545–579.

Hammen, Constance. 1991. *Depression Runs in Families: The Social Context of Risk and Resilience in Children of Depressed Mothers.* New York: Springer-Verlag.

Harrington, Michael. 1984. *The New American Poverty.* New York: Penguin.

Harrison, L. and E. Gardiner. 1999. "Do the Rich Really Die Young? Alcohol-related Mortality and Social Class in Great Britain, 1988–94." *Addiction* 94 (12): 1871–1880.

Hartigan, John Jr. 1997. "Name Calling." In *White Trash: Race and Class in America,* edited by Matt Wray and Annalee Newitz. New York: Routledge.

Hartmann, Heidi. 1981. "The Family as a Locus of Gender, Class and Political Struggle: The Example of Housework." *Signs* 6 (3): 366–394.

Hartmann, Heidi. 1981. "The Unhappy Marriage of Marxism and Feminism: Towards a More Progressive Union." In *Women and Revolution: A Discussion of the Unhappy Marriage of Marxism and Feminism,* edited by Lydia Sargent. Boston: South End Press.

Hertz, Rosanna. 1986. *More Equal Than Others.* Berkeley: University of California Press.

Hochschild, Arlie Russell. 1983. *The Managed Heart: Commercialization of Human Feeling.* Berkeley: University of California Press.

Hochschild, Arlie. 1989. *The Second Shift: Working Parents and the Revolution at Home.* New York: Viking.

Hodson, Randy. 1989. "Gender Differences in Job Satisfaction: Why Aren't Women More Dissatisfied?" *The Sociological Quarterly* 30 (3): 385–399.

hooks, bell. 2001. *Where We Stand: Class Matters.* New York: Routledge.

Hopkins, Eric. 1994. *Childhood Transformed: Working-Class Children in Nineteenth Century England.* Manchester: Manchester University Press.

Hughes, Everett C. 1958. *Men and Their Work.* Glencoe, Ill.: The Free Press.

Jencks, Christopher, Lauri Perlman, and Lee Rainwater. 1988. "What Is a Good Job? A New Measure of Labor Market Success." *American Journal of Sociology* 93 (6): 1322–1357.

Joyce, Patrick. 1987. *The Historical Meanings of Work.* Cambridge: Cambridge University Press.

Judge, Timothy A., Edwin A. Locke, Cathy C. Durham, and Avraham N. Kluger. 1998. "Dispositional Effects on Job and Life Satisfaction: The Role of Core Evaluations." *Journal of Applied Psychology* 83 (1): 17–34.

Kalleberg, Arne. 1977. "Work Values and Job Rewards: A Theory of Job Satisfaction." *American Sociological Review* 42: 124–143.

Kanter, Rosabeth Moss. 1977. *Men and Women of the Corporation.* New York: Basic Books.

Karasek, Robert et al. 1981. "Job Decision Latitude, Job Demands, and Cardiovascular-Disease: A Prospective-study of Swedish Men." *American Journal of Public Health* 71 (7): 694–705.

Karasek, Robert et al. 1987. "Work and Non-Work Correlates of Illness and Behavior for Male and Female Swedish White-Collar Workers." *Journal of Occupational Behavior* 8: 187–207.

Karasek, Robert et al. 1979. "Job Demands, Job Decision Latitude, and Mental Strain: Implications for Job Redesign." *Administrative Science Quarterly* 24: 285–309.

Katzman, David M. 1978. *Seven Days a Week: Women and Domestic Service in Industrializing America.* New York: Oxford University Press.

Kessler-Harris, Alice. 1981. *Women Have Always Worked: A Historical Overview.* New York: McGraw-Hill.

Kibria, N., R. Barnett, G. Baruch, N. Marshall, and J. Pleck. 1990. "Homemaking Role Quality and the Psychological Well-Being and Distress of Employed Women." *Sex Roles* 22: 327–347.

Kohn, Melvin, L. 1990. "Unresolved Issues in the Relationship between Work and Personality." In *The Nature of Work: Sociological Perspectives*, edited by Kai Erickson and Steven Vallas. New Haven: Yale University Press.

Kohn, Melvin and Carmi Schooler. 1983. *Work and Personality: An Inquiry into the Impact of Social Stratification.* Norwood, N.J.: Ablex Publishing.

Komarovsky, Mirra. 1967. *Blue Collar Marriage.* New York: Vintage Books.

Kornhauser, A. 1965. *Mental Health of the Industrial Worker: A Detroit Study.* New York: John Wiley and Sons.

Kronick, Robert F. and Charles B. Hargis. 1990. *Dropouts: Who Drops Out and Why? And the Recommended Action.* Springfield, Ill.: Charles Thomas.

Kutscher. Ronald E. 1993. "The American Work Force, 1992–2005: Historical Trends, 1950–1992, and Current Uncertainties." *Monthly Labor Review*, November: 3–10.

Lamphere, Louise, Patricia Zavella, and Felipe Gonzalez with Peter B. Evans. 1993. *Sunbelt Working Mothers: Reconciling Family and Factory.* Ithaca: Cornell University Press.

Lawler, Steph. 1999. "Getting Out and Getting Away: Women's Narratives of Class Mobility." *Feminist Review* 63: 3–24.

Lehmann, Nicholas. 1996. "With College for All." *Time*, June 10, vol. 147, no. 24.

Lenski, Gerhard. 1966. *Power and Privilege: A Theory of Social Stratification.* New York: McGraw-Hill.

Lopata, Helena Z. 1994. *Circles and Settings: Role Changes of American Women.* Albany: SUNY Press.

Lopata, Helena Z., Cheryl Miller, and Debra Barnewolt. 1986. *City Women in America.* New York: Praeger.

Loscocco, Karen. 1990. "Reactions to blue-collar work: A comparison of women and men." *Work and Occupations* 17 (2): 152–177.

Luker, Kristin. 1984. *Abortion and the Politics of Motherhood.* Berkeley: University of California Press.

MacMillan, H. L., J. E. Fleming, N. Trocme, M. H. Boyle, M. Wong, Y. A. Racine, W. R. Beardslee, and D. R. Offord. 1997. "Prevalence of Child Physical and Sexual Abuse in the Community. Results from the Ontario Health Supplement." *Journal of the American Medical Association* 278: 131–135.

Marshall, Nancy L. and Rosalind C. Barnett. 1991. "Race, Class and Multiple Role Strains and Gains Among Women Employed in the Service Sector." *Women and Health* 1 (17): 1–19.

Martin, Jack C. and Constance L. Shehan. 1989. "Education and Job Satisfaction: The Influences of Gender, Wage-Earning Status, and Job Values." *Work and Occupations* 16 (2): 184–199.

Maryland Department of Labor. 2001. *Industry Outlook 1996–2006—Personnel Supply Services.* September.

Maryland Department of Labor. 2001. *Maryland Occupational Wages: All Industries in Baltimore City.* September.

Marx, Karl. 1959. *Economic and Philosophic Manuscripts of 1844.* Translated by Martin Milligan. Moscow: Foreign Languages Publishing House.

Marx, Karl. 1987. *The Eighteenth Brumaire of Louis Bonaparte.* New York: International Publishers.

Marx, Karl and Friedrich Engels, 1959. *The Communist Manifesto.* In *Capital and Other Writings by Karl Marx,* edited by Max Eastman. New York: Random House.

Mather, Cotton. 1702. *Two Brief Discourses: The One Offering Methods and Motives for Parents, The Other Offering Some Instructions for Children.* Boston: T. Green for Benjamin Eliot.

McCall, Leslie. 2001. *Complex Inequality.* New York: Routledge.

McDill, Edward L., Gary Natriello, and Aaron M. Pallas. 1986. "A Population at Risk: Potential Consequences of Tougher School Standards for Student Dropouts." *American Journal of Education* 94 (2): 135–181.

McNally, Fiona. 1979. *Women for Hire: A Study of the Female Office Worker.* New York: St. Martin's Press.

Merriwether-de-Vries, Cynthia et al. 1996. "Early Parenting and Intergenerational Family Relationships among African-American Families." In *Transitions Through Adulthood: Interpersonal Domains and Contexts,* edited by Julia A. Gruber, Jeanne Brooks-Gunn, and Anne C. Petersen. New Jersey: Lawrence Erlbaum and Associates.

Miller, Jean Baker. 1976. *Toward a New Psychology of Women.* Boston: Beacon Press.

Miller, Joanne. 1980. "Individual and Occupational Determinants of Job Satisfaction: A Focus on Gender Differences." *Sociology of Work and Occupations* 7: 337–366.

Mills, C. Wright. 1951. *White Collar: The American Middle Class.* New York: Oxford University Press.

Mills, C. Wright. 1956. *The Power Elite.* London: Oxford University Press.

Mills, C. Wright. 1959. *The Sociological Imagination*. New York: Oxford University Press.

Mishel, L. and J. Bernstein. 1994. *The State of Working America*. New York: Economic Policy Institute.

Moen, Phyllis. 1992. *Women's Two Roles: A Contemporary Dilemma*. New York: Auburn House.

Moen, Phyllis and Ken R. Smith. 1986. "Women at Work: Commitment and Behavior over the Life Course." *Sociological Forum* 1: 450–474.

Mott, Frank L. and Lois B. Shaw. 1986. "The Employment Consequences of Different Fertility Behaviors." In *Midlife Women at Work: A Fifteen-Year Perspective*, edited by Lois Banfill Shaw. Lexington, Mass.: D.C. Heath and Company.

Motz, Jane. 1968. *Baltimore Civil Disorders, April 1968*. American Friends Service Committee, Middle Atlantic Region.

Murdoch, D., R. O. Pihl, and D. Ross. 1990. "Alcohol and Crimes of Violence: Present Issues." *International Journal of the Addictions* 25 (9): 1065–1081.

Musil, Carol M., Susan Schrader, and John Mutikani. 2000. "Social Support, Stress and Special Coping Tasks of Grandmother Caregivers." In *To Grandmother's House We Go and Stay: Perspectives on Custodial Grandparents*, edited by Carole B. Cox. New York: Springer Publishing.

Neff, Wanda F. 1929. *Victorian Working Women*. New York: Columbia University Press.

Neil, C. and W. Snizek. 1988. "Gender as a Moderator of Job Satisfaction." *Work and Occupations* 15: 201–219.

Nelson, Margaret K. 1990. *Negotiated Care: The Experience of Family Day Care Providers*. Philadelphia: Temple University Press.

Nippert-Eng, Christena E. 1996. *Home and Work: Negotiating Boundaries through Everyday Life*. Chicago: The University of Chicago Press.

Odulana, J. A., L. D. Camblin, and P. White. 1996. "Cultural Roles and Health Status of Contemporary African-American Young Grandmothers." *The Journal of Multicultural Nursing and Health* 2: 28–35.

Pareto, Wilfredo. 1935. *The Mind and Society*. Translated by A. Bongiorno and Arthur Livingston. Edited by Arthur Livingston. New York: Harcourt.

Peng, S. S. 1985. *High School Dropout: A National Concern*. Washington, D.C.: U.S. Government Printing Office.

Phelan, Jo. 1994. "The Paradox of the Contented Female Worker: An Assessment of Alternative Explanations." *Social Psychology Quarterly* 57 (2): 95–107.

Potuchek, Jean L. 1997. *Who Supports the Family? Gender and Breadwinning in Dual-earner Marriages*. Stanford: Stanford University Press.

Quinn, Robert P. and Linda J. Shepard. 1974. *The 1972–73 Quality of Employment Survey*. Ann Arbor: Institute of Social Research, University of Michigan.

Radke-Yarrow, Marian in collaboration with Pedro Martinez, Anne Mayfield, and

Donna Ronsaville. 1998. *Children of Depressed Mothers: From Early Childhood to Maturity*. Cambridge: Cambridge University Press.

Rapoport, R. and P. Rapoport. 1971. *Dual Career Families*. Baltimore: Penguin.

Rapoport, R. and P. Rapoport. 1976. *Dual-Career Families Re-Examined*. New York: Harper and Row.

Repetti, Reta. 1993. "The Effects of Workload and the Social Environment at Work on Health." In *Handbook of Stress: Theoretical and Clinical Aspects*, edited by Leo Goldberger and Shlomo Breznitz. New York: The Free Press.

Rodgers, D. 1978. *The Work Ethic in Industrial America, 1850–1920*. London: University of Chicago Press.

Rodin, J. and J. Ickovics. 1990. "Women's Health: Review and Research Agenda as We Approach the Twenty-First Century." *American Psychologist* 45: 1018–1034.

Rollins, Judith. 1985. *Between Women: Domestics and their Employers*. Philadelphia: Temple University Press.

Rosen, Ellen. 1982. *"The Changing Jobs of American Women Factory Workers."* A paper presented at the Conference on the Changing Jobs of American Women Workers, sponsored by the Professional and Business Women's Foundation, George Washington University, and the Service Employees Union, Washington, D.C.

Rossi, Alice S. and Bhavani Sitaraman. 1988. "Abortion in Context: Historical Trends and Future Changes." *Family Planning Perspectives* 20 (6): 273–281.

Rubin, Lillian Breslow. 1976. *Worlds of Pain: Life in the Working-Class Family*. New York: Basic Books.

Rutter, Michael. 1979. "Protective Factors in Children's Responses to Stress and Disadvantage." In *Primary Prevention of Psychopathology*. Vol. 3, edited by M. W. Kent and J. E. Rolf. Hanover, N.H.: University Free Press of New England.

Ryan, Barbara. 1992. *Feminism and the Women's Movement: Dynamics of Change in Social Movement Ideology and Activism*. New York: Routledge.

Ryan, J. and C. Sackrey. 1984. *Strangers in Paradise: Academics from the Working Class*. Boston: South End Press.

Ryder, Norman. 1965. "The Cohort as a Concept in the Study of Social Change." *American Sociological Review* 30: 843–861.

Safilios-Rothschild, Constantina. 1970. "The Influence of Wife's Degree of Work Commitment upon Some Aspects of Family Organization and Dynamics." *Journal of Marriage and the Family*. November: 681–686.

Saluter, A. F. 1992. "Marital Status and Living Arrangements: March 1991." *Current Population Reports*, Series P-20, No. 461. Washington, D.C.: U.S. Government Printing Office.

Schutz, Alfred. 1967. *The Phenomenology of the Social World*. Translated by George Walsh and Frederick Lehnert. Chicago: Northwestern University Press.

Schutz Alfred and Thomas Luckmann. 1973. *Structures of the Life World*. Translated by

Richard M. Zaner and H. Tristam Engelhardt Jr. Evanston: Northwestern University Press.

Sedlak, A. J. and D. D. Broadhurst. 1996. "Executive Summary of the Third National Incidence Study of Child Abuse and Neglect." Washington, D.C.: U.S. Department of Health and Human Services, Administration for Children and Families, National Center for Child Abuse and Neglect.

Sennett, Richard and J. Cobb. 1973. *The Hidden Injuries of Class.* New York, Vintage Books.

Shakur, Assata. 1987. *Assata.* Chicago: Lawrence Hill Books.

Singh, G. K. and D. L. Hoyert. 2000. "Social Epidemiology of Chronic Liver Disease and Cirrhosis Mortality in the United States,1935–1997: Trends and Differentials by Ethnicity, Socioeconomic Status, and Alcohol Consumption." *Human Biology* 72 (5): 801–820.

Sisley, A., L. Jacobs, G. Poole, S. Campbell, and T. Esposito. 1996. "Violence in America: A Public Health Crisis-domestic Violence." *Journal of Trauma* 46: 1105–1112.

Smith, T. 1984. "School Grades and Responsibility for Younger Siblings: An Empirical Study of the 'Teaching Function.'" *American Sociological Review* 49: 248–260.

Solinger, Rickie. 2000. *Wake Up Little Susie.* New York: Routledge.

Starr, Paul. 1982. *The Social Transformation of American Medicine.* New York: Basic Books.

Stinchcombe, Arthur. 1964. *Rebellion in a High School.* Chicago: Chicago University Press.

Terkel, Studs. 1972. *Working.* New York: Ballantine Books.

Teixeira, Ruy and Joel Rogers. 2000. *Why the White Working Class Still Matters: America's Forgotten Majority.* New York: Basic Books.

Tilly, Louise A. and Joan W. Scott. 1978. *Women, Work and Family.* New York: Holt, Rinehart & Winston.

Towle, L. H. 1997. "Grandma, Where's Mommy?" *Carolina Parent.*

U.S. Census Bureau. Issued October 1999. *Trends in Premarital Childbearing: 1930–1994.*

U.S. Commerce Department, Bureau of the Census. 1991. *Statistical Abstracts of the United States.* Washington, D.C.: Government Printing Office.

U.S. Commerce Department, Bureau of the Census, *Census 2000.* http://www.census.gov.

U.S. Department of Education. 2001. *Dropout Rates in the United States, 2000.* Washington, D.C.: U.S. Government Printing Office.

U.S. Department of Health and Human Services. 1999. *Child Maltreatment 1998: Reports from the States to the National Child Abuse and Neglect Data System.* Washington, D.C.: U.S. Government Printing Office.

U.S. Department of Labor, Women's Bureau. 1994. *Working Women Count! A Report to the Nation, 1994.* Washington, D.C.: Government Printing Office.

U.S. Department of Labor, Women's Bureau. 1998. *Equal Pay: A Thirty-five Year Perspective*. Washington, D.C.: Government Printing Office.

U.S. Department of Labor, Women's Bureau. 1998. *Women's Jobs, 1964–1997: Thirty Years of Progress* (Washington, D.C.: Government Printing Office.

U.S. Department of Labor, Women's Bureau. *20 Leading Occupations of Employed Women: 2000 Annual Averages*. http://www.dol.gov/dol/wb.

Walker, Dollie, Arthur L. Stinchcombe, and Mary S. McDill. 1967. *School Desegregation in Baltimore*. Center for the Study of the Social Organization of Schools, The Johns Hopkins University, Report Number 3.

Walshok, Mary L. 1978. "Occupational Values and Family Roles: A Descriptive Study of Women Working in Blue-Collar and Service Occupations." *Urban and Social Change Review* 11: 12–20.

Weber, Max. 1964. *The Theory of Social and Economic Organization*, edited by Talcott Parsons. New York: Free Press.

Weich, Scott and Glyn Lewis. 1998. "Material Standard of Living, Social Class, and the Prevalence of the Common Mental Disorders in Great Britain." *Journal of Epidemiology and Community Health* 52 (8): 8–14.

Welter, Barbara. 1966. "The Cult of True Womanhood, 1820–1860," *American Quarterly* 18: 151–174.

West, Jackie. 1982. "New Technology and Women's Office Work." In *Work, Women and the Labour Market*, edited by Jackie West. London: Routledge and Kegan Paul.

Wheeler, S. 1990. "Double Lives." In *The Nature of Work: Sociological Perspectives*. Edited by Kai Erikson and S. Vallas. New Haven: Yale University Press.

Wilt, S. and S. Olson. 1996. "Prevalence of domestic violence in the United States." *Journal of the American Medical Women's Association* 51: 77–82.

Wolf, Wendy C. and Neil D. Fligstein. 1979. "Sex and Authority in the Workplace," *American Sociological Review* 44: 235–252.

Wolfson, Michael C and Brian B. Murphy. 1998. "New Views on Inequality Trends in Canada and the United States." *Monthly Labor Review* April: 3–23.

Wright, Erik Olin. 1985. *Classes*. Thetford: Verso.

Yans-McLaughlin, Virginia. 1971. *Family and Community: Italian Immigrants in Buffalo, 1880–1930*. Ithaca: Cornell University Press.

Zal, Michael H. 1992. *The Sandwich Generation: Caught Between Growing Children and Aging Parents*. New York: Insight Books.

Zelizer, Viviana. 1985. *Pricing the Priceless Child: The Changing Social Value of Children*. New York: Basic Books.

Index